Introduction to

Handbook of
American Indian Languages

Indian Linguistic Families
of America North of Mexico

FRANZ BOAS

Introduction to
Handbook of
American Indian Languages

J. W. POWELL

Indian Linguistic Families
of America North of Mexico

Edited by Preston Holder

UNIVERSITY OF NEBRASKA PRESS · LINCOLN

First Bison Book printing September, 1966
Second Bison Book printing September, 1968
Third Bison Book printing April, 1970
Fourth Bison Book printing July, 1971
Fifth Bison Book printing May, 1973

Manufactured in the United States of America

Preface

This volume contains two fundamental contributions to the study of American Indian languages. Although both bear on the problem of the exact nature of North American native language, they are of quite different intent: Franz Boas, in his Introduction to the *Handbook of American Indian Languages* (1911), is concerned with basic linguistic characteristics,[1] while J. W. Powell, in "Indian Linguistic Families of America North of Mexico" (1891), treats the classification of languages in terms of lexical elements.[2] Both works have been relatively difficult of access, yet both are of immediate and continuing value, not only to students of linguistics but to all Americanists and anthropologists in general.

Boas's essay presents some of his fundamental ideas concerning language as of the end of the first decade of the present century. Originally intended to lay the groundwork for the series of grammatical sketches presented in the four-volume *Handbook of American Indian Languages*, it gives a clear statement of fundamental theory and of basic methodological principles which demonstrate the inadequacy of the old methods and point to new paths of research which were to lead to impressive results. In later essays—his Introduction to the *International Journal of American Linguistics* (1917), "The Classification of American Languages" (1920), and "Classification of American Indian Languages" (1929)[3]— Boas presented further ideas concerning the theory and methods of linguistic analysis and classification. These essays must be consulted by the student for a thorough understanding of the growth of linguistic studies, but nowhere in them will he find that Boas's original stand is seriously modified.

J. W. Powell's work following Gallatin's original efforts, is based on contributions by Horatio Hale, James C. Pilling, George Gibbs, Stephen Powers, Albert S. Gatschet, Stephen R. Riggs, J. Owen Dorsey, and many other ethnologists and linguists associated with the Bureau of American Ethnology during the nineteenth century. The long-continued study of North American native languages seems to have grown out of a central and vexing problem facing the United States government: how to adequately identify, classify, and locate the various indigenous peoples of North America, especially those of the United States and Alaska.

Powell explains his methodology in considerable detail. While the weakness of classifying languages on the basis of brief vocabularies is self-evident—its dangers are fully explored in Boas's essays—nonetheless, the linguistic families determined by Powell represent a very real configuration. The passing years have seen some consolidation of originally separate elements, a few changes in orthography, and various additions, but the main outlines remain unchanged. Boas paid a deserved tribute in 1917 when he said that "the classification of North American languages, that we owe to Major Powell, . . . will form the basis of all future work. . . ."[4]

In a more recent appraisal, Harry Hoijer stated: "Though a number of far-reaching modifications of this classification have been suggested since, the groups set up by Powell still retain their validity. In no case has a stock established by Powell been discredited by later work; the modifications that have been suggested are all concerned with the establishment of larger stocks to include two or more of Powell's groupings.[5] Thus Powell's fifty-eight families are reduced to fifty-four in Hoijer's listing. In the present volume, modern spellings are indicated by listing Hoijer's labels in a table following the text.

The student will find that many of the ethnological and linguistic generalizations in Powell's preliminary discussion are no longer tenable. That we are able today to criticize and discard these generalizations is a measure of the growth of our field and the increase in our understanding of the complexities of cultural processes.

The past two decades have seen great interest in the problems of classification raised by these lists, especially concerning relationships suggested by Edward Sapir at the super-family, stock, and phylum levels.[6] The development of lexicostatistics and glottochronology under Swadesh's leadership has led to suggestions of relationships far beyond the level of the family and at the same time has given some indication of the time intervals involved in the differentiation of the languages within families. The student must familiarize himself with this extensive literature if he is to understand the current direction of research in this field.[7] Again it must be stressed that all of this later work stems directly out of the pioneering papers here presented.

PRESTON HOLDER
University of Nebraska

1. Franz Boas, Introduction, *Handbook of American Indian Languages*, Bulletin 40, Part I, Bureau of American Ethnology (Washington, D. C.: Government Printing Office, 1911), pp. 1–83.

2. J. W. Powell, "Indian Linguistic Families of America North of Mexico," *Seventh Annual Report*, Bureau of American Ethnology (Washington, D. C.: Government Printing Office, 1891), pp. 1–142.

3. All are reprinted in Franz Boas, *Race, Language and Culture* (New York: Macmillan, 1940).

4. Franz Boas, Introduction, *International Journal of American Linguistics*, in *Race, Language and Culture*, p. 202.

5. Harry Hoijer, Introduction, "Linguistic Structures of Native North America," *Viking Fund Publications in Anthropology* No. 6, ed. C. Osgood (New York, 1956), p. 10.

6. Sapir's original presentation, updated by Hoijer in recent printings, is to be found in the 14th edition of the Encyclopaedia Britannica under "Central and North American Languages," Vol. V, pp. 138–141. The table of relationships gives some idea of the suggested changes:

Proposed Classification of American Indian Languages North of Mexico (and Certain Languages of Mexico and Central America)

I. *Eskimo-Aleut*

II. *Algonkin-Wakashan*

A. Algonkin-Ritwan
  1. Algonkin
  2. Beothuk
  3. Ritwan
    a. Wiyot
    b. Yurok

B. Kootenay
C. Mosan (Wakashan-Salish)
  1. Wakashan (Kwakiutl-Nootka)
  2. Chimakuan
  3. Salish

III. *Nadene*

A. Haida

B. Continental Nadene
  1. Tlingit
  2. Athapaskan

IV. *Penutian*

A. Californian Penutian
  1. Miwok-Costanoan
  2. Yokuts
  3. Maidu
  4. Wintun
B. Oregon Penutian
  1. Takelma
  2. Coast Oregon Penutian
    a. Coos
    b. Siuslaw
    c. Yakonan
  3. Kalapuya

C. Chinook
D. Tsimshian
E. Plateau Penutian
  1. Sahaptin
  2. Waiilatpuan (Molala-Cayuse)
  3. Lutuami (Klamath-Modoc)
F. Mexican Penutian
  1. Mixe-Zoque
  2. Huave

V. *Hokan-Siouan*

A. Hokan-Coahuiltecan
  1. Hokan
    a. Northern Hokan
      (1) Karok / Chimariko / Shasta-Achomawi
      (2) Yana
      (3) Pomo
    b. Washo
    c. Esselen-Yuman
      (1) Esselen

    b. Coahuilteco
      (1) Coahuilteco proper
      (2) Cotoname
      (3) Comecrudo
    c. Karankawa
B. Yuki
C. Keres
D. Tunican
  1. Tunica-Atakapa
  2. Chitimacha

(2) Yuman
d. Salinan-Seri
(1) Salinan
(2) Chumash
(3) Seri
e. Tequistlatecan
(Chontal)
2. Subtiaba-Tlappanec
3. Coahuiltecan
a. Tonkawa

E. Iroquois-Caddoan
1. Iroquoian
2. Caddoan
F. Eastern group
1. Siouan-Yuchi
a. Siouan
b. Yuchi
2. Natchez-Muskogian
a. Natchez
b. Muskogian
c. Timucua (?)

VI. *Aztec-Tanoan*

A. Uto-Aztecan
1. Nahuatl
2. Piman
3. Shoshonean

B. Tanoan-Kiowa
1. Tanoan
2. Kiowa
C. Zuñi (?)

7. For a review of contributions following Swadesh's original suggestions, see: Swadesh, Morris, "Lexicostatistic Dating of Prehistoric Ethnic Contacts," *Proceedings of the American Philosophical Society*, Vol. XCVI, No. 4 (1952); Gudschinsky, Sarah C., "The ABC's of lexicostatistics (Glottochronology)," *Word*, 12, 175–210 (1956); Swadesh, Morris, "Linguistic Overview," in *Prehistoric Man in the New World*, edd. Jennings and Norbeck (Chicago: University of Chicago Press, 1964); and Hymes, Dell H., "Lexicostatistics So Far," *Current Anthropology*, I, 1 (1960). The last-named contains an extensive bibliography indicating relevant current literature in specialized journals.

The "Languages of the World" project, launched under Voegelin's direction in the journal *Anthropological Linguistics* (Archives of Languages of the World, Anthropology Department, Indiana University) promises a new list of New World Languages as well as a revised map. The result to date will confuse the beginning student but should be consulted for recent trends.

Introduction to

Handbook of
American Indian Languages

Introduction

By Franz Boas

I. RACE AND LANGUAGE

Early Attempts to Determine the Position of the American Race

When Columbus started on his journey to reach the Indies, sailing westward, and discovered the shores of America, he beheld a new race of man, different in type, different in culture, different in language, from any known before that time. This race resembled neither the European types, nor the negroes, nor the better-known races of southern Asia. As the Spanish conquest of America progressed, other peoples of our continent became known to the invaders, and all showed a certain degree of outer resemblance, which led the Spaniards to designate them by the term "Indios" (Indians), the inhabitants of the country which was believed to be part of India. Thus the mistaken geographical term came to be applied to the inhabitants of the New World; and owing to the contrast of their appearance to that of other races, and the peculiarities of their cultures and their languages, they came to be in time considered as a racial unit.

The same point of view still prevailed when the discoveries included more extended parts of the New World. The people with whom the Spaniards and Portuguese came into contact in South America, as well as the inhabitants of the northern parts of North America, all seemed to partake so much of the same characteristics, that they were readily classed with the natives first discovered, and were considered as a single race of mankind.

It was only when our knowledge of the Indian tribes increased, that differences between the various types of man inhabiting our continent became known. Differences in degree of culture, as well as differences in language, were recognized at an early time. Much later came a recognition of the fact that the Indians of our continent differ in type as much among themselves as do the members of other races.

As soon as investigators began to concern themselves with these questions, the problem of the position of the natives of America among the races of mankind came to be of considerable interest, and speculations in regard to their origin and relationships occur even in the early descriptions of the New World.

Among the earlier attempts we find particularly endeavors to prove that certain parts of the beliefs and customs of the Indians agree with those of the Old World. Such agreements were considered proof that the Indians belong to one of the races enumerated in biblical history; and the theory that they represent the lost tribes of Israel was propounded frequently, and has held its own for a long time. In a similar way were traced analogies between the languages of the New World and those of the Old World, and many investigators believe even now that they have established such relationships. Attempts were also made to prove similarities in appearance between the American races and other races, and thus to determine their position among the races of the Old World.

Classifications based on Physical Type, Language, and Customs

The problems involved in the determination of the relations of the various races have been approached from two different points of view—either the attempt has been made to assign a definite position to a race in a classificatory system of the races of man, or the history of the race has been traced as far back as available data may permit.

The attempts to classify mankind are numerous. Setting aside the classifications based on biblical tradition, and considering only those that are based on scientific discussion, we find a number of attempts based on comparisons of the anatomical characteristics of mankind, combined with geographical considerations; others are based on the discussion of a combination of anatomical and cultural characteristics—traits which are considered as characteristic of certain groups of mankind; while still others are based primarily on the study of the languages spoken by people representing a certain anatomical type.

The attempts that have thus been made have led to entirely different results. Blumenbach, one of the first scientists who attempted to classify mankind, first distinguished five races—the Caucasian, Mongolian, Ethiopian, American, and Malay. It is fairly clear that this classification is based as much on geographical as on anatomical considerations, although the description of each race is primarily an anatomical one. Cuvier distinguished three races—the white, yellow, and black. Huxley proceeds more strictly on a biological basis. He combines part of the Mongolian and American races of Blumenbach into one, assigns part of the South Asiatic peoples to the Australian type, and subdivides the European races into a dark and a light division. The numerical preponderance of the European types has evidently led him to make finer distinctions in this race, which he divides into the xanthochroic and melanochroic races. It would be easy to make subdivisions of equal value in other races. Still clearer is the influence of cultural points of view in classifications like those of Gobineau and Klemm (who distinguishes the active and passive races), according to the cultural achievements of the various types of man.

The most typical attempt to classify mankind from a consideration of both anatomical and linguistic points of view is that of Friederich Müller, who takes as the basis of his primary divisions the form of hair, while all the minor divisions are based on linguistic considerations.

Relations between Physical Type, Language, and Customs

An attempt to correlate the numerous classifications that have been proposed shows clearly a condition of utter confusion and contradiction. If it were true that anatomical form, language, and culture are all closely associated, and that each subdivision of mankind is characterized by a certain bodily form, a certain culture, and a certain language, which can never become separated, we might expect that the results of the various investigations would show better agreement. If, on the other hand, the various phenomena which were made the leading points in the attempt at classification are not closely associated, then we may naturally expect such contradictions and lack of agreement as are actually found.

It is therefore necessary, first of all, to be clear in regard to the significance of anatomical characteristics, language, and culture, as characteristic of any subdivision of mankind.

It seems desirable to consider the actual development of these various traits among the existing races.

Permanence of Physical Type; Changes in Language and Culture

At the present period we may observe many cases in which a complete change of language and culture takes place without a corresponding change in physical type. This is true, for instance, among the North American negroes, a people by descent largely African; in culture and language, however, essentially European. While it is true that certain survivals of African culture and language are found among our American negroes, their culture is essentially that of the uneducated classes of the people among whom they live, and their language is on the whole identical with that of their neighbors—English, French, Spanish, and Portuguese, according to the prevalent language in various parts of the continent. It might be objected that the transportation of the African race to America was an artificial one, and that in earlier times extended migrations and transplantations of this kind have not taken place.

The history of medieval Europe, however, shows clearly that extended changes in language and culture have taken place many times without corresponding changes in blood.

Recent investigations of the physical types of Europe have shown with great clearness that the distribution of types has remained the same for a long period. Without considering details, it may be said that an Alpine type can easily be distinguished from a north-European type on the one hand, and a south-European type on the other. The Alpine type appears fairly uniform over a large territory, no matter what language may be spoken and what national culture may prevail in the particular district. The central-European Frenchmen, Germans, Italians, and Slavs are so nearly of the same type that we may safely assume a considerable degree of blood relationship, notwithstanding their linguistic differences.

Instances of similar kind, in which we find permanence of blood with far-reaching modifications of language and culture, are found in other parts of the world. As an example may be mentioned the Veddah of Ceylon, a people fundamentally different in type from the neighboring Singhalese, whose language they seem to have adopted, and from whom they have also evidently borrowed a number of cultural traits. Still other examples are the Japanese of the northern part of Japan, who are undoubtedly, to a considerable extent, Ainu in blood; and the Yukaghir of Siberia, who, while retaining to a great extent the old blood, have been assimilated in culture and language by the neighboring Tungus.

Permanence of Language; Changes of Physical Type

While it is therefore evident that in many cases a people, without undergoing a considerable change in type by mixture, have changed completely their language and culture, still other cases may be adduced in which it can be shown that a people have retained their language while undergoing material changes in blood and culture, or in both. As an example of this may be mentioned the Magyar of Europe, who have retained their old language, but have become mixed with people speaking Indo-European languages, and who have, to all intents and purposes, adopted European culture.

Similar conditions must have prevailed among the Athapascans, one of the great linguistic families of North America. The great body of people speaking languages belonging to this linguistic stock live in the northwestern part of America, while other dialects are spoken by small tribes in California, and still others by a large body of people in Arizona and New Mexico. The relationship between all these dialects is so close that they must be considered as branches of one large group, and it must be assumed that all of them have sprung from a language once spoken over a continuous area. At the present time the people speaking these languages differ fundamentally in type, the inhabitants of the Mackenzie river region being quite different from the tribes of California, and these, again, differing from the tribes of New Mexico. The forms of culture in these different regions are also quite distinct; the culture of the California Athapascans resembles that of other Californian tribes, while the culture of the Athapascans of New Mexico and Arizona is influenced by that of other peoples of that area. It seems most plausible to assume in this case that branches of this stock migrated from one part of this large area to another, where they intermingled with the neighboring people, and thus changed their physical characteristics, while at the same time they retained their speech. Without historical evidence this process can not, of course, be proved. I shall refer to this example later on.

Changes of Language and Type

These two phenomena—a retention of type with a change of language, and a retention of language with a change of type— apparently opposed to each other, are still very closely related, and in many cases go hand in hand. An example of this is, for instance, the distribution of the Arabs along the north coast of Africa. On the whole, the Arab element has retained its language; but at the same time intermarriages with the native races were common, so that the descendants of the Arabs have often retained the old language and have changed their type. On the other hand, the natives have to a certain extent given up their own languages, but have continued to intermarry among themselves and have thus preserved their type. So far as any change of this kind is connected with intermixture, both types of changes must always occur at the same time, and will be classed as a change of type or a change of language, as our attention is directed to the one people or the other, or, in some cases, as the one or the other change is more pronounced. Cases of complete assimilation without any mixture of the people involved seem to be rare, if not entirely absent.

Permanence of Type and Language; Change of Culture

Cases of permanence of type and language and of change of culture are much more numerous. As a matter of fact, the whole historical development of Europe, from prehistoric times on, is one endless series of examples of this process, which seems to be much easier, since assimilation of cultures occurs everywhere without actual blood mixture, as an effect of imitation. Proof of diffusion of cultural elements may be found in every single cultural area which covers a district in which many languages are spoken. In North America, California offers a good example of this kind; for here many languages are spoken, and there is a certain degree of differentiation of type, but at the same time a considerable uniformity of culture prevails. Another case in point is the coast of New Guinea, where, notwithstanding strong local differentiations, a certain fairly characteristic type of culture prevails, which goes hand in hand with a strong differentiation of languages. Among more highly civilized peoples, the whole area which is under the influence of Chinese culture might be given as an example.

These considerations make it fairly clear that, at least at the present time, anatomical type, language, and culture have not necessarily the same fates; that a people may remain constant in type and language and change in culture; that they may remain constant in type, but change in language; or that they may remain constant in language and change in type and culture. If this is true, then it is obvious that attempts to classify mankind, based on the present distribution of type, language, and culture, must lead to different results, according to the point of view taken; that a classification based primarily on type alone will lead to a system which represents, more or less accurately, the blood relationships of the people, which do not need to coincide with their cultural relationships; and that, in the same way, classifications based on language and culture do not need at all to coincide with a biological classification.

If this be true, then a problem like the much discussed Aryan problem really does not exist, because the problem is primarily a linguistic one, relating to the history of the Aryan languages; and the assumption that a certain definite people whose members have always been related by blood must have been the carriers of this language throughout history; and the other assumption, that a certain cultural type must have always belonged to this people—are purely arbitrary ones and not in accord with the observed facts.

Hypothesis of Original Correlation of Type, Language, and Culture

Nevertheless, it must be granted, that in a theoretical consideration of the history of the types of mankind, of languages, and of cultures, we are led back to the assumption of early conditions during which each type was much more isolated from the rest of mankind than it is at the present time. For this reason, the culture and the language belonging to a single type must have been much more sharply separated from those of other types than we find them to be at the present period. It is true that such a condition has nowhere been observed; but the knowledge of historical developments almost compels us to assume its existence at a very early period in the development of mankind. If this is true, the question would arise, whether an isolated group, at an early period, was necessarily characterized by a single type, a single language, and a single culture, or whether in such a group different types, different languages, and different cultures may have been represented.

The historical development of mankind would afford a simpler and clearer picture, if we were justified in assuming that in primitive communities the three phenomena had been intimately associated. No proof, however, of such an assumption can be given. On the contrary, the present distribution of languages, as compared with the distribution of types, makes it plausible that even at the earliest times the biological units may have been wider than the linguistic units, and presumably also wider than the cultural units. I believe that it may be safely said that all over the world the biological unit is much larger than the linguistic unit: in other words, that groups of men who are so closely related in bodily appearance that we must consider them as representatives of the same variety of mankind, embrace a much larger number of individuals than the number of men speaking languages which we know to be genetically related. Examples of this kind may be given from many parts of the world. Thus, the European race—including under this term roughly all those individuals who are without hesitation classed by us as members of the white race—would include peoples speaking Indo-European, Basque, and Ural-Altaic languages. West African negroes would represent individuals of a certain negro type, but speaking the most diverse languages; and the same would be true, among Asiatic types, of Siberians; among American types, of part of the Californian Indians.

So far as our historical evidence goes, there is no reason to believe that the number of distinct languages has at any time been less than it is now. On the contrary, all our evidence goes to show that the number of apparently unrelated languages has been much greater in earlier times than at present. On the other hand, the number of types that have presumably become extinct seems to be rather small, so that there is no reason to suppose that at an early period there should have been a nearer correspondence between the number of distinct linguistic and anatomical types; and we are thus led to the conclusion that presumably, at an early time, each human type may have existed in a number of small isolated groups, each of which may have possessed a language and culture of its own.

However this may be, the probabilities are decidedly in favor of the assumption that there is no necessity to assume that originally each language and culture were confined to a single type, or that each type and culture were confined to one language: in short, that there has been at any time a close correlation between these three phenomena.

The assumption that type, language, and culture were originally closely correlated would entail the further assumption that these three traits developed approximately at the same period, and that they developed conjointly for a considerable length of time. This assumption does not seem by any means plausible. The fundamental types of man which are represented in the negroid race and in the mongoloid race must have been differentiated long before the formation of those forms of speech that are now recognized in the linguistic families of the world. I think that even the differentiation of the more important subdivisions of the great races antedates the formation of the existing linguistic families. At any rate, the biological differentiation and the formation of speech were, at this early period, subject to the same causes that are acting upon them now, and our whole experience shows that these causes act much more rapidly on language than on the human body. In this consideration lies the principal reason for the theory of lack of correlation of type and language, even during the period of formation of types and of linguistic families.

What is true of language is obviously even more true of culture. In other words, if a certain type of man migrated over a considerable area before its language assumed the form which can now be traced in related linguistic groups, and before its culture assumed the definite type the further development of which can now be recognized, there would be no possibility of ever discovering a correlation of type, language, and culture, even if it had ever existed; but it is quite possible that such correlation has really never occurred.

It is quite conceivable that a certain racial type may have scattered over a considerable area during a formative period of speech, and that the languages which developed among the various groups of this racial type came to be so different that it is now impossible to prove them to be genetically related. In the same way, new developments of culture may have taken place which are so entirely disconnected with older types that the older genetic relationships, even if they existed, can no longer be discovered.

If we adopt this point of view, and thus eliminate the hypothetical assumption of correlation between primitive type, primitive language, and primitive culture, we recognize that any attempt at classification which includes more than one of these traits can not be consistent.

It may be added that the general term "culture" which has been used here may be subdivided from a considerable number of points of view, and different results again might be expected when we consider the inventions, the types of social organization, or beliefs, as leading points of view in our classification.

Artificial Character of All Classifications of Mankind

We recognize thus that every classification of mankind must be more or less artificial, according to the point of view selected, and here, even more than in the domain of biology, we find that classification can only be a substitute for the genesis and history of the now existing types.

Thus we recognize that the essential object in comparing different types of man must be the reconstruction of the history of the development of their types, their languages, and their cultures. The history of each of these various traits is subject to a distinct set of modifying causes, and the investigation of each may be expected to contribute data toward the solution of our problem. The biological investigation may reveal the blood-relationships of types and their modifications under social and geographical environment. The linguistic investigation may disclose the history of languages, the contact of the people speaking them with other people, and the causes that led to linguistic differentiation and integration; while the history of civilization deals with the contact of a people with neighboring peoples, as well as with the history of its own achievements.

II. THE CHARACTERISTICS OF LANGUAGE

Definition of Language

The discussions of the preceding chapter have shown that a consideration of the human languages alone must not be understood to yield a history of the blood-relationships of races and of their component elements, but that all that we can hope to obtain is a clear understanding of the relationship of the languages, no matter by whom they may be spoken.

Before discussing the extent to which we may reconstruct the history of languages, it seems necessary to describe briefly the essential traits of human speech.

In our present discussion we do not deal with gesture-language or musical means of communication, but confine ourselves to the discussion of articulate speech; that is, to communication by means of groups of sounds produced by the articulating organs—the larynx, oral cavity, tongue, lips, and nose.

Character of Phonetics

Speech consists of groups of sounds produced by the articulating organs, partly noises made by opening and closing certain places in the larynx, pharynx, mouth, or nose, or by restricting certain parts of the passage of the breath; partly resonant sounds produced by the vocal chords.

Number of Sounds Unlimited

The number of sounds that may be produced in this manner is unlimited. In our own language we select only a limited number of all possible sounds; for instance, some sounds, like *p*, are produced by the closing and a sudden opening of the lips; others, like *t*, by bringing the tip of the tongue into contact with the anterior portion of the palate, by producing a closure at this point, and by suddenly expelling the air. On the other hand, a sound might be produced by placing the tip of the tongue between the lips, making a closure in this manner, and by expelling the air suddenly. This sound would to our ear partake of the character of both our *t* and our *p*, while it would correspond to neither of these. A comparison of the sounds of the well-known European languages—like English, French, and German; or even of the different dialects of the same

languages, like those of Scotch and of the various English dialects—
reveals the fact that considerable variation occurs in the manner of
producing sounds, and that each dialect has its own characteristic
phonetic system, in which each sound is nearly fixed, although subject to slight modifications which are due to accident or to the effects
of surrounding sounds.

Each Language Uses a Limited Number of Sounds

One of the most important facts relating to the phonetics of
human speech is, that every single language has a definite and
limited group of sounds, and that the number of those used in any
particular dialect is never excessively large.

It would seem that this limitation in the use of sounds is necessary in order to make possible rapid communication. If the number of sounds that are used in any particular language were unlimited, the accuracy with which the movements of the complicated
mechanism required for producing the sounds are performed would
presumably be lacking, and consequently rapidity and accuracy of
pronunciation, and with them the possibility of accurate interpretation of the sounds heard, would be difficult, or even impossible.
On the other hand, limitation of the number of sounds brings it about
that the movements required in the production of each become
automatic, that the association between the sound heard and the
muscular movements, and that between the auditory impression and
the muscular sensation of the articulation, become firmly fixed.
Thus it would seem that limited phonetic resources are necessary
for easy communication.

Alleged Lack of Differentiation of Sounds in Primitive Languages

It has been maintained that this is not a characteristic found in
more primitive types of languages, and particularly, examples of
American languages have often been brought forward to show that
the accuracy of their pronunciation is much less than that found in
the languages of the civilized world.

It would seem that this view is based largely on the fact that certain sounds that occur in American languages are interpreted by
observers sometimes as one European sound, sometimes as another.
Thus the Pawnee language contains a sound which may be heard

more or less distinctly sometimes as an *l*, sometimes an *r*, sometimes as *n*, and again as *d*, which, however, without any doubt, is throughout the same sound, although modified to a certain extent by its position in the word and by surrounding sounds. It is an exceedingly weak *r*, made by trilling with the tip of the tongue at a point a little behind the roots of the incisors, and in which the tongue hardly leaves the palate, the trill being produced by the lateral part of the tongue adjoining the tip. As soon as the trill is heard more strongly, we receive the impression of an *r*. When the lateral movement prevails and the tip of the tongue does not seem to leave the palate, the impression of an *l* is strongest, while when the trill is almost suppressed and a sudden release of the tongue from the palate takes place, the impression of the *d* is given. The impression of an *n* is produced because the sound is often accompanied by an audible breathing through the nose. This peculiar sound is, of course, entirely foreign to our phonetic system; but its variations are not greater than those of the English *r* in various combinations, as in *broth, mother, where.* The different impression is brought about by the fact that the sound, according to its prevailing character, associates itself either with our *l*, or our *r*, *n*, or *d*.

Other examples are quite common. Thus, the lower Chinook has a sound which is readily perceived as a *b*, *m*, or *w*. As a matter of fact, it is a *b* sound, produced by a very weak closure of the lips and with open nose, the breath passing weakly both through the mouth and through the nose, and accompanied by a faint intonation of the vocal chords. This sound associates itself with our *b*, which is produced by a moderately weak release of the lips; with our *m*, which is a free breath through the nose with closed lips; and with our *w*, which is a breath through the lips, which are almost closed, all accompanied by a faint intonation of the vocal chords. The association of this sound with *w*, is particularly marked when it appears in combination with a *u* vowel, which imitates the characteristic *u* tinge of our *w*. Still another example is the *b* sound, which is produced with half-closed nose by the Indians of the Strait of Fuca, in the State of Washington. In this case the characteristic trait of the sound is a semiclosure of the nose, similar to the effect produced by a cold in the head. Not less common are sounds intermediate between our vowels. Thus we seem to find in a number of Indian languages a vowel which is sometimes perceived as *o*, sometimes as *u* (continental pronunciation), and which is in reality pronounced in a position intermediate between these two sounds.

The correctness of this interpretation of Indian phonetics is perhaps best proved by the fact that observers belonging to different nationalities readily perceive the sounds in accordance with the system of sounds with which they are familiar. Often it is not difficult to recognize the nationality of a recorder from the system selected by him for the rendering of sounds.

Still another proof of the correctness of this view of Indian phonetics is given by the fact that, wherever there is a greater number of Indian sounds of a class represented by a single sound in English, our own sounds are misinterpreted in similar manner. Thus, for instance, the Indians of the North Pacific coast have a series of *l* sounds, which may be roughly compared to our sounds *tl*, *cl*, *gl*. Consequently, a word like *close* is heard by the Indians sometimes one way, sometimes another; our *cl* is for them an intermediate sound, in the same way as some Indian sounds are intermediate sounds to our ears. The alternation of the sounds is clearly an effect of perception through the medium of a foreign system of phonetics, not that of a greater variability of pronunciation than the one that is characteristic of our own sounds.

While the phonetic system of each language is limited and fixed, the sounds selected in different types of languages show great differences, and it seems necessary to compare groups of languages from the point of view of their constituent phonetic elements.

Brief Description of Phonetics

A complete discussion of this subject can not be given at this place; but a brief statement of the characteristics of articulate sounds, and the manner of rendering them by means of symbols, seems necessary.

All articulate sounds are produced by the vibrations of the articulating organs, which are set in motion by breathing. In the vast majority of cases it is the outgoing breath which causes the vibrations; while in a few languages, as in those of South Africa, the breath, while being drawn in, is used for producing the sound.

One group of sounds is produced by the vibration of the vocal chords, and is characterized by the form given to the cavities of mouth and nose. These are the vowels. When the nose is closed, we have pure vowels; when the posterior part of the nose is more or less open, more or less nasalized vowels. The character of the vowel depends upon the form given to the oral cavity. The timbre of the vowels changes according to the degree to which the larynx is raised; the epiglottis lowered or raised; the tongue retracted or brought forward and its back rounded or flattened; and the lips rounded and brought forward, or an elongated opening of the mouth produced by retracting the corners of the mouth. With open lips and the tongue and pharynx at rest, but the soft palate (velum) raised, we have the pure vowel *a*, similar to the *a* in *father*. From this sound the vowels vary in two principal directions. The one extreme is *u* (like *oo* in English *fool*), with small round opening of the protruding lips, tongue retracted, and round opening between tongue and palate, and large opening between larynx and pharynx, the larynx still being almost at rest. The transitional sounds pass through *â* (*aw* in English *law*) and *o* (as in *most*), but the range of intermediate positions is continuous. In another direction the vowels pass from *a* through *e* (*a* in English *mane*) to *i* (*ee* in *fleet*). The *i* is pronounced with extreme retraction of the corners of the mouth and elongated opening of the lips, with very narrow flat opening between tongue and palate, and the posterior part of the tongue brought forward, so that there is a wide opening in the back part of the mouth, the larynx being raised at the same time.

Variations of vowels may be produced by a different grouping of the movements of the articulating organs. Thus, when the lips are in *i* position, the tongue and pharynx and larynx in *u* position, we have the sound *ü*, which is connected with the *a* by a series passing through *ö*. These sounds are similar to the German umlaut.

Other combinations of positions of the tongue and of the lips occur, although the ones here described seem to be the most frequent vowel-sounds. All vowels may become very much weakened in strength of articulation, and dwindle down to a slight intonation of the vocal chords, although retaining the peculiar vowel timbre, which depends upon the position of mouth, nose, and lips. When this articulation becomes very weak, all the vowels tend to become quite similar in character, or may be influenced in their timbre by neighboring consonants, as will be described later.

All sounds produced by vibrations in any part of the articulating organs other than the vocal chords are consonants. These vibrations may be produced either by closing the air-passages completely and then suddenly opening the closure, or by producing a narrowing or stricture at any point. The former series of sounds are called "stops" (like our *p, t, k*). In all of these there is a complete closure before the air is expelled. The latter are called "spirants" or "continued" (like our *s* and *f*), in which there is a continuous escape of breath. When a stop is made and is followed by a breathing through a stricture at the same place, sounds develop like our *ts*. These are called "affricatives." When the mouth is completely stopped, and the air escapes through the nose, the sound is called a "nasal consonant" (like our *m* and *n*). There may also be stricture and nasal opening. A rapidly repeated series of stops, a trill, is represented by our *r*. The character of the sound depends largely upon the parts of the articulating organs that produce the closure or stricture, and upon the place where these occur. Closure or stricture may be made by the lips, lips and tongue, lips and teeth, tongue and teeth, tongue and hard palate, tongue and soft palate (velum), by the vocal chords, and in the nose.

In the following table, only the principal groups of consonants are described. Rare sounds are omitted. According to what has been said before, it will be recognized that here also the total number of possible sounds is infinitely large.

Bilabial stop . . . . p
Linguo-palatal stops:
    Apical (dental, alveolar, post-alveolar) . . . t
    Cerebral (produced with the tip of the tongue
      turned backward) . . . . t
    Dorsal:
      Anterior palatal . . . . k·
      Medial . . . . k
      Velar . . . . q
Glottal (a stop produced with the vocal chords) . . ε
Nasal . . . . N

Almost all these stops may be modified by giving to the closure a different degree of stress. In English we have two principal degrees of stress, represented, for instance, by our *b* and *p* or *d* and *t*. In many languages, as, for instance, in Sioux and in the languages of the Pacific coast, there are three degrees of stress that may be readily differentiated. The strongest of these we call the "fortis," and indicate it by following the consonant by an ! (*p!*, *t!*).

When these stops are not accompanied by any kind of vibration of the vocal chords, they are called "surds."

It is, of course, also possible that more than one stop may be made at one time. Thus it might be possible to close at the same time the lips and the posterior part of the mouth with the tongue. This type of combination is, however, rare; but we find very frequently articulation of the vocal chords with stops. This results in the voiced consonants, or sonants. In English we find that almost always the stress of articulation of the voiced sound is less than the stress of articulation of the unvoiced sound, or surd; but this correlation is not necessary. In American languages particularly, we find very commonly the same degree of stress used with voicing and without voicing, which brings it about that to the European ear the surd and sonant are difficult to distinguish.

A third modification of the consonants is brought about by the strength of breathing accompanying the release of the closure. In a sound like *t*, for instance, the sound may be simply produced by closing the mouth, by laying the tip of the tongue firmly against the palate, producing a slightly increased amount of air-pressure behind the tongue, and then releasing the closure. On the other hand, the sound may be produced by bringing about the closure and combining the release with the expiration of a full breath. Sounds which are accompanied by this full breathing may be called "aspirates," and we will designate the aspiration by ʽ, the symbol of the Greek spiritus asper. This full breathing may follow the stop, or may begin even before the completion of the closure. With the increased stress of closure of the fortis is connected a closure of the glottis or of the posterior part of the tongue, so that only the air that has been poured into the vocal cavity is expelled.

In the case of voiced consonants, the voicing may either be entirely synchronous with the consonant, or it may slightly precede or follow it. In both of these cases we may get the impression of a preceding or following exceedingly weak vowel, the timbre of which will depend essentially upon the accompanying consonant. When the timbre is very indefinite, we write this vowel *E;* when it is more definite, *A*, *I*, *O*, *U*, etc. In other cases, where the release at the closure is made without a full breath going out, and simply by compressing the air slightly in the space behind the closure, a break is very liable to originate between the stop and the following sound of the word. Such a hiatus in the word is indicated by an apostrophe ('). It seems likely that, where such a hiatus occurs following a vowel, it is generally due to a closing of the glottis.

Most of the phenomena here described may also occur with the spirants and nasals, which, however, do not seem to differ so much in regard to strength; while the character of the outgoing breath, the voicing and the breaking-off, show traits similar to those observed among the stops.

All the stops may be changed into nasals by letting the air escape through the nose while the closure is continued. In this manner originate our n and m. The nasal opening may also differ in width, and the stricture of the upper nares may produce semi-nasalized consonants.

In the spirant sounds before described, the escape of the air is along the middle line of the palate. There are a number of other sounds in which the air escapes laterally. These are represented by our l. They also may vary considerably, according to the place and form of the opening through which the air escapes and the form of closure of the mouth.

It seems that the peculiar timbre of some of the consonants depends also upon the resonance of the oral opening. This seems to be particularly the case in regard to the t and k sounds. In pronouncing the t sounds, one of the essential characteristics seems to be that the posterior part of the mouth is open, while the anterior portion of the mouth is filled by the tongue. In the k series, on the other hand, the posterior portion of the mouth is filled by the tongue, while the anterior portion remains open. Sounds produced with both the posterior and anterior portion of the mouth open partake of the character of both the k and t series.[1]

Two of the vowels show a close affiliation to consonants of the continuant series. These are i and u, owing largely to the fact that in i the position of the tongue is very nearly a stricture in the anterior portion of the mouth, while in u the position of the lips is quite near to a stricture. Thus originate the semi-vowels y and w. The last sound that must be mentioned is the free breathing h, which, in its

---

[1] See P. W. Schmidt, Anthropos, II, 834.

most characteristic form, is produced by the expiration of the breath with all the articulating organs at rest.

In tabular form we obtain thus the following series of the most important consonantic sounds:

	Stops.			Spirants.		Nasals.		Trill.	
	Sonant.	Surd.	Fortis.	Sonant.	Surd.	Sonant.	Surd.	Sonant.	Surd.
Bilabial...........	b	p	p!	v	f	m	m̥	....	....
Labio-dental......	....	....	....	v	f	....	....	....	....
Linguo-labial	d	t	t!	ç	¢	n	ṇ	....	....
Linguo-dental.....	d	t	t!	ç	¢	n	ṇ	....	....
Dental...........	....	....	....	j	c	....	....	....	....
Lingual—									
Apical .... Cerebral.......	d	t	t!	z	ş	n	ṇ	r	ɽ
Dorsal—									
Medial....	ɟ	k	k!	γ	x̣	ñ	ŋ̊	r	ɽ
Velar.....	g	q	q!	ɣ	x	ñ̄	ŋ̃̊	ɽ	R
Lateral.......	ʎ	L	L!	l	ɫ	....	....	....	....
Glottal...........	ɛ	....	....	....	....	....	....	....	....
Nasal.............	N	....	....	....	....	....	....	....	....

Semi-vowels y, w.   Breath, 'h.   Hiatus '.

The vocalic tinge of consonants is expressed by superior vowels following them: ^{a} ^{e} ^{i} ^{o} ^{u}. The series of affricatives which begin with a stop and end with a continued sound have been omitted from this table.

It will be noticed that in the preceding table the same symbols are used in several columns. This is done, because, ordinarily, only one, or at most two, series of these groups occur in one language, so that these differences can be expressed in each special case by diacritical marks. Attempts have been made by other authors to give a general system of sound representation. For any particular language, these are liable to become cumbersome, and are therefore not used in the sketches contained in this volume.

Unconsciousness of Phonetic Elements

In the preceding pages we have briefly discussed the results of an analysis of the phonetic elements of human speech. It must, however, be remembered that the single sound as such has no independent existence, that it never enters into the consciousness of the speaker, but that it exists only as a part of a sound-complex which conveys a definite meaning. This will be easily recognized, if we consider for a moment grammatical forms in the English language in which the modification of the idea is expressed by a single sound. In the word *hills,* the terminal *s* does not enter our consciousness as a separate element with separate significance, expressing the idea of plurality,—except, perhaps, in so far as our grammatical training has taught us the fact that plurals may be formed by the use of a terminal *s,*—but the word forms a firm unit, which conveys a meaning only as a whole. The variety of uses of the terminal *s* as a plural, possessive, and third person singular of the verb, and the strong effort required to recognize the phonetic identity of these terminal elements, may be adduced as a further proof of the fact that the single phonetic elements become conscious to us only as a result of analysis. A comparison of words that differ only in a single sound, like *mail* and *nail, snake* and *stake,* makes it also clear that the isolation of sounds is a result of secondary analysis.

Grammatical Categories

Differences in Categories of Different Languages

In all articulate speech the groups of sounds which are uttered serve to convey ideas, and each group of sounds has a fixed meaning. Languages differ not only in the character of their constituent phonetic elements and sound-clusters, but also in the groups of ideas that find expression in fixed phonetic groups.

Limitation of the Number of Phonetic Groups Expressing Ideas

The total number of possible combinations of phonetic elements is also unlimited; but only a limited number are used to express ideas. This implies that the total number of ideas that are expressed by distinct phonetic groups is limited in number.

Since the total range of personal experience which language serves to express is infinitely varied, and its whole scope must be expressed by a limited number of phonetic groups, it is obvious that an extended classification of experiences must underlie all articulate speech.

This coincides with a fundamental trait of human thought. In our actual experience no two sense-impressions or emotional states are identical. Nevertheless we classify them, according to their similarities, in wider or narrower groups the limits of which may be determined from a variety of points of view. Notwithstanding their individual differences, we recognize in our experiences common elements, and consider them as related or even as the same, provided a sufficient number of characteristic traits belong to them in common. Thus the limitation of the number of phonetic groups expressing distinct ideas is an expression of the psychological fact that many different individual experiences appear to us as representatives of the same category of thought.

This trait of human thought and speech may be compared in a certain manner to the limitation of the whole series of possible articulating movements by selection of a limited number of habitual movements. If the whole mass of concepts, with all their variants, were expressed in language by entirely heterogeneous and unrelated sound-complexes, a condition would arise in which closely related ideas would not show their relationship by the corresponding relationship of their phonetic symbols, and an infinitely large number of distinct phonetic groups would be required for expression. If this were the case, the association between an idea and its representative sound-complex would not become sufficiently stable to be reproduced automatically without reflection at any given moment. As the automatic and rapid use of articulations has brought it about that a limited number of articulations only, each with limited variability, and a limited number of sound-clusters, have been selected from the infinitely large range of possible articulations and clusters of articulations, so the infinitely large number of ideas have been reduced by classification to a lesser number, which by constant use have established firm associations, and which can be used automatically.

It seems important at this point of our considerations to emphasize the fact that the groups of ideas expressed by specific phonetic groups show very material differences in different languages, and do not conform by any means to the same principles of classification. To take again the example of English, we find that the idea of WATER is expressed in a great variety of forms: one term serves to express water as a LIQUID; another one, water in the form of a large expanse (LAKE); others, water as running in a large body or in a small body (RIVER and BROOK); still other terms express water in the form of RAIN, DEW, WAVE, and FOAM. It is perfectly conceivable that this variety of ideas, each of which is expressed by a single independent term in English, might be expressed in other languages by derivations from the same term.

Another example of the same kind, the words for SNOW in Eskimo, may be given. Here we find one word, *aput*, expressing SNOW ON

THE GROUND; another one, *qana*, FALLING SNOW; a third one, *piq-sirpoq*, DRIFTING SNOW; and a fourth one, *qimuqsuq*, A SNOWDRIFT.

In the same language the SEAL in different conditions is expressed by a variety of terms. One word is the general term for SEAL; another one signifies the SEAL BASKING IN THE SUN; a third one, a SEAL FLOATING ON A PIECE OF ICE; not to mention the many names for the seals of different ages and for male and female.

As an example of the manner in which terms that we express by independent words are grouped together under one concept, the Dakota language may be selected. The terms *naxta'ka* TO KICK, *paxta'ka* TO BIND IN BUNDLES, *yaxta'ka* TO BITE, *ic'a'xtaka* TO BE NEAR TO, *boxta'ka* TO POUND, are all derived from the common element *xtaka* TO GRIP, which holds them together, while we use distinct words for expressing the various ideas.

It seems fairly evident that the selection of such simple terms must to a certain extent depend upon the chief interests of a people; and where it is necessary to distinguish a certain phenomenon in many aspects, which in the life of the people play each an entirely independent rôle, many independent words may develop, while in other cases modifications of a single term may suffice.

Thus it happens that each language, from the point of view of another language, may be arbitrary in its classifications; that what appears as a single simple idea in one language may be characterized by a series of distinct phonetic groups in another.

The tendency of a language to express a complex idea by a single term has been styled "holophrasis," and it appears therefore that every language may be holophrastic from the point of view of another language. Holophrasis can hardly be taken as a fundamental characteristic of primitive languages.

We have seen before that some kind of classification of expression must be found in every language. This classification of ideas into groups, each of which is expressed by an independent phonetic group, makes it necessary that concepts which are not readily rendered by a single one among the available sound-complexes should be expressed by combinations or by modifications of what might be called the elementary phonetic groups, in accordance with the elementary ideas to which the particular idea is reduced.

This classification, and the necessity of expressing certain experiences by means of other related ones, which by limiting one another define the special idea to be expressed, entail the presence of certain formal elements which determine the relations of the single phonetic groups. If each idea could be expressed by a single phonetic group, languages without form would be possible. Since, however, ideas must be expressed by being reduced to a number of related ideas, the kinds of relation become important elements in articulate speech; and it follows that all languages must contain formal elements, and that their number must be the greater, the fewer the elementary phonetic groups that define special ideas. In a language which commands a very large, fixed vocabulary, the number of formal elements may become quite small.

Grammatical Processes

It is important to note that, in the languages of the world, the number of processes which are utilized to express the relations of terms is limited. Presumably this is due to the general characteristics of articulate speech. The only methods that are available for expressing the relations between definite phonetic groups are their composition in definite order, which may be combined with a mutual phonetic influence of the component elements upon one another, and inner modification of the phonetic groups themselves. Both these methods are found in a great many languages, but sometimes only the method of composition occurs.

Word and Sentence

In order to understand the significance of the ideas expressed by independent phonetic groups and of the elements expressing their mutual relations, we have to discuss here the question, What forms the unit of speech? It has been pointed out before that the phonetic elements as such can be isolated only by analysis, and that they occur in speech only in combinations which are the equivalents of definite concepts.

Since all speech is intended to serve for the communication of ideas, the natural unit of expression is the sentence; that is to say, a group of articulate sounds which convey a complete idea. It might seem that speech can readily be further subdivided, and that the word also forms a natural unit from which the sentence is built up. In most cases, however, it is easy to show that such is not the case, and that the word as such is known only by analysis. This is particularly clear in the case of words like prepositions, conjunctions, or verbal forms which belong to subordinate clauses. Thus it would be exceedingly difficult to imagine the use of words like *and, for, to, were,* expressed in such a way that they would convey a clear idea, except perhaps in forms like the Laconic *If,* in which all the rest of the sentence is implied, and sufficiently indicated by the *if.* In the same way, however, we who are grammatically trained may use a simple ending to correct an idea previously expressed. Thus the statement *He sings beautifully* might elicit a reply, *sang;* or a laconically inclined person might even remark, in reply to the statement *He plays well, -ed,* which by his friends might be well understood. It is clear that in all these cases the single elements are isolated by a secondary process from the complete unit of the sentence.

Less clear appears the artificiality of the word as a unit in those cases in which the word seems to designate a concept that stands out clearly from others. Such is the case, for instance, with nouns; and it might seem that a word like *stone* is a natural unit. Nevertheless it will be recognized that the word *stone* alone conveys at most an objective picture, not a complete idea.

Thus we are led to the important question of the relation of the word to the sentence. Basing our considerations on languages differing fundamentally in form, it would seem that we may define the word as *a phonetic group which, owing to its permanence of form, clearness of significance, and phonetic independence, is readily separated from the whole sentence.* This definition obviously contains a considerable number of arbitrary elements, which may induce us, according to the general point of view taken, sometimes to designate a certain unit as a word, sometimes to deny its independent existence. We shall see later on, in the discussion of American languages, that this practical difficulty confronts us many times, and that it is not possible to decide with objective certainty whether it is justifiable to consider a certain phonetic group as an independent word or as a subordinate part of a word.

Nevertheless there are certain elements contained in our definition which seem to be essential for the interpretation of a sound-complex as an independent word. From the point of view of grammatical form, the least important; from the point of view of phonetics, however, the most fundamental, is the phonetic independence of the element in question. It has been pointed out before how difficult it is to conceive the independence of the English *s*, which expresses the plural, the possessive, and the third person singular of the verb. This is largely due to the phonetic weakness of this grammatical element. If the idea of plurality were expressed by an element as strong phonetically as the word *many;* the possessive part of the word, by an element as strong as the preposition *of;* and the third person singular, by an element like *he*—we might, perhaps, be much more ready to recognize the character of these elements as independent words, and we actually do so. For example, *stones, John's, loves*, are single words; while *many sheep, of stone, he went*, are each considered as two words. Difficulties of this kind are met with constantly in American languages. Thus we find in a language like the Chinook that modifying elements are expressed by single sounds which phonetically enter into clusters which are pronounced without any break. To give an example: The word *aniā'lōt* I GIVE HIM TO HER may be analyzed into the following elements: *a* (tense), *n* I, *i* HIM, *a* HER, *l* TO, *ō* (direction away), *t* TO GIVE. Here, again, the weakness of the component elements and their close phonetic association forbid us to consider them independent words; while the whole expression appears to us as a firm unit.

Whenever we are guided by this principle alone, the limitation of the word unit appears naturally exceedingly uncertain, on account of the difference in impression of the phonetic strength of the component elements.

It also happens that certain elements appear sometimes with such phonetic weakness that they can not possibly be considered as independent units of the sentence, while closely related forms, or even the same forms in other combinations, may gain the strength which they are lacking in other cases. As an example of this kind may be given the Kwakiutl, in which many of the pronominal forms appear as exceedingly weak phonetic elements. Thus the expression HE STRIKES HIM WITH IT is rendered by *mîx·ᵉī'dᴇqs*, in which the two terminal elements mean: *q* HIM, *s* WITH IT. When, however, substantives are introduced in this expression for object and instrument, the *q* assumes the fuller form *xa*, and the *s* the fuller form *sa*, which we might quite readily write as independent words analogous to our articles.

I doubt very much whether an investigator who would record French in the same way as we do the unwritten American languages would be inclined to write the pronominal elements which enter into the transitive verb as independent words, at least not when recording the indicative forms of a positive verb. He might be induced to do so on discovering their freedom of position which appears in the negative and in some interrogative forms.

The determining influence of the freedom of position of a phonetically fixed part of the sentence makes it necessary to include it in our definition of the word.

Whenever a certain phonetic group appears in a variety of positions in a sentence, and always in the same form, without any, or at least without material, modifications, we readily recognize its individuality, and in an analysis of the language we are inclined to consider it as a separate word. These conditions are fully realized only in cases in which the sound-complex in question shows no modifications at all.

It may, however, happen that minor modifications occur, particularly at the beginning and at the end, which we may be ready to disregard on account of their slight significance as compared to the permanence of the whole word. Such is the case, for instance, in the Dakota language, in which the terminal sound of a permanent word-complex which has a clearly defined significance will automatically modify the first sound of the following word-complex which has the same characteristics of permanence. The reverse may also occur. Strictly speaking, the line of demarcation between what we should commonly call two words is lost in this case; but the mutual influence of the two words in connection is, comparatively speaking, so slight that the concept of the individuality of the word outweighs their organic connection.

In other cases, where the organic connection becomes so firm that either both or one of the component elements may never occur without signs marking their close coupling, they will appear to us as a single unit. As an example of this condition may be mentioned the Eskimo. This language contains a great many elements which are quite clear in their significance and strong in phonetic character, but which in their position are so limited that they always follow other definite parts of the sentence, that they can never form the beginning of a complete phonetic group, and that the preceding phonetic group loses its more permanent phonetic form whenever they appear added to it. To give an example: *takuvoq* means HE SEES; *takulerpoq* means HE BEGINS TO SEE. In the second form the idea of seeing is contained in the element *taku-*, which by itself is incomplete. The following element, *-ler*, can never begin a sentence, and attains the significance of BEGINNING only in connection with a preceding phonetic group, the terminal sound of which is to a certain extent determined by it. In its turn, it requires an ending, which expresses, in the example here selected, the third person singular, *-poq;* while the word expressing the idea of SEEING requires the ending *-voq* for the same person. These also can not possibly begin a sentence, and their initial sounds, *v* and *p*, are determined solely by the terminal sounds of the preceding elements. Thus it will be seen that this group of sound-complexes forms a firm unit, held together by the formal incompleteness of each part and their far-reaching phonetic influences upon one another. It would seem that, in a language in which the elements are so firmly knit together as in Eskimo, there could not be the slightest doubt as to what constitutes the word in our ordinary sense of the term. The same is true in many cases in Iroquois, a language in which conditions quite similar to those in the Eskimo prevail. Here an example may be given from the Oneida dialect. *Watgajijanegale* THE FLOWER BREAKS OPEN consists of the formal elements *wa-*, *-t-*, and *-g-*, which are temporal, modal, and pronominal in character; the vowel *-a-*, which is the character of the stem *-jija* FLOWER, which never occurs alone; and the stem *-negale* TO BREAK OPEN, which also has no independent existence.

In all these cases the elements possess great clearness of significance, but the lack of permanence of form compels us to consider them as parts of a longer word.

While in some languages this gives us the impression of an adequate criterion for the separation of words, there are other cases in which certain parts of the sentence may be thus isolated, while the others retain their independent form. In American languages this is particularly the case when nouns enter the verbal complex without any modification of their component elements. This is the case, for instance, in Pawnee: *tā'tuk^{u}t* I HAVE CUT IT FOR THEE, and *rīks* ARROW, combine into *tatū'riksk^{u}t* I CUT THY ARROW. The closeness of connection of these forms is even clearer in cases in which far-reaching phonetic modifications occur. Thus the elements *ta-t-ru^{ɛ}n* combine into *ta'hu^{ɛ}n* I MAKE (because *tr* in a word changes to *h*); and *ta-t-rīks-ru^{ɛ}n* becomes *tahīkstu^{ɛ}n* I MAKE AN ARROW (because *r* after *s* changes to *t*). At the same time *rīks* ARROW occurs as an independent word.

If we follow the principle laid down in the preceding remarks, it will readily be seen that the same element may appear at one time as an independent noun, then again as a part of a word, the rest of which has all the characteristics before described, and which for this reason we are not inclined to consider as a complex of independent elements.

Ambiguity in regard to the independence of parts of the sentence may also arise either when in their significance they become dependent upon other parts of the sentence, or when their meaning is so vague and weak as compared to the other parts of the sentence that we are led to regard them as subordinate parts. Words of this kind, when phonetically strong, will generally be considered as independent particles; when, on the other hand, they are phonetically weak, they will generally be considered as modifying parts of other words. A good example of this kind is contained in the Ponca texts by the Rev. James Owen Dorsey,[1] in which the same elements are often treated as independent particles, while in other cases they appear as subordinate parts of words. Thus we find *ɸéama* THESE (p. 23, line 17), but *jábe amá* THE BEAVER (p. 553, line 7).

The same is true in regard to the treatment of the grammar of the Sioux by the Rev. S. R. Riggs. We find in this case, for instance, the element *pi* always treated as the ending of a word, probably owing to the fact that it represents the plural, which in the Indo-European languages is almost always expressed by a modification of the word to which it applies. On the other hand, elements like *kta* and *śni*, signifying the future and negation respectively, are treated as independent words, although they appear in exactly the same form as the *pi* mentioned before.

Other examples of this kind are the modifying elements in Tsimshian, a language in which innumerable adverbial elements are expressed by fairly weak phonetic groups which have a definite position. Here, also, it seems entirely arbitrary whether these phonetic groups are considered as separate words, or whether they

---

[1] Contributions to North American Ethnology, VI.

are combined with the verbal expressions into a single word. In these cases the independent existence of the word to which such particles are joined without any modification will generally determine us to consider these elements as independent particles, provided they are phonetically strong enough; while whenever the verbal expression to which they are joined is modified either by the insertion of these elements between its component parts, or in some other way, we are inclined to consider them as parts of the word.

It seemed important to discuss somewhat fully the concept of the word in its relation to the whole sentence, because in the morphological treatment of American languages this question plays an important rôle.

Stem and Affix

The analytic treatment of languages results in the separation of a number of different groups of the elements of speech. When we arrange these according to their functions, it appears that certain elements recur in every single sentence. These are, for instance, the forms indicating subject and predicate, or, in modern European languages, forms indicating number, tense, and person. Others, like terms expressing demonstrative ideas, may or may not occur in a sentence. These and many others are treated in our grammars. According to the character of these elements, they seem to modify the material contents of the sentence; as, for instance, in the English sentences *he strikes him*, and *I struck thee*, where the idea of striking somebody appears as the content of the communication; while the ideas *he, present, him*, and *I, past, thee*, appear as modifications.

It is of fundamental importance to note that this separation of the ideas contained in a sentence into material contents and formal modifications is an arbitrary one, brought about, presumably, first of of all, by the great variety of ideas which may be expressed in the same formal manner by the same pronominal and tense elements. In other words, the material contents of the sentence may be represented by subjects and predicates expressing an unlimited number of ideas, while the modifying elements—here the pronouns and tenses—comprise, comparatively speaking, a very small number of ideas. In the discussion of a language, the parts expressing the material contents of sentences appear to us as the subject-matter of lexicography; parts expressing the modifying relations, as the subject-matter of grammar. In modern Indo-European languages the number of ideas which are expressed by subordinate elements is, on the whole, limited, and for this reason the dividing-line between grammar and dictionary appears perfectly clear and well drawn. In a wider sense, however, all etymological processes and word compositions must be considered as parts of the grammar; and, if we include those, we find that, even in Indo-European languages, the number of classifying ideas is quite large.

In American languages the distinction between grammar and lexicography often becomes quite obscure, owing to the fact that the number of elements which enter into formal compositions becomes very large. It seems necessary to explain this somewhat more fully by examples. In the Tsimshian language we find a very great number of adverbial elements which can not be considered as entirely independent, and which, without doubt, must be considered as elements modifying verbal ideas. On account of the very large number of these elements, the total number of verbs of motion seems to be somewhat restricted, although the total number of verbs that may be combined with these adverbial ideas is much larger than the total number of the adverbial ideas themselves. Thus, the number of adverbs appears to be fixed, while the number of verbs appears unlimited; and consequently we have the impression that the former are modifying elements, and that their discussion belongs to the grammar of the language, while the latter are words, and their discussion belongs to the lexicography of the language. The number of such modifying elements in Eskimo is even larger; and here the impression that the discussion of these elements belongs to the grammar of the language is increased by the fact that they can never take an initial position, and that they are not placed following a complete word, but are added to an element which, if pronounced by itself, would not give any sense.

Now, it is important to note that, in a number of languages, the number of the modifying elements may increase so much that it may become doubtful which element represents a series of ideas limited in number, and which represents an almost unlimited series of words belonging to the vocabulary. This is true, for instance, in Algonquian, where in almost all verbs several elements appear in conjunction, each in a definite position, but each group so numerous that it would be entirely arbitrary to designate the one group as words modified by the other group, or vice versa.

The importance of this consideration for our purposes lies in the fact that it illustrates the lack of definiteness of the terms *stem* and *affix*. According to the ordinary terminology, affixes are elements attached to stems or words, and modifying them. This definition is perfectly acceptable as long as the number of modifying ideas is limited. When, however, the number of modifying elements becomes exceedingly large, we may well doubt which of the two is the modifier and which the modified, and the determination finally becomes entirely arbitrary. In the following discussions the attempt has been made to confine the terms *prefix*, *suffix*, and *affix* entirely to those cases where the number of ideas expressed by these elements is strictly limited. Wherever the number of combined elements becomes so large that they can not be properly classified, these terms have not been used, but the elements have been treated as co-ordinate.

Discussion of Grammatical Categories

From what has been said it appears that, in an objective discussion of languages, three points have to be considered: first, the constituent phonetic elements of the language; second, the groups of ideas expressed by phonetic groups; third, the methods of combining and modifying phonetic groups.

It seems desirable to discuss the second of these points somewhat more fully before taking up the description of the characteristics of American languages.

Grammarians who have studied the languages of Europe and western Asia have developed a system of categories which we are inclined to look for in every language. It seems desirable to show here in how far the system with which we are familiar is characteristic only of certain groups of languages, and in how far other systems may be substituted for it. It seems easiest to illustrate this matter by discussing first some of the characteristics of the Indo-European noun, pronoun, and verb, and then by taking up the wider aspects of this subject.

Nominal Categories

In the treatment of our noun we are accustomed to look for a number of fundamental categories. In most Indo-European languages, nouns are classified according to gender, they are modified by forms expressing singular and plural, and they also appear in syntactic combinations as cases. None of these apparently fundamental aspects of the noun are necessary elements of articulate speech.

GENDER

The history of the English language shows clearly that the gender of a noun may practically be suppressed without interfering with the clearness of expression. While we still find traces of gender in English, practically all inanimate objects have come to belong to one single gender. It is interesting to note that, in the languages of the world, gender is not by any means a fundamental category, and that nouns may not be divided into classes at all, or the point of view of classification may be an entirely different one. Thus the Bantu languages of Africa classify words into a great many distinct groups the significance of most of which is not by any means clear. The Algonquian of North America classify nouns as animate and inanimate, without, however, adhering strictly to the natural classification implied in these terms. Thus the small animals may be classified as inanimate, while certain plants may appear as animate. Some of the Siouan languages classify nouns by means of articles, and strict distinctions are made between animate moving and animate at rest, inanimate long, inanimate round, inanimate high, and inanimate collective objects. The Iroquois distinguish strictly between nouns designating men and other nouns. The latter may again be subdivided into a definite and indefinite group. The Uchee distinguish between members of the tribe and other human beings. In America, true gender is on the whole rare; it is found, perhaps, among a few of the languages of the lower Mississippi; it occurs in the same way as in most Indo-European languages in the Chinook of Columbia river, and to a more limited extent among some of the languages of the state of Washington and of British Columbia. Among North American languages, the Eskimo and Athapascan have no trace of a classification of nouns. The examples here given show clearly that the sex principle, which underlies the classification of nouns in European languages, is merely one of a great many possible classifications of this kind.

PLURAL

Of a somewhat different character is the plural of Indo-European nouns. Because, for the purpose of clear expression, each noun must be expressed either as a singular or as a plural, it might seem that this classification is almost indispensable; but it is not difficult to show, by means of sentences, that, even in English, the distinction is not always made. For instance, in the sentence *The wolf has devoured the sheep*, it is not clear whether a single sheep is meant, or a plurality of sheep are referred to. Nevertheless, this would not, on the whole, be felt as an inconvenience, since either the context would show whether singular or plural is meant, or an added adjective would give the desired information.

While, according to the structure of our European languages, we always tend to look for the expression of singularity or plurality for the sake of clearness of expression, there are other languages that are entirely indifferent towards this distinction. A good example of this kind is the Kwakiutl. It is entirely immaterial to the Kwakiutl whether he says, *There is a house* or *There are houses*. The same form is used for expressing both ideas, and the idea of singularity and plurality must be understood either by the context or by the addition of a special adjective. Similar conditions prevail in the Athapascan languages and in Haida. In Siouan, also, a distinction between singularity and plurality is made only in the case of animate objects. It would seem that, on the whole, American languages are rather indifferent in regard to the clear expression of plurality, but that they tend to express much more rigidly the ideas of collectivity or distribution. Thus the Kwakiutl, who are rather indifferent to the expression of plurality, are very particular in denoting whether the objects spoken of are distributed here or there. When this is the case, the distribution is carefully expressed. In the same way, when speaking of fish, they express by the same term a single fish and a quantity of fish. When, however, they desire to say that these fish belong to different species, a distributive

form expressing this idea is made use of. A similar indifference to
the idea of singular and plural may be observed in the pronouns of
several languages, and will be noted later on.

On the other hand, the idea of number may be much more strongly
emphasized than it is in the modern languages of Europe. The dual,
as in Greek, is of common occurrence the world over; but it happens
also that a trialis and paucalis—expressions for *three* and *a few*—are
distinguished.

CASE

What is true of number is no less true of case. Psychologically,
the substitution of prepositional expressions for cases would hardly
represent a complete absence of the concept of cases. This is rather
found in those languages in which the whole group of relations of the
nouns of a sentence is expressed in the verb. When, for instance, in
Chinook, we find expressions like *he her it with cut, man, woman,
knife*, meaning *The man cut the woman with the knife*, we may safely
say that the nouns themselves appear without any trace of case-
relationship, merely as appositions to a number of pronouns. It is
true that in this case a distinction is made in the pronoun between
subject and object, and that, in this sense, cases are found, although
not as nominal cases, but still as pronominal cases. The case-
relation, however, is confined to the two forms of subject and
object, since the oblique cases are expressed by pronominal objects,
while the characteristic of each particular oblique relation is
expressed by adverbial elements. In the same language, the genitive
relation is eliminated by substituting for it possessive expressions,
like, for instance, *the man, his house*, instead of *the man's house*.
While, therefore, case-expressions are not entirely eliminated, their
number, which in some European languages is considerable, may be
largely reduced.

Thus we find that some of our nominal categories either do not
occur at all, or occur only in very much reduced forms. On the other
hand, we must recognize that other new categories may occur which
are entirely foreign to our European languages. Classifications like
those referred to before—such as animate and inanimate, or of nouns
designating men, and other nouns; and, further, of nouns according
to form—are rather foreign to us, although, in the connection of verb

and noun, form-classifications occur. Thus we do not say, *a tree is somewhere*, but *a tree stands;* not, *the river is in New York*, but *the river flows through New York*.

TENSE

Tense classes of nouns are not rare in American languages. As we may speak of *a future husband* or of *our late friend*, thus many Indian languages express in every noun its existence in presence, past, or future, which they require as much for clearness of expression as we require the distinction of singular and plural.

Personal Pronouns

The same lack of conformity in the principles of classification may be found in the pronouns. We are accustomed to speak of three persons of the pronoun, which occur both in the singular and in the plural. Although we make a distinction of gender for the third person of the pronoun, we do not carry out this principle of classification consistently in the other persons. The first and second persons and the third person plural have the same form for masculine, feminine, and neuter. A more rigid application of the sex system is made, for instance, in the language of the Hottentots of South Africa, in which sex is distinguished, not only in the third person, but also in the first and second persons.

Logically, our three persons of the pronoun are based on the two concepts of self and not-self, the second of which is subdivided, according to the needs of speech, into the two concepts of person addressed and person spoken of. When, therefore, we speak of a first person plural, we mean logically either self and person addressed, or self and person or persons spoken of, or, finally, self, person or persons addressed, and person or persons spoken of. A true first person plural is impossible, because there can never be more than one self. This logical laxity is avoided by many languages, in which a sharp distinction is made between the two combinations self and person or persons spoken to, or self and person or persons spoken of. I do not know of any language expressing in a separate form the combination of the three persons, probably because this idea readily coalesces with the idea of self and persons spoken to. These two forms are generally designated by the rather inaccurate term of "inclusive" and "exclusive first person plural," by which is meant the first person plural, including or excluding the person addressed. The second and third persons form true plurals.. Thus the principle of division of the pronouns is carried through in many languages more rigidly than we find it in the European group.

On the other hand, the lack of clear distinction between singular and plural may be observed also in the pronominal forms of a number of languages. Thus the Sioux do not know any pronominal distinction between the singular and plural of the second person, and only a very imperfect distinction between the third person singular and plural; while the first person singular and plural, according to the fundamental difference in their significance, are sharply distinguished. In some Siouan dialects we may well say that the pronominal object has only a first person singular, first person plural, and a second person, and that no other pronoun for the object occurs. Thus the system of pronouns may be reduced to a mere fragment of what we are accustomed to find.

Demonstrative Pronouns

In many cases, the analogy of the personal pronouns and of the demonstrative pronouns is rigid, the demonstrative pronoun having three persons in the same way as the personal pronoun. Thus the Kwakiutl will say, *the house near me* (this house), *the house near thee* (that house), *the house near him* (that house).

But other points of view are added to the principle of division corresponding to the personal pronoun. Thus, the Kwakiutl, and many other American languages, add to the pronominal concept just discussed that of visibility and invisibility, while the Chinook add the concepts of present and past. Perhaps the most exuberant development of the demonstrative idea is found among the Eskimo, where not only the ideas corresponding to the three personal pronouns occur, but also those of position in space in relation to the speaker,—which are specified in seven directions; as, center, above, below, in front, behind, right, left,—and expressing points of the compass in relation to the position of the speaker.

It must be borne in mind that the divisions which are mentioned here are all *necessary* parts of clear expression in the languages mentioned. For instance, in Kwakiutl it would be inconceivable to use an expression like our *that house*, which means in English *the single house away from the speaker.* The Kwakiutl must express this idea in one of the following six forms:

The (singular or plural) house visible near me
invisible near me
visible near thee
invisible near thee
visible near him
invisible near him

while the Eskimo would express a term like *this man* as

This man near me
near thee
near him
behind me
in front of me
to the right of me
to the left of me
above me
below me, etc.

Verbal Categories

We can follow out similar differences in the verb. In our Indo-European languages we have expressions signifying persons, tenses, moods, and voices. The ideas represented by these groups are quite unevenly developed in various languages. In a great many cases the forms expressing the persons are expressed simply by a combination of the personal pronoun and the verb; while in other cases the phonetic complexes expressing personal relations are developed in an astonishing manner. Thus the Algonquian and the Eskimo possess special phonetic groups expressing definite relations between the subject and object which occur in transitive verbs. For example, in sentences like *I strike thee*, or *They strike me*, the combination of the pronouns *I — thee*, and *they — me*, are expressed by special phonetic equivalents. There are even cases in which the indirect objects (as in the sentence, *I send him to you*) may be expressed by a single form. The characteristic trait of the forms here referred to is, that the combined pronoun can not be reduced to its constituent elements, although historically it may have originated from combinations of separate forms. It is obvious that in cases in which the development of the pronoun is as weak as in the Siouan languages, to which I have referred before, the definiteness of the pronominal forms of the verb, to which we are accustomed, is entirely lost. Thus it happens that in the Sioux the verb alone may be used as well for the more or less abstract idea of verbal action as for the third person of the indicative.

Much more fundamental are the existing differences in regard to the occurrence of tenses and modes. We are accustomed to verbal forms in which the tense is always expressed with perfect definiteness. In the sentence *The man is sick* we really express the idea, *The single definite man is sick at the present time.* This strict expression of the time relation of the occurrence is missing in many languages. The Eskimo, for instance, in expressing the same idea, will simply say, *single man sick*, leaving the question entirely open whether the man was sick at a previous time, is sick at the present time, or is going to be sick in the future. The condition here is similar to the one described before in relation to plurality. The Eskimo can, of course, express whether the man is sick at the present time, was sick, or is going to be sick, but the grammatical form of his sentences does not *require* the expression of the tense relation. In other cases the temporal ideas may be expressed with much greater nicety than we find in our familiar grammars. Generally, languages in which a multiplicity of tenses are found include in their form of expression certain modifications of the tense concept which might be called "semi-temporal," like inchoatives, which express the beginning of an action; duratives, which express the extent of time during which the action lasts; transitionals, which express the change of one state of being into another; etc. There is very little agreement in regard to the occurrence of such tenses, and the characteristics of many languages show that tenses are not by any means required for clear expression.

What is true of tenses is also true of modes. The number of languages which get along with a single mode, or at most with the indicative and imperative, is considerable; although, in this case also, the idea of subordination may be expressed if it seems desirable to do so.

The few examples that I have given here illustrate that many of the categories which we are inclined to consider as essential may be absent in foreign languages, and that other categories may occur as substitutes.

Interpretation of Grammatical Categories

When we consider for a moment what this implies, it will be recognized that in each language only a part of the complete concept that we have in mind is expressed, and that each language has a peculiar tendency to select this or that aspect of the mental image which is conveyed by the expression of the thought. To use again the example which I mentioned before, *The man is sick.* We express by this sentence, in English, the idea, *a definite single man at present sick.* In Kwakiutl this sentence would have to be rendered by an expression which would mean, in the vaguest possible form that could be given to it, *definite man near him invisible sick near him invisible.* Visibility and nearness to the first or second person might, of course, have been selected in our example in place of invisibility and nearness to the third person. An idiomatic expression of the sentence in this language would, however, be much more definite, and would require an expression somewhat like the following, *That invisible man lies sick on his back on the floor of the absent house.* In Eskimo, on the other hand, the same idea would be expressed by a form like *(single) man sick,* leaving place and time entirely indefinite. In Ponca, one of the Siouan dialects, the same idea would require a decision of the question whether the man is at rest or moving, and we might have a form like *the moving single man sick.* If we take into consideration further traits of idiomatic expression, this example might be further expanded by adding modalities of the verb; thus the Kwakiutl, whose language I have used several times as an example, would require a form indicating whether this is a new subject introduced in conversation or not; and, in case the speaker had not seen the sick person himself, he would have to express whether he knows by hearsay or by evidence that the person is sick, or whether he has dreamed it. It seems, however, better not to complicate our present discussion by taking into consideration the possibilities of exact expression that may be required in idiomatic forms of speech, but rather to consider only those parts of the sentence which, according to the morphology of the language, *must* be expressed.

We conclude from the examples here given that in a discussion of the characteristics of various languages different fundamental categories will be found, and that in a comparison of different languages it will be necessary to compare as well the phonetic characteristics as the characteristics of the vocabulary and those of the grammatical concepts in order to give each language its proper place.

III. CLASSIFICATION OF LANGUAGES

Origin of Dialects

In many cases the determination of the genetic relationship of languages is perfectly simple. Wherever we find close similarities in phonetics, in vocabularies, and in details of grammar, there can not be the slightest doubt that the languages that are being studied are varieties of the same ancestral form.

To a certain extent the differentiation of a single language into a number of dialects is spontaneous. When communication between peoples speaking the same tongue ceases, peculiarities of pronunciation will readily manifest themselves in one region or the other and may become permanent. In some cases these modifications of pronunciation may gradually increase and may become so radical that several quite different forms of the original language develop. At the same time words readily assume a new significance, and if the separation of the people should be accompanied by a differentiation of culture, these changes may proceed at a very rapid rate.

In cases of such phonetic changes and of modifications in the significance of words, a certain degree of regularity may always be observed, and for this reason the historical relationship between the new dialects and the older forms can always be readily established and may be compared to the modifications that take place in a series of generations of living beings.

Another form of modification may occur that is also analogous to biological transformations. We must recognize that the origin of language must not be looked for in human faculties that have once been active, but which have disappeared. As a matter of fact, new additions to linguistic devices and to linguistic material are constantly being made. Such spontaneous additions to a language may occur in one of the new dialects, while they do not occur in the other. These, although related to the structure of the older language, will be so entirely new in their character that they can not be directly related to the ancestral language.

It must also be considered that each of these dialects may incorporate new material. Nevertheless in all cases where the older material constitutes the bulk of the material of the language, its close relationship to the ancestral tongue will readily be recognized. In all these cases, phonetics, details of grammatical structure, and vocabulary will show far-reaching similarities.

Comparison of Distinct Languages

The problem becomes much more difficult when the similarities in any of these traits become less pronounced. With the extension of our knowledge of primitive languages, it has been found that cases are not rare in which languages spoken in certain continuous areas show radical differences in vocabulary and in grammatical form, but close similarity in their phonetic elements. In other cases the similarity of phonetic elements may be less pronounced, but there may exist a close similarity in structural details. Again, many investigators have pointed out peculiar analogies in certain words without being able to show that grammatical form and general phonetic character coincide. Many examples of such conditions may be given. In America, for instance, the phonetic similarity of the languages spoken between the coast of Oregon and Mount St. Elias is quite striking. All these languages are characterized by the occurrence of a great many peculiar k sounds and peculiar l sounds, and by their tendency towards great stress of articulation, and, in most cases, towards a clustering of consonants. Consequently to our ear these languages sound rough and harsh. Notwithstanding these similarities, the grammatical forms and the vocabularies are so utterly distinct that a common origin of the languages of this area seems entirely out of the question. A similar example may be given from South Africa, where the Bantu negroes, Bushmen, and Hottentots utilize some peculiar sounds which are produced by inspiration— by drawing in the breath, not by expelling it—and which are ordinarily called "clicks." Notwithstanding this very peculiar common trait in their languages, there is no similarity in grammar and hardly any in vocabulary.

We might also give the example of the Siouan and the Iroquois languages of North America, two stocks that have been in proximity, and which are characterized by the occurrence of numerous nasalized vowels; or the phonetic characteristics of Californian languages, which sound to our ear euphonious, and are in strong contrast to the languages of the North Pacific coast.

It must be said that, on the whole, such phonetic characteristics of a limited area appear in their most pronounced form when we compare the whole region with the neighboring districts. They form a unit rather by contrast with foreign phonetics than when compared among themselves, each language having its own peculiar characteristics in a group of this kind. Thus, the Tlingit of the North Pacific coast differs very much from the Chinook of Columbia river. Nevertheless, when both languages are compared to a language of southern California, the Sioux or the Algonquian, traits that are common to both of them appear to quite a marked degree.

What is true of phonetics is also true of grammatical form, and this is evidently a characteristic trait of the languages of the whole world. In North America particularly such groups of languages can be readily recognized. A more detailed discussion of this problem will be given in another place, and it will be sufficient to state here, that languages—like, for instance, the Athapascan, Tlingit, and Haida—which are spoken in one continuous area on the northwest coast of our continent show certain common characteristics when compared with neighboring languages like the Eskimo, Algonquian, and Tsimshian. In a similar way, a number of Californian languages, or languages of southern British Columbia, and languages like the Pawnee and Iroquois, each form a group characterized by certain traits which are not found in other languages.

In cases where such morphological similarities occur without a corresponding similarity of vocabulary, it becomes exceedingly difficult to determine whether these languages may be considered as descendants of one parent language; and there are numerous cases in which our judgment must be suspended, because, on the one hand, these similarities are far-reaching, while, on the other hand, such radical differences are found that we can not account for them without assuming the introduction of an entirely foreign element.

Similar phenomena have recently induced P. W. Schmidt to consider the languages of Farther India and of Malaysia as related; and the same problem has been discussed by Lepsius, and again by Meinhoff, in reference to the relation of the languages of the Hottentot to a number of east African languages and to the languages of the Hamitic peoples of North Africa.

Difficulties also arise in cases where a considerable number of similar words are found without a corresponding similarity of grammatical forms, so that we may be reluctant to combine two such languages, notwithstanding their similarities of vocabulary.

The comparison of vocabularies offers peculiar difficulties in American languages. Unfortunately, our knowledge of American languages is very limited, and in many cases we are confined to collections of a few hundred words, without any information in regard to grammatical forms. Owing to the strong tendency of many American languages to form compound words or derivatives of various kinds, it is very difficult in vocabularies of this kind to recognize the component elements of words, and often accidental similarities may obtrude themselves which a thorough knowledge of the languages would prove to be of no significance whatever.

Setting aside this practical difficulty, it may happen quite often that in neighboring languages the same term is used to designate the same object, owing, not to the relationship of the languages, but to the fact that the word may be a loan word in several of them. Since the vocabularies which are ordinarily collected embrace terms for objects found in most common use, it seems most likely that among these a number of loan words may occur.

Even when the available material is fuller and more thoroughly analyzed, doubt may arise regarding the significance of the apparent similarities of vocabulary.

Mutual Influences of Languages

In all these cases the final decision will depend upon the answer to the questions in how far distinct languages may influence one another, and in how far a language without being subject to foreign influences may deviate from the parental type. While it seems that the time has hardly come when it is possible to answer these questions in a definite manner, the evidence seems to be in favor of the existence of far-reaching influences of this kind.

Phonetic Influences

This is perhaps most clearly evident in the case of phonetics. It is hardly conceivable why languages spoken in continuous areas, and entirely distinct in vocabulary and in grammatical structure, should partake of the same phonetic characteristics, unless, by imitation, certain phonetic traits may be carried beyond a single linguistic stock. While I do not know that historical evidence of such occurrences has been definitely given, the phenomenon as it occurs in South Africa, among the Bantu and Hottentot, admits of hardly any other explanation. And the same is true, to a more or less pronounced extent, among other distinct but neighboring languages.

The possibility of such a transfer of sounds can not be denied. Among the American Indians, for instance—where intermarriages between individuals belonging to different tribes are frequent; where slave women raise their own and their masters' children; and where, owing to the small number of individuals constituting the tribe, individuals who have mastered several distinct languages are not by any means rare—ample opportunity is given for one language to exert its phonetic influence over another. Whether this explanation is adequate, is a question that remains to be decided by further historical studies.[1]

Grammatical Influences

Influence of the syntax of one language upon another, and even, to a certain extent, of the morphology of one language upon another, is also probable. The study of the languages of Europe has proved clearly the deep influence exerted by Latin upon the syntax of all the modern European languages. We can also recognize how certain syntactic forms of expression occur in neighboring languages on our American continent. To give an instance of this kind, we find that, in the most diverse languages of the North Pacific coast, commands are given in the periphrastic form, *It would be good if you did so and so;* and in many cases this periphrastic form has been substituted entirely for the ordinary imperative. Thus it may well be that groups of psychological concepts which are expressed by means of grammatical forms have developed in one language under the influence of another; and it is difficult to say, if we once admit such influence, where the limit may be to the modifications caused by such processes.

On the other hand, it seems exceedingly difficult to understand why the most fundamental morphological traits of a language should disappear under the influence of another form of thought as exhibited in another language. This would mean that the greater number of grammatical forms would disappear, and entirely new categories develop. It certainly can not be denied that far-reaching modifications of this kind are possible, but it will require the most cautious proof in every single case before their existence can be accepted.

[1] See also p. 53.

Cases of the introduction of new suffixes in European languages are not by any means rare. Thus, the ending -*able* of French words has been adopted so frequently into English that the ending itself has attained a certain independence, and we can form words like *eatable*, or even *get-at-able*, in which the ending, which was originally French, is added to an English word. In a similar way the French verbal ending -*ir*, combined with the German infinitive ending in -*en*, is used in a large number of German words as though it were a purely German ending. I do not know, however, of any observations which would point to a radical modification of the morphological traits of a language through the influence of another language.

Lexicographic Influences

While the phonetic influence of distinct languages upon one another and the modification of morphological traits in different languages are still obscure, the borrowing of words is very common, and sometimes reaches to an enormous extent. The vocabulary of English is an excellent example of such extensive amalgamation of the vocabularies of quite distinct languages, and the manner by which it has been attained is instructive. It is not only that Anglo - Saxon adopted large parts of the vocabulary of the Norman conquerors, that it took over a few terms of the older Celtic language, and adopted some words from the Norse invaders; but we find also, later, introductions from Latin and Greek, which were introduced through the progress of the arts and sciences, and which filtered down from the educated to the uneducated classes. Furthermore, numerous terms were adopted from the less civilized peoples with whom the English-speaking people came into contact in different parts of the world. Thus, the Australian and the Indian-English have each adopted a great many native terms, quite a number of which have found their way into colloquial and written modern English. This phenomenon is so common, and the processes by which new words enter into a language are so obvious, that a full discussion is not required. Another example that may be mentioned here is that of the Turkish language, which has adopted a very large number of Arab words.

In such a transfer of the vocabulary of one language into another, words undergo, of course, far-reaching changes. These may be partly due to phonetic difficulties, and consist in the adaptation of an unfamiliar group of sounds to the familiar similar sounds of the language by which the word has been adopted. There may be assimilations by which the grammatical form of a word is made similar to more familiar forms. Furthermore, changes in the significance of the word are common, and new derivations may be formed from the word after it has once become entirely familiar, like other native words.

In this respect a number of American languages seem to behave curiously when compared with European languages. Borrowing of words in Europe is particularly common when a new object is first introduced. In almost all these cases the foreign designation is taken over with more or less fundamental phonetic modifications. Examples of this kind are the words *tobacco, canoe, maize, chocolate*—to take as illustration a few words borrowed from American languages. American natives, on the other hand, do not commonly adopt words in this manner, but much more frequently invent descriptive words by which the new object is designated. Thus the Tsimshian of British Columbia designate rice by a term meaning *looking like maggots*. The Kwakiutl call a steamboat *fire on its back moving on the water*. The Eskimo call cut tobacco *being blown upon*. Words of this type are in wide use; nevertheless, loan words taken from English are not by any means rare. The terms *biscuit, dollar, coffee, tea*, are found in a great many Indian languages. The probable reason why descriptive words are more common in American languages than in European languages lies in the frequent occurrence of descriptive nouns.

We find, therefore, that there are two sets of phenomena which must be considered in the classification of languages: (1) differences which can easily be proved to be derived from modifications of a single ancestral language; and (2) similarities which can not be thus explained, and some of which may be due to the effects of mixture.

Origin of Similarities; by Dissemination or by Parallel Development

Before we proceed with this consideration, we have to discuss the two logical possibilities for such similarities. Either they may be due to dissemination from a common source, so that they originated only a single time, and were diffused by the influence of one people upon another; or it may be that they are due to an independent origin in many parts of the world.

This alternative is present in the explanation of all ethnic phenomena, and is one of the fundamental questions in regard to which the ethnologist, as well as the investigator of languages, must be clear. In the older considerations of the position of the American race among the races of man, for instance, it has always been assumed that occurrence of similar phenomena among the peoples of the Old World and of the New proved genetic relationship. It is obvious that this method of proving relationship assumes that, wherever similarities occur, they must have been carried by the same people over different parts of the world, and that therefore they may be considered as proof of common descent. The method thus applied does not take into consideration the possibility of a gradual diffusion of cultural elements from one people to another, and the other more fundamental one of a parallel but independent development of similar phenomena among different races in remote parts of the world. Since such development is a logical possibility, proofs of genetic relationship must not be based on the occurrence of sporadic resemblances alone.

A final decision of this vexed problem can be given only by historical evidence, which is hardly ever available, and for this reason the systematic treatment of the question must always proceed with the greatest caution.

The cases in which isolated similarities of ethnic phenomena in remote parts of the world have been recorded are numerous, and many of these are of such a character that transmission cannot be proved at all. If, for instance, the Indians of South America use sacred musical instruments, which must not be seen by women, and if apparently the same custom prevails among the Australian aborigines, it is inadmissible to assume the occurrence of what seems to be the same custom in these two remote districts as due to transmission. It is perfectly intelligible that the custom may have developed independently in each continent. On the other hand, there are many cases in which certain peculiar and complex customs are distributed over large continuous areas, and where transmission over large portions of this area is plausible. In this case, even if independent origin had taken place in different parts of the district in question, the present distribution is fully explained by the assumption of extended dissemination.

It is true, for instance, in the case of similar traditions which are found distributed over large districts. An example of this is the story of two girls who noticed two stars, a bright one and a small one, and wished these stars for their husbands. The following morning they found themselves in the sky, married to the stars, and later on tried to return to the earth by letting themselves down through a hole in the sky. This rather complex tale is found distributed over the American continent in an area extending from Nova Scotia to the mouth of the Mississippi river and westward to the Rocky mountains, and in places even on the Pacific ocean, for instance, in Alaska and in the state of Washington. It would seem difficult to assume, in a case of this kind, the possibility of an independent invention of the tale at a number of distinct points; but it must be assumed that, after the tale had once attained its present form, it spread by dissemination over that part of the continent where it is now found.

In extreme cases the conclusions drawn from these two types of explanation seem quite unassailable; but there are naturally a very large number of others in which the phenomenon in question is neither sufficiently complex, nor distributed over a sufficiently large continuous area, to lead with certainty to the conclusion of an origin by dissemination; and there are others where the sporadic distributions seem curiously arranged, and where vague possibilities of contact occur. Thus it happens often that a satisfactory conclusion cannot be reached.

We must also bear in mind that in many cases a continuous distribution may once have existed, but may have become discontinuous, owing to the disappearance of the phenomena in question in intermediate regions. If, however, we want to follow a safe method, we must not admit such causes for sporadic distribution, unless they can be definitely proved by other evidence; otherwise, the way is open to attempts to bring into contact practically every part of the world with all others.

The general occurrence of similar ethnic phenomena in remote parts of the world admits also of the explanation of the existence of a certain number of customs and habits that were common to large parts of mankind at a very early period, and which have maintained themselves here and there up to the present time. It can not be denied that this point of view has certain elements in its favor; but in the present state of our knowledge we can hardly say that it would be possible to prove or to disprove it.

We meet the same fundamental problem in connection with similarities of languages which are too vague to be considered as proofs of genetic relationship. That these exist is obvious. Here we have not only the common characteristics of all human language, which have been discussed in the preceding chapter, but also certain other similarities which must here be considered.

Influence of Environment on Language

It has often been suggested that similarities of neighboring languages and customs may be explained by the influence of environment. The leading thought in this theory is, that the human mind, under the stress of similar conditions, will produce the same results; that consequently, if the members of the same race live in the same surroundings, they will produce, for instance, in their articulate speech, the same kind of phonetics, differing perhaps in detail according to the variations of environment, but the same in their essential traits. Thus it has been claimed that the moist and stormy climate of the North Pacific coast caused a chronic catarrhal condition among the inhabitants, and that to this condition is due the guttural pronunciation and harshness of their languages; while, on the other hand, the mildness of the California climate has been made responsible for the euphonious character of the languages of that district.

I do not believe that detailed investigations in any part of the world would sustain this theory. We might demand proof that the same language, when distributed over different climates, should produce the same kind of modifications as those here exemplified; and we might further demand that, wherever similar climates are found, at least a certain approach to similarity in the phonetics of the languages should occur. It would be difficult to prove that this is the case, even if we should admit the excuse that modifying influences have obscured the original similarity of phonetic character. Taking, for instance, the arctic people of the Old and New Worlds as a unit, we find fundamentally different traits in the phonetics of the Eskimo, of the Chukchee of eastern Siberia, and of other arctic Asiatic and European peoples. The phonetics of the deserts of Asia and South

Africa and of southwestern North America are not by any means the same. The prairie tribes of North America, although living in nearly the same climate, over a considerable area, show remarkable differences in the phonetics of their languages; and, on the other hand, the tribes belonging to the Salish family who live east of the Rocky mountains, in the interior of British Columbia, speak a language that is not less harsh than that of their congeners on the northern coast of the state of Washington. In any attempt at arranging phonetics in accordance with climate, the discrepancies would be so numerous, that an attempt to carry out the theory would lead to the necessity of explaining exceptions rather than examples corroborating its correctness.

What is true in regard to phonetics is no less true in regard to morphology and vocabulary. I do not think that it has ever been claimed that similar words must necessarily originate under the stress of the same conditions, although, if we admit the correctness of the principle, there is no reason for making an exception in regard to the vocabulary.

I think this theory can be sustained even less in the field of linguistics than in the field of ethnology. It is certainly true that each people accommodates itself to a certain extent to its surroundings, and that it even may make the best possible use of its surroundings in accordance with the fundamental traits of its culture, but I do not believe that in any single case it will be possible to explain the culture of a people as due to the influence of its surroundings. It is self-evident that the Eskimo of northern arctic America do not make extended use of wood, a substance which is very rare in those parts of the world, and that the Indians of the woodlands of Brazil are not familiar with the uses to which snow may be put. We may even go further, and acknowledge that, after the usefulness of certain substances, plants, and animals—like bamboo in the tropics, or the cedar on the North Pacific coast of America, or ivory in the arctic regions, or the buffalo on the plains of North America—has once been recognized, they will find the most extended use, and that numerous inventions will be made to expand their usefulness. We may also recognize that the distribution of the produce of a country, the difficulties and ease of travel, the necessity of reaching certain points, may deeply influence the habits of the people. But with all this, to geographical conditions cannot be ascribed more than a modifying influence upon the fundamental traits of culture. If this were not true, the peculiar facts of distribution of inventions, of beliefs, of habits, and of other ethnological phenomena, would be unintelligible.

For instance, the use of the underground house is distributed, in America and Asia, over the northern parts of the plateaus to parts of the Great Plains, northward into the arctic region; and crossing Bering strait we find it in use along the Pacific coast of Asia and as far south as northern Japan, not to speak of the subterranean dwellings of Europe and North Africa. The climate of this district shows very considerable differences, and the climatic necessity for underground habitations does not exist by any means in many parts of the area where they occur.

In a similar area we find the custom of increasing the elasticity of the bow by overlaying it with sinew. While this procedure may be quite necessary in the arctic regions, where no elastic wood is available, it is certainly not necessary in the more southern parts of the Rocky mountains, or along the east coast of Asia, where a great many varieties of strong elastic wood are available. Nevertheless the usefulness of the invention seems to have led to its general application over an extended district.

We might also give numerous examples which would illustrate that the adaptation of a people to their surroundings is not by any means perfect. How, for instance, can we explain the fact that the Eskimo, notwithstanding their inventiveness, have never thought of domesticating the caribou, while the Chukchee have acquired large reindeer-herds? Why, on the other hand, should the Chukchee, who are compelled to travel about with their reindeer-herds, use a tent which is so cumbersome that a train of many sledges is required to move it, while the Eskimo have reduced the frame of their tents to such a degree that a single sledge can be used for conveying it from place to place?

Other examples of a similar kind are the difference in the habitations of the arctic Athapascan tribes and those of the Eskimo. Notwithstanding the rigor of the climate, the former live in light skin tents, while the Eskimo have succeeded in protecting themselves efficiently against the gales and the snows of winter.

What actually seems to take place in the movements of peoples is, that a people who settle in a new environment will first of all cling to their old habits and only modify them as much as is absolutely necessary in order to live fairly comfortably, the comfort of life being generally of secondary importance to the inertia or conservatism which prevents a people from changing their settled habits, that have become customary to such an extent that they are more or less automatic, and that a change would be felt as something decidedly unusual.

Even when a people remain located in the same place, it would seem that historical influences are much stronger than geographical influences. I am inclined, for instance, to explain in this manner the differences between the cultures of the tribes of arctic Asia and of arctic America, and the difference in the habits of the tribes of the southern plateaus of North America when compared with those of the northern plateaus of North America. In the southern regions the influence of the Pueblos has made itself felt, while farther to the north the simpler culture of the Mackenzie basin gives the essential tone to the culture of the people.

While fully acknowledging the importance of geographical conditions upon life, I do not believe that they can be given a place at all comparable to that of culture as handed down, and to that of the historical influence exerted by the cultures of surrounding tribes; and it seems likely that the less direct the influence of the surroundings is, the less also can it be used for accounting for peculiar ethnological traits.

So far as language is concerned, the influence of geographical surroundings and of climate seems to be exceedingly remote; and as long as we are not even able to prove that the whole organism of man, and with it the articulating organs, are directly influenced by geographical environment, I do not think we are justified in considering this element as an essential trait in the formation or modification of human speech, much less as a cause which can be used to account for the similarities of human speech in neighboring areas.

Influence of Common Psychic Traits

Equally uncertain seems to be the resort to the assumption of peculiar psychic traits that are common to geographical divisions of the same race. It may be claimed, for instance, that the languages of the Athapascan, Tlingit, and Haida, which were referred to before as similar in certain fundamental morphological traits, are alike, for the reason that these three peoples have certain psychical traits in common which are not shared in by other American tribes.

It seems certainly admissible to assume slight differences in the psychical make-up among groups of a race which are different in regard to their physical type. If we can prove by means of anatomical investigations that the bodily form, and with it the nervous system and the brain of one part of a race show differences from the analogous traits of another part of the race, it seems justifiable to conclude that the physical differentiation may be accompanied by psychic differences. It must, however, be borne in mind that the extent of physical difference is always exceedingly slight, and that, within the limits of each geographical type, variations are found which are great as compared to the total differences between the averages of the types. To use a diagram:

If a represents the middle point of one type and b and c its extremes, a' the average of another type and b' and c' its extremes, and if these types are so placed, one over the other, that types in the second series correspond to those in the first series vertically over them, then it will be seen that the bulk of the population of the two types will very well coincide, while only the extremes will be more frequent in the one group than in the other. That is to say, the physical difference is not a difference in kind, but a difference more or less in degree, and a considerable overlapping of the types necessarily takes place.

If this is true in regard to the physical type, and if, furthermore, the difference in psychical types is inferred only from the observed differences of the physical types, then we must assume that the same kind of overlapping will take place in the psychical types. The differences with which we are dealing can, therefore, be only very slight, and it seems hardly likely that these slight differences could lead to radically diverse results.

As a matter of fact, the proof which has been given before,[1] that the same languages may be spoken by entirely distinct types, shows clearly how slight the effect of difference in anatomical type upon

[1] See p. 9.

language is at the present time, and there is no reason to presume that it has ever been greater. Viewing the matter from this standpoint, the hereditary mental differences of various groups of mankind, particularly within the same race, seem to be so slight that it would be very difficult to believe that they account in any way for the fundamental differences in the traits of distinct languages.

Uncertainty of Definition of Linguistic Families

The problem thus remains unsolved how to interpret the similarities of distinct languages in cases where the similarities are no longer sufficient to prove genetic relationship. From what has been said we may conclude that, even in languages which can easily be proved to be genetically related, independent elements may be found in various divisions. Such independent elements may be due partly to new tendencies which develop in one or the other of the dialects, or to foreign influence. It is quite conceivable that such new tendencies and foreign influences may attain such importance that the new language may still be considered as historically related to the ancestral family, but that its deviations, due to elements that are not found in the ancestral language, have become so important that it can no longer be considered as a branch of the older family.

Thus it will be seen that the concept of a linguistic family can not be sharply defined; that even among the dialects of one linguistic family, more or less foreign material may be present, and that in this sense the languages, as has been pointed out by Paul,[1] are not, in the strict sense of the term, descendants of a single ancestral family.

Thus the whole problem of the final classification of languages in linguistic families that are without doubt related, seems destined to remain open until our knowledge of the processes by which distinct languages are developed shall have become much more thorough than it is at the present time. Under these circumstances we must confine ourselves to classifying American languages in those linguistic families for which we can give a proof of relationship that can not possibly be challenged. Beyond this point we can do no more than give certain definite classifications in which the traits common to certain groups of languages are pointed out, while the decision as to the significance of these common traits must be left to later times.

---

[1] Paul, Principien der Sprachgeschichte.

IV. LINGUISTICS AND ETHNOLOGY

It seems desirable to say a few words on the function of linguistic researches in the study of the ethnography of the Indians.

Practical Need of Linguistic Studies for Ethnological Purposes

First of all, the purely practical aspect of this question may be considered. Ordinarily, the investigator who visits an Indian tribe is not able to converse with the natives themselves and to obtain his information first-hand, but he is obliged to rely more or less on data transmitted by interpreters, or at least by the help of interpreters. He may ask his question through an interpreter, and receive again through his mouth the answer given by the Indians. It is obvious that this is an unsatisfactory method, even when the interpreters are good; but, as a rule, the available men are either not sufficiently familiar with the English language, or they are so entirely out of sympathy with the Indian point of view, and understand the need of accuracy on the part of the investigator so little, that information furnished by them can be used only with a considerable degree of caution. At the present time it is possible to get along in many parts of America without interpreters, by means of the trade-jargons that have developed everywhere in the intercourse between the whites and the Indians. These, however, are also a very unsatisfactory means of inquiring into the customs of the natives, because, in some cases, the vocabulary of the trade-languages is extremely limited, and it is almost impossible to convey information relating to the religious and philosophic ideas or to the higher aspects of native art, all of which play so important a part in Indian life. Another difficulty which often develops whenever the investigator works with a particularly intelligent interpreter is, that the interpreter imbibes too readily the views of the investigator, and that his information, for this reason, is strongly biased, because he is not so well able to withstand the influence of formative theories as the trained investigator ought to be. Anyone who has carried on work with intelligent Indians will recall instances of this kind, where the interpreter may have formulated a theory based on the questions that have been put through him, and has interpreted his answers under the guidance of his preconceived notions. All this is so obvious that it hardly requires a full discussion. Our needs become particularly apparent when we compare the methods that we expect from any investigator of cultures of the Old World with those of the ethnologist who is studying primitive tribes. Nobody would expect authoritative accounts of the civilization of China or of Japan from a man who does not speak the languages readily, and who has not mastered their literatures. The student of antiquity is expected to have a thorough mastery of the ancient languages. A student of Mohammedan life in Arabia or Turkey would hardly be considered a serious investigator if all his knowledge had to be derived from second-hand accounts. The ethnologist, on the other hand, undertakes in the majority of cases to elucidate the innermost thoughts and feelings of a people without so much as a smattering of knowledge of their language.

It is true that the American ethnologist is confronted with a serious practical difficulty, for, in the present state of American society, by far the greater number of customs and practices have gone out of existence, and the investigator is compelled to rely upon accounts of customs of former times recorded from the mouths of the old generation who, when young, still took part in these performances. Added to this he is confronted with the difficulty that the number of trained investigators is very small, and the number of American languages that are mutually unintelligible exceedingly large, probably exceeding three hundred in number. Our investigating ethnologists are also denied opportunity to spend long continuous periods with any particular tribe, so that the practical difficulties in the way of acquiring languages are almost insuperable. Nevertheless, we must insist that a command of the language is an indispensable means of obtaining accurate and thorough knowledge, because much information can be gained by listening to conversations of the natives and by taking part in their daily life, which, to the observer who has no command of the language, will remain entirely inaccessible.

It must be admitted that this ideal aim is, under present conditions, entirely beyond our reach. It is, however, quite possible for the ethnographer to obtain a theoretical knowledge of native languages that will enable him to collect at least part of the information that could be best obtained by a practical knowledge of the language. Fortunately, the Indian is easily misled, by the ability of the observer

to read his language, into thinking that he is also able to understand
what he reads. Thus, in taking down tales or other records in the
native language, and reading them to the Indians, the Indian always
believes that the reader also understands what he pronounces, because
it is quite inconceivable to him that a person can freely utter the sentences in his language without clearly grasping their meaning. This
fact facilitates the initial stages of ethnographic information in the
native languages, because, on the whole, the northern Indians are
eager to be put on record in regard to questions that are of supreme
interest to them. If the observer is capable of grasping by a rapid
analysis the significance of what is dictated to him, even without being
able to express himself freely in the native language, he is in a position
to obtain much information that otherwise would be entirely unob-
tainable. Although this is wholly a makeshift, still it puts the
observer in an infinitely better position than that in which he would
be without any knowledge whatever of the language. First of
all, he can get the information from the Indians first-hand, without
employing an interpreter, who may mislead him. Furthermore, the
range of subjects on which he can get information is considerably
increased, because the limitations of the linguistic knowledge of the
interpreter, or those of the trade-language, are eliminated. It
would seem, therefore, that under present conditions we are more or
less compelled to rely upon an extended series of texts as the safest
means of obtaining information from the Indians. A general review
of our ethnographic literature shows clearly how much better is the
information obtained by observers who have command of the language, and who are on terms of intimate friendship with the natives,
than that obtained through the medium of interpreters.

The best material we possess is perhaps contained in the naïve out-
pourings of the Eskimo, which they write and print themselves, and
distribute as a newspaper, intended to inform the people of all the
events that are of interest. These used to contain much mythological matter and much that related to the mode of life of the people.
Other material of similar character is furnished by the large text
collections of the Ponca, published by the late James Owen Dorsey;
although many of these are influenced by the changed conditions
under which the people now live. Some older records on the Iroquois, written by prominent members of the tribe, also deserve attention; and among the most recent literature the descriptions of the

Sauk and Fox by Dr. William Jones are remarkable on account of the thorough understanding that the author has reached, owing to his mastery of the language. Similar in character, although rendered entirely in English, are the observations of Mr. James Teit on the Thompson Indians.

In some cases it has been possible to interest educated natives in the study of their own tribes and to induce them to write down in their own language their observations. These, also, are much superior to English records, in which the natives are generally hampered by the lack of mastery of the foreign language.

While in all these cases a collector thoroughly familiar with the Indian language and with English might give us the results of his studies without using the native language in his publications, this is quite indispensable when we try to investigate the deeper problems of ethnology. A few examples will show clearly what is meant. When the question arises, for instance, of investigating the poetry of the Indians, no translation can possibly be considered as an adequate substitute for the original. The form of rhythm, the treatment of the language, the adjustment of text to music, the imagery, the use of metaphors, and all the numerous problems involved in any thorough investigation of the style of poetry, can be interpreted only by the investigator who has equal command of the ethnographical traits of the tribe and of their language. The same is true in the investigation of rituals, with their set, more or less poetic phrases, or in the investigation of prayers and incantations. The oratory of the Indians, a subject that has received much attention by ethnologists, is not adequately known, because only a very few speeches have been handed down in the original. Here, also, an accurate investigation of the method of composition and of the devices used to reach oratorical effect, requires the preservation of speeches as rendered in the original language.

There are also numerous other features of the life of the Indians which can not be adequately presented without linguistic investigation. To these belong, for instance, the discussion of personal, tribal, and local names. The translations of Indian names which are popularly known—like Sitting-Bull, Afraid-Of-His-Horse, etc.—indicate that names possess a deeper significance. The translations, however, are so difficult that a thorough linguistic knowledge is required in order to explain the significance adequately.

In all the subjects mentioned heretofore, a knowledge of Indian languages serves as an important adjunct to a full understanding of the customs and beliefs of the people whom we are studying. But in all these cases the service which language lends us is first of all a practical one—a means to a clearer understanding of ethnological phenomena which in themselves have nothing to do with linguistic problems.

Theoretical Importance of Linguistic Studies

Language a Part of Ethnological Phenomena in General

It seems, however, that a theoretical study of Indian languages is not less important than a practical knowledge of them; that the purely linguistic inquiry is part and parcel of a thorough investigation of the psychology of the peoples of the world. If ethnology is understood as the science dealing with the mental phenomena of the life of the peoples of the world, human language, one of the most important manifestations of mental life, would seem to belong naturally to the field of work of ethnology, unless special reasons can be adduced why it should not be so considered. It is true that a practical reason of this kind exists, namely, the specialization which has taken place in the methods of philological research, which has progressed to such an extent that philology and comparative linguistics are sciences which require the utmost attention, and do not allow the student to devote much of his time to other fields that require different methods of study. This, however, is no reason for believing that the results of linguistic inquiry are unimportant to the ethnologist. There are other fields of ethnological investigation which have come to be more or less specialized, and which require for their successful treatment peculiar specialization. This is true, for instance, of the study of primitive music, of primitive art, and, to a certain extent, of primitive law. Nevertheless, these subjects continue to form an important part of ethnological science.

If the phenomena of human speech seem to form in a way a subject by itself, this is perhaps largely due to the fact that the laws of language remain entirely unknown to the speakers, that linguistic phenomena never rise into the consciousness of primitive man, while all other ethnological phenomena are more or less clearly subjects of conscious thought.

The question of the relation of linguistic phenomena to ethnological phenomena, in the narrower sense of the term, deserves, therefore, special discussion.

Language and Thought

First of all, it may be well to discuss the relation between language and thought. It has been claimed that the conciseness and clearness of thought of a people depend to a great extent upon their language. The ease with which in our modern European languages we express wide abstract ideas by a single term, and the facility with which wide generalizations are cast into the frame of a simple sentence, have been claimed to be one of the fundamental conditions of the clearness of our concepts, the logical force of our thought, and the precision with which we eliminate in our thoughts irrelevant details. Apparently this view has much in its favor. When we compare modern English with some of those Indian languages which are most concrete in their formative expression, the contrast is striking. When we say *The eye is the organ of sight,* the Indian may not be able to form the expression *the eye,* but may have to define that the eye of a person or of an animal is meant. Neither may the Indian be able to generalize readily the abstract idea of an eye as the representative of the whole class of objects, but may have to specialize by an expression like *this eye here.* Neither may he be able to express by a single term the idea of *organ,* but may have to specify it by an expression like *instrument of seeing,* so that the whole sentence might assume a form like *An indefinite person's eye is his means of seeing.* Still, it will be recognized that in this more specific form the general idea may be well expressed. It seems very questionable in how far the restriction of the use of certain grammatical forms can really be conceived as a hindrance in the formulation of generalized ideas. It seems much more likely that the lack of these forms is due to the lack of their need. Primitive man, when conversing with his fellow-man, is not in the habit of discussing abstract ideas. His interests center around the occupations of his daily life; and where philosophic problems are touched upon, they appear either in relation to definite individuals or in the more or less anthropomorphic forms of religious beliefs. Discourses on qualities without connection with the object to which the qualities belong, or of activities or states disconnected from the idea of the actor or the subject being in a certain state, will hardly occur in primitive speech. Thus the Indian will not speak of goodness as such, although he may very well speak of the goodness of a person. He will not speak of a state of bliss apart from the person who is in such a state. He will not refer to the power of seeing without designating an individual who has such power. Thus it happens that in languages in which the idea of possession is expressed by elements subordinated to nouns, all abstract terms appear always with possessive elements. It is, however, perfectly conceivable that an Indian trained in philosophic thought would proceed to free the underlying nominal forms from the possessive elements, and thus reach abstract forms strictly corresponding to the abstract forms of our modern languages. I have made this experiment, for instance, with the Kwakiutl language of Vancouver Island, in which no abstract term ever occurs without its possessive elements. After some discussion, I found it perfectly easy to develop the idea of the abstract term in the mind of the Indian, who will state that the word without a possessive pronoun gives a sense, although it is not used idiomatically. I succeeded, for instance, in this manner, in isolating the terms for *love* and *pity*, which ordinarily occur only in possessive forms, like *his love for him* or *my pity for you*. That this view is correct may also be observed in languages in which possessive elements appear as independent forms, as, for instance, in the Siouan languages. In these, pure abstract terms are quite common.

There is also evidence that other specializing elements, which are so characteristic of many Indian languages, may be dispensed with when, for one reason or another, it seems desirable to generalize a term. To use the example of the Kwakiutl language, the idea *to be seated* is almost always expressed with an inseparable suffix expressing the place in which a person is seated, as *seated on the floor of the house, on the ground, on the beach, on a pile of things,* or *on a round thing,* etc. When, however, for some reason, the dea of the state of sitting is to be emphasized, a form may be used which expresses simply *being in a sitting posture*. In this case, also, the device for generalized expression is present, but the opportunity for its application arises seldom, or perhaps never. I think what is true in these cases is true of the structure of every single language. The fact that generalized forms of expression are not

44877—Bull. 40, pt 1—10——5

used does not prove inability to form them, but it merely proves that the mode of life of the people is such that they are not required; that they would, however, develop just as soon as needed.

This point of view is also corroborated by a study of the numeral systems of primitive languages. As is well known, many languages exist in which the numerals do not exceed two or three. It has been inferred from this that the people speaking these languages are not capable of forming the concept of higher numbers. I think this interpretation of the existing conditions is quite erroneous. People like the South American Indians (among whom these defective numeral systems are found), or like the Eskimo (whose old system of numbers probably did not exceed ten), are presumably not in need of higher numerical expressions, because there are not many objects that they have to count. On the other hand, just as soon as these same people find themselves in contact with civilization, and when they acquire standards of value that have to be counted, they adopt with perfect ease higher numerals from other languages and develop a more or less perfect system of counting. This does not mean that every individual who in the course of his life has never made use of higher numerals would acquire more complex systems readily, but the tribe as a whole seems always to be capable of adjusting itself to the needs of counting. It must be borne in mind that counting does not become necessary until objects are considered in such generalized form that their individualities are entirely lost sight of. For this reason it is possible that even a person who has a flock of domesticated animals may know them by name and by their characteristics without ever desiring to count them. Members of a war expedition may be known by name and may not be counted. In short, there is no proof that the lack of the use of numerals is in any way connected with the inability to form the concepts of higher numbers.

If we want to form a correct judgment of the influence that language exerts over thought, we ought to bear in mind that our European languages as found at the present time have been moulded to a great extent by the abstract thought of philosophers. Terms like *essence* and *existence*, many of which are now commonly used, are by origin artificial devices for expressing the results of abstract thought. In this they would resemble the artificial, unidiomatic abstract terms that may be formed in primitive languages.

Thus it would seem that the obstacles to generalized thought inherent in the form of a language are of minor importance only, and that presumably the language alone would not prevent a people from advancing to more generalized forms of thinking if the general state of their culture should require expression of such thought; that under these conditions the language would be moulded rather by the cultural state.   It does not seem likely, therefore, that there is any direct relation between the culture of a tribe and the language they speak, except in so far as the form of the language will be moulded by the state of culture, but not in so far as a certain state of culture is conditioned by morphological traits of the language.

Unconscious Character of Linguistic Phenomena

Of greater positive importance is the question of the relation of the unconscious character of linguistic phenomena to the more conscious ethnological phenomena.   It seems to my mind that this contrast is only apparent, and that the very fact of the unconsciousness of linguistic processes helps us to gain a clearer understanding of the ethnological phenomena, a point the importance of which can not be underrated.   It has been mentioned before that in all languages certain classifications of concepts occur.   To mention only a few: we find objects classified according to sex, or as animate and inanimate, or according to form.   We find actions determined according to time and place, etc.   The behavior of primitive man makes it perfectly clear that all these concepts, although they are in constant use, have never risen into consciousness, and that consequently their origin must be sought, not in rational, but in entirely unconscious, we may perhaps say instinctive, processes of the mind.   They must be due to a grouping of sense-impressions and of concepts which is not in any sense of the term voluntary, but which develops from quite different psychological causes.   It would seem that the essential difference between linguistic phenomena and other ethnological phenomena is, that the linguistic classifications never rise into consciousness, while in other ethnological phenomena, although the same unconscious origin prevails, these often rise into consciousness, and thus give rise to secondary reasoning and to re-interpretations.   It would, for instance, seem very plausible that the fundamental religious notions—like the idea of the voluntary power of inanimate objects, or of the anthropomorphic character of animals, or of the existence of powers that are superior to the mental and physical powers of man—are in their origin just as little conscious as are the fundamental ideas of language. While, however, the use of language is so automatic that the opportunity never arises for the fundamental notions to emerge into consciousness, this happens very frequently in all phenomena relating to religion. It would seem that there is no tribe in the world in which the religious activities have not come to be a subject of thought. While the religious activities may have been performed before the reason for performing them had become a subject of thought, they attained at an early time such importance that man asked himself the reason why he performed these actions. With this moment speculation in regard to religous activities arose, and the whole series of secondary explanations which form so vast a field of ethnological phenomena came into existence.

It is difficult to give a definite proof of the unconscious origin of ethnic phenomena, because so many of them are, or have come to be, subjects of thought. The best evidence that can be given for their unconscious origin must be taken from our own experience, and I think it is not difficult to show that certain groups of our activities, whatever the history of their earlier development may have been, develop at present in each individual and in the whole people entirely sub-consciously, and nevertheless are most potent in the formation of our opinions and actions. Simple examples of this kind are actions which we consider as proper and improper, and which may be found in great numbers in what we call good manners. Thus table manners, which on the whole are impressed vigorously upon the child while it is still young, have a very fixed form. Smacking of the lips and bringing the plate up to the mouth would not be tolerated, although no esthetic or other reason could be given for their rigid exclusiou; and it is instructive to know that among a tribe like the Omaha it is considered as bad taste, when invited to eat, not to smack one's lips, because this is a sign of appreciation of the meal. I think it will readily be recognized that the simple fact that these habits are customary, while others are not, is sufficient reason for eliminating those acts that are not customary, and that the idea of propriety simply arises from the continuity and automatic repetition of these acts, which brings about the notion that manners contrary to custom are unusual, and therefore not the proper manners. It may be observed in this connection that bad manners are always accompanied by rather intense feelings of displeasure, the psychological reason for which can be found only in the fact that the actions in question are contrary to those which have become habitual. It is fairly evident that in our table manners this strong feeling of propriety is associated with the familiar modes of eating. When a new kind of food is presented, the proper manner of eating which is not known, practically any habit that is not in absolute conflict with the common habits may readily establish itself.

The example of table manners gives also a fairly good instance of secondary explanation. It is not customary to bring the knife to the mouth, and very readily the feeling arises, that the knife is not used in this manner because in eating thus one would easily cut the lips. The lateness of the invention of the fork, and the fact that in many countries dull knives are used and that a similar danger exists of pricking the tongue or the lips with the sharp-pointed steel fork which is commonly used in Europe, show readily that this explanation is only a secondary rationalistic attempt to explain a custom that otherwise would remain unexplained.

If we are to draw a parallel to linguistic phenomena in this case, it would appear that the grouping of a number of unrelated actions in one group, for the reason that they cause a feeling of disgust, is brought about without any reasoning, and still sets off these actions clearly and definitely in a group by themselves.

On account of the importance of this question, it seems desirable to give another example, and one that seems to be more deeply seated than the one given before. A case of this kind is presented in the group of acts which we characterize as modest. It requires very little thought to see that, while the feelings of modesty are fundamental, the particular acts which are considered modest or immodest show immense variation, and are determined entirely by habits that develop unconsciously so far as their relation to modesty is concerned, and which may have their ultimate origin in causes of an entirely different character. A study of the history of costume proves at once that at different times and in different parts of the world it has been considered immodest to bare certain parts of the body. What parts of the body these are, is to a great extent a matter of accident. Even at the present time, and within a rather narrow range, great variations in this respect may be found. Examples are the use of the veil in Turkey, the more or less rigid use of the glove in our own society, and the difference between street costume and evening dress. A lady in full evening dress in a street-car, during the daytime, would hardly appear in place.

We all are at once conscious of the intensity of these feelings of modesty, and of the extreme repugnance of the individual to any act that goes counter to the customary concepts of modesty. In a number of cases the origin of a costume can readily be traced, and in its development no considerations of modesty exert any influence. It is therefore evident that in this respect the grouping-together of certain customs again develops entirely unconsciously, but that, nevertheless, they stand out as a group set apart from others with great clearness as soon as our attention is directed toward the feelings of modesty.

To draw a parallel again between this ethnological phenomenon and linguistic phenomena, it would seem that the common feature of both is the grouping-together of a considerable number of activities under the form of a single idea, without the necessity of this idea itself entering into consciousness. The difference, again, would lie in the fact that the idea of modesty is easily isolated from other concepts, and that then secondary explanations are given of what is considered modest and what not. I believe that the unconscious formation of these categories is one of the fundamental traits of ethnic life, and that it even manifests itself in many of its more complex aspects; that many of our religious views and activities, of our ethical concepts, and even our scientific views, which are apparently based entirely on conscious reasoning, are affected by this tendency of distinct activities to associate themselves under the influence of strong emotions. It has been recognized before that this is one of the fundamental causes of error and of the diversity of opinion.

It seems necessary to dwell upon the analogy of ethnology and language in this respect, because, if we adopt this point of view, language seems to be one of the most instructive fields of inquiry in an investigation of the formation of the fundamental ethnic ideas. The great advantage that linguistics offer in this respect is the fact that, on the whole, the categories which are formed always remain unconscious, and that for this reason the processes which lead to their formation can be followed without the misleading and disturbing factors of secondary explanations, which are so common in ethnology, so much so that they generally obscure the real history of the development of ideas entirely.

Cases are rare in which a people have begun to speculate about linguistic categories, and these speculations are almost always so clearly affected by the faulty reasoning that has led to secondary explanations, that they are readily recognized as such, and can not disturb the clear view of the history of linguistic processes. In America we find this tendency, for instance, among the Pawnee, who seem to have been led to several of their religious opinions by linguistic similarities. Incidentally such cases occur also in other languages, as, for instance, in Chinook mythology, where the Culture Hero discovers a man in a canoe who obtains fish by dancing, and tells him that he must not do so, but must catch fish with the net, a tale which is entirely based on the identity of the two words for *dancing*, and *catching with a net*. These are cases which show that Max Müller's theory of the influence of etymology upon religious concepts explains some of the religious phenomena, although, of course, it can be held to account for only a very small portion.

Judging the importance of linguistic studies from this point of view, it seems well worth while to subject the whole range of linguistic concepts to a searching analysis, and to seek in the peculiarities of the grouping of ideas in different languages an important characteristic in the history of the mental development of the various branches of mankind. From this point of view, the occurrence of the most fundamental grammatical concepts in all languages must be considered as proof of the unity of fundamental psychological processes. The characteristic groupings of concepts in American languages will be treated more fully in the discussion of the single linguistic stocks. The ethnological significance of these studies lies in the clear definition of the groupings of ideas which are brought out by the objective study of language.

There is still another theoretical aspect that deserves special attention. When we try to think at all clearly, we think, on the whole, in words; and it is well known that, even in the advancement of science, inaccuracy of vocabulary has often been a stumbling-block which has made it difficult to reach accurate conclusions. The same words may be used with different significance, and by assuming the word to have the same significance always, erroneous conclusions may be reached. It may also be that the word expresses only part of an idea, so that owing to its use the full range of the subject-matter discussed may not be recognized. In the same manner the words may be too wide in their significance, including a number of distinct ideas the differences of which in the course of the development of the language were not recognized. Furthermore, we find that, among more primitive tribes, similarities of sound are misunderstood, and that ideas expressed by similar words are considered as similar or identical, and that descriptive terms are misunderstood as expressing an identity, or at least close relationship, between the object described and the group of ideas contained in the description.

All these traits of human thought, which are known to influence the history of science and which play a more or less important rôle in the general history of civilization, occur with equal frequency in the thoughts of primitive man. It will be sufficient to give a few examples of these cases.

One of the most common cases of a group of views due to failure to notice that the same word may signify divers objects, is that based on the belief of the identity of persons bearing the same name. Generally the interpretation is given that a child receives the name of an ancestor because he is believed to be a re-incarnation of the individuality of the ancestor. It seems, however, much more likely that this is not the real reason for the views connected with this custom, which seems due to the fact that no distinction is made between the name and the personality known under the name. The association established between name and individual is so close that the two seem almost inseparable; and when a name is mentioned, not only the name itself, but also the personality of its bearer, appears before the mind of the speaker.

Inferences based on peculiar forms of classification of ideas, and due to the fact that a whole group of distinct ideas are expressed by a single term, occur commonly in the terms of relationship of various languages; as, for instance, in our term *uncle*, which means the two distinct classes of father's brother and mother's brother. Here, also, it is commonly assumed that the linguistic expression is a secondary reflex of the customs of the people; but the question is quite open in how far the one phenomenon is the primary one and the other the secondary one, and whether the customs of the people have not rather developed from the unconsciously developed terminology.

Cases in which the similarity of sound of words is reflected in the views of the people are not rare, and examples of these have been given before in referring to Max Müller's theory of the origin of religions.

Finally, a few examples may be given of cases in which the use of descriptive terms for certain concepts, or the metaphorical use of terms, has led to peculiar views or customs. It seems plausible to my mind, for instance, that the terms of relationship by which some of the eastern Indian tribes designate one another were originally nothing but a metaphorical use of these terms, and that the further elaboration of the social relations of the tribes may have been largely determined by transferring the ideas accompanying these terms into practice.

More convincing are examples taken from the use of metaphorical terms in poetry, which, in rituals, are taken literally, and are made the basis of certain rites. I am inclined to believe, for instance, that the frequently occurring image of *the devouring of wealth* has a close relation to the detailed form of the winter ritual among the Indians of the North Pacific coast, and that the poetical simile in which the chief is called the *support of the sky* has to a certain extent been taken literally in the elaboration of mythological ideas.

Thus it appears that from practical, as well as from theoretical, points of view, the study of language must be considered as one of the most important branches of ethnological study, because, on the one hand, a thorough insight into ethnology can not be gained without practical knowledge of language, and, on the other hand, the fundamental concepts illustrated by human languages are not distinct in kind from ethnological phenomena; and because, furthermore, the peculiar characteristics of languages are clearly reflected in the views and customs of the peoples of the world.

V. CHARACTERISTICS OF AMERICAN LANGUAGES

In older treatises of the languages of the world, languages have often been classified as isolating, agglutinating, polysynthetic, and inflecting languages. Chinese is generally given as an example of an isolating language. The agglutinating languages are represented by the Ural-Altaic languages of northern Asia; polysynthetic languages, by the languages of America; and inflecting languages, by the Indo-European and Semitic languages. The essential traits of these four groups are: That in the first, sentences are expressed solely by the juxtaposition of unchangeable elements; in the agglutinating languages, a single stem is modified by the attachment of numerous formative elements which modify the fundamental idea of the stem; in polysynthetic languages, a large number of distinct ideas are amalgamated by grammatical processes and form a single word, without any morphological distinction between the formal elements in the sentence and the contents of the sentence; and in the inflecting languages, on the other hand, a sharp distinction is made between formal elements and the material contents of the sentence, and stems are modified solely according to the logical forms in which they appear in the sentence.

An example of what is meant by polysynthesis is given, for instance, in the following Eskimo word: *takusariartorumagaluarnerpâ?* DO YOU THINK HE REALLY INTENDS TO GO TO LOOK AFTER IT? (*takusar[pâ]* he looks after it; *-iartor[poq]* he goes to; *-uma[voq]* he intends to; *-[g]aluar[poq]* he does so—but; *-ner[poq]* do you think he—; *-â*, interrogation, third person.) It will be recognized here, that there is no correspondence between the suffixed elements of the fundamental stem and the formal elements that appear in the Indo-European languages, but that a great variety of ideas are expressed by the long series of suffixes. Another example of similar kind is the Tsimshian word *t-yuk-ligi-lo-d'ɛp-dāʟɛt* HE BEGAN TO PUT IT DOWN SOMEWHERE INSIDE (*t*, he; *yuk* to begin; *ligi* somewhere; *lo* in; *d'ɛp* down; *dāʟ* to put down; *-t* it).

American languages have also been designated as incorporating languages, by which is meant a tendency to incorporate the object of the sentence, either nominal or pronominal, in the verbal expression. Examples of this tendency are the Mexican *ni-petla-tšiwa* I MAKE MATS (*petla-tl* mat); or the Pawnee *tʌ-t-i'tka'wit* I DIG DIRT (*tʌ-* indicative; *t-* I; *i'tkãr^u* dirt; *-pĩt* to dig [*rp* in contact, form *'w*]); or the Oneida *g-nagla'-sl-i-zak-s* I SEARCH FOR A VILLAGE (*g-* I; *-nagla'* to live; *-sl-* abstract noun; *-i-* verbal character; *-zak* to search; *-s* continuative).

A more thorough knowledge of the structure of many American languages shows that the general designation of all these languages as polysynthetic and incorporating is not tenable. We have in America a sufficiently large number of cases of languages in which the pronouns are not incorporated, but joined loosely to the verb, and we also have numerous languages in which the incorporation of many elements into a single word hardly occurs at all. Among the languages treated here, the Chinook may be given as an example of lack of polysynthesis. There are very few, if any, cases in which a single Chinook word expresses an extended complex of ideas, and we notice particularly that there are no large classes of ideas which are expressed in such form that they may be considered as subordinate. An examination of the structure of the Chinook grammar will show that each verbal stem appears modified only by pronominal and a few adverbial elements, and that nouns show hardly any tendency to incorporate new ideas such as are expressed by our adjectives. On the other hand, the Athapascan and the Haida and Tlingit may be taken as examples of languages which, though polysynthetic in the sense here described, do not readily incorporate the object, but treat both pronominal subject and pronominal object as independent elements. Among the languages of northern North America, the Iroquois alone has so strong a tendency to incorporate the nominal object into the verb, and at the same time to modify so much its independent form, that it can be considered as one of the characteristic languages that incorporate the object. To a lesser extent this trait belongs also to the Tsimshian, Kutenai, and Shoshone. It is strongly developed in the Caddoan languages. All the other incorporating languages treated here, like the Eskimo, Algonquian, and Kwakiutl, confine themselves to a more or less close incorporation of the pronominal object. In Shoshone, the incorporation of the pronominal object and of the nominal object is so weak that it is almost arbitrary whether we consider these forms as incorporated or not. If we extend our view over other parts of America, the same facts appear clearly, and it is not possible to consider these two traits as characteristics of all American languages.

On the other hand, there are certain traits that, although not common to all American languages, are at least frequent, and which are not less characteristic than the tendency to objective incorporation and to polysynthesis. The most important of these is the tendency to divide the verb sharply into an active and a neutral class, one of which is closely related to the possessive forms of the noun, while the other is treated as a true verb. We might perhaps say that American languages have a strong tendency to draw the dividing line between denominating terms and predicative terms, not in the same way that we are accustomed to do. In American languages many of our predicative terms are closely related to nominal terms, most frequently the neutral verbs expressing a state, like *to sit, to stand*. These, also, often include a considerable number of adjectives. On the other hand, terms expressing activities—like *to sing, to eat, to kill*—are treated as true predicative terms. The differentiation of these two classes is generally expressed by the occurrence of an entirely or partially separated set of pronouns for the predicative terms.

Beyond these extremely vague points, there are hardly any characteristics that are common to many American languages. A number of traits, however, may be enumerated which occur with considerable frequency in many parts of America.

The phonetic systems of American languages differ very considerably, but we find with remarkable frequency a peculiar differentiation of voiced and unvoiced stops,—corresponding to our *b, p; d, t; g, k,*—which differ in principle from the classification of the corresponding sounds in most of the European languages. An examination of American vocabularies and texts shows very clearly that all observers have had more or less difficulty in differentiating these sounds. Although there is not the slightest doubt that they differ in character, it would seem that there is almost everywhere a tendency to pronounce the voiced and unvoiced sounds with very nearly equal stress of articulation, not as in European languages, where the unvoiced sound is generally pronounced with greater stress. This equality of stress of the two sounds brings it about that their differences appear rather slight. On the other hand, there are frequently sounds, particularly in the languages of the Pacific coast, in which a stress of articulation is used which is considerably greater than any stresses occurring in the languages with which we are familiar. These sounds are generally unvoiced; but a high air-pressure in the oral cavity is secured by closing the glottis and nares, or by closing the posterior part of the mouth with the base of the tongue. The release at the point of articulation lets out the small amount of strongly compressed air, and the subsequent opening of glottis and nares or base of tongue produces a break in the continuity of sound.

We find also with particular frequency the occurrence of a number of lingual stops corresponding more or less strictly to our k sounds which, however, are more finely differentiated than our k sounds. Thus the velar k, which is so characteristic of Semitic languages, occurs with great frequency in America. On the other hand, the labio-dental f seems to be rather rare, and where a similar sound occurs it is often the bilabial sound.

The same may be said of the r, which on the whole is a rare sound in American languages, and the trill of which is almost always so weak that it merges into the d, n, l, or y, as the case may be.

On the whole, the system of consonants of American languages is well developed, particularly owing to the occurrence of the three stresses to which I referred before, instead of the two with which we are more familiar. In some groups of languages we have also a quite distinct set of stops accompanied by full breathing, which correspond to the English surds. Furthermore, a peculiar break, produced by closing the vocal chords, occurs quite commonly, not only in connection with sonants, but also following or preceding vowels or affricative consonants. This intonation is sometimes quite audible, and sometimes merely a break or hiatus in the continuity of pronunciation. Sometimes it seems related to the pronunciation of a voiced consonant in which the voicing is preceded by a closure of the vocal chords. In other cases it seems related to the production of the great stress of articulation to which I referred before. For instance, in a strong t the tongue may be pressed so firmly against the palate that all the articulating organs, including the vocal chords, take part in the tension, and that the sudden expulsion of the air is accompanied also by a sudden relaxation of the vocal chords, so that for this reason the strong, exploded sound appears to be accompanied by an intonation of the vocal chords.

As stated before, these traits are not by any means common to all American languages, but they are sufficiently frequent to deserve mention in a generalized discussion of the subject.

On the other hand, there are languages which are exceedingly deficient in their phonetic system. Among these may be mentioned, for instance, the Iroquois, which possesses not a single true labial consonant; or the Haida, in which the labials are confined to a few sounds, which are rather rare.

The vocalic systems of the northern languages seem peculiarly uncertain. The cases are very numerous in which obscure vowels occur, which are evidently related to fuller vowels, but whose affiliations often can not be determined. It would seem that in the southern languages these weak vowels are not so prominent. We also find very frequently a lack of clear distinction between o and u on the one hand, and e and i on the other. Although the variability of vowels in some of the languages seems beyond doubt, there are others in which the vocalic system is very definite and in which distinctions are expressed, not only by the timbre of the vowel, but also by its rising or falling tone. Among these may be mentioned the Pawnee and the Takelma. The Pawnee seems to have at least two tones, a sinking tone and a rising tone, while in Takelma there seem to be three tones. Nasalized vowels are very common in some languages, and entirely absent in others. This nasalization occurs both with open lips and with closed lips. An example of the latter is the Iroquois u^m.

It is not possible to give any general characterization of American languages with regard to the grouping of sounds. While in some languages consonantic clusters of incredible complexity are formed, others avoid such clusters altogether. There is, however, a habit of pronunciation which deserves attention, and which is found very widely distributed. This is the slurring of the ends of words, which is sometimes so pronounced, that, in an attempt to write the words, the terminations, grammatical or other, may become entirely inaudible. The simplest form in which this tendency expresses itself is in the suppression of terminal consonants, which are only articulated, but not pronounced. In the Nass river dialect of the Tsimshian, for instance, the terminal n of the word *gan* TREE is indicated by the position of the tongue, but is entirely inaudible, unless the word is followed by other words belonging to the same sentence. In that language the same is true of the sounds l and m. Vowels are suppressed in a similar manner by being only indicated by the position of the mouth, without being articulated. This happens frequently to the u following a k, or with an i in the same position.

Thus, the Kwakiutl pronounce $w\bar{a}'d_Ek^u$. If, however, another vowel follows, the u which is not articulated appears as a w, as in the form $w\bar{a}'d_Ekwa$.

The slurring, however, extends over whole syllables, which in these cases may appear highly modified. Thus, in the Oneida dialect of the Iroquois, a peculiar l sound is heard, which presumably occurs only in such slurred syllables. It is very remarkable that the Indians of all tribes are perfectly conscious of the phonetic elements which have thus been suppressed, and can, when pressed to do so, pronounce the words with their full endings.

Another trait that is characteristic of many American languages, and that deserves mention, is the tendency of various parts of the population to modify the pronunciation of sounds. Thus we find that among some Eskimo tribes the men pronounce the terminal p, t, k, and q distinctly, while the women always transform these sounds into m, n, $\tilde{n}$, and $\tilde{\eta}$. In some dialects the men have also adopted this manner of pronouncing, so that the pronunciation has become uniform again. Such mannerisms, that are peculiar to certain social groups, are of course not entirely foreign to us, but they are seldom developed in so striking a manner as in a few of the Indian languages.

In many American languages we find highly developed laws of euphony,—laws by which, automatically, one sound in a sentence requires certain other sounds either to precede or to follow it. In the majority of cases these laws of euphony seem to act forward in a manner that may be compared to the laws of vowel harmony in the Ural-Altaic languages. Particularly remarkable among these laws is the influence of the o upon following vowels, which occurs in a few languages of the Pacific coast. In these, the vowels following an o in the same word must, under certain conditions, be transformed into o vowels, or at least be modified by the addition of a w. Quite different in character are the numerous influences of contact of sounds, which are very pronounced in the Siouan languages, and occur again in a quite different form in the Pawnee. It may be well to give an example of these also. Thus, in Dakota, words ending with an a and followed by a word beginning with a k transform the former into e, the latter into $\check{c}$. In Pawnee, on the other hand, the combination tr is always transformed into an h; b following an i is generally changed into a *w; rp* becomes *hw,* etc. While in some languages these phonetic changes do not occupy a prominent place, they are exceedingly important in others. They correspond in a way to the laws of euphony of Sanskrit.

Just as much variety as is shown in phonetic systems is found in the use of grammatical devices. In discussing the definition of the word, it has been pointed out that in some American languages the word-unit seems to be perfectly clear and consistent, while in others the structure of the sentence would seem to justify us in considering it as composed of a number of independent elements combined by juxtaposition. Thus, languages which have a polysynthetic character have the tendency to form firmly knit word-units, which may be predicative sentences, but may also be used for denominative purposes. For example, the Chinook may say, *He runs into the water,* and may designate by this term *the mink;* or the Hupa may say *They have been laid together,* meaning by this term *a fire.* On the other hand, there are innumerable languages in America in which expressions of this kind are entirely impossible.

In forming words and sentences, affixes are used extensively, and we find prefixes, as well as suffixes and infixes. It is not absolutely certain that cases occur in America where true infixing into a stem takes place, and where it might not be better explained as an insertion of the apparently infixed element into a compound stem, or as due to secondary phonetic phenomena, like those of metathesis; but in the Siouan languages at least, infixion in bisyllabic stems that are apparently simple in their origin occurs. Otherwise, suffixing is, on the whole, more extensively used than prefixing; and in some languages only one of these two methods is used, in others both. There are probably no languages in which prefixing alone occurs.

Change of stem is also a device that is used with great frequency. We find particularly that methods of reduplication are used extensively. Modifications of single sounds of the stem occur also, and sometimes in peculiar form. Thus we have cases, as in Tsimshian, where the lengthening of a vowel indicates plurality; or, as in Algonquian, where modality is expressed by vocalic modification; and, as in Chinook, where diminutive and augmentative are expressed by increasing the stress of consonants. Sometimes an exuberance of reduplicated forms is found, the reduplicated stem being reduplicated a second and even a third time. On the other hand, we find numerous languages in which the stem is entirely unchangeable, excepting so far as it may be subject to phonetic contact phenomena.

The following grammatical sketches have been contributed by investigators, each of whom has made a special study of the linguistic stock of which he treats. The attempt has been made to adopt, so far as feasible, a uniform method of treatment, without, however, sacrificing the individual conception of each investigator.

In accordance with the general views expressed in the introductory chapters, the method of treatment has been throughout an analytical one. No attempt has been made to compare the forms of the Indian grammars with the grammars of English, Latin, or even among themselves; but in each case the psychological groupings which are given depend entirely upon the inner form of each language. In other words, the grammar has been treated as though an intelligent Indian was going to develop the forms of his own thoughts by an analysis of his own form of speech.

It will be understood that the results of this analysis can not be claimed to represent the fundamental categories from which the present form of each language has developed. There is not the slightest doubt that, in all Indian languages, processes have occurred analogous to those processes which are historically known and to which the modern forms of Indo-European languages owe their present forms. Grammatical categories have been lost, and new ones have developed. Even a hasty comparison of the dialects of various American linguistic families gives ample proof that similar processes have taken place here. To give an example, we find that, in the Ponca dialect of the Siouan languages, nouns are classified according to form, and that there is a clear formal distinction between the subject and the object of the sentence. These important features have disappeared entirely in the Dakota dialect of the same group of languages. To give another example, we find a pronominal sex gender in all the dialects of the Salishan stock that are spoken west of the Coast range in the states of Washington and in British Columbia, while in the dialects of the interior there is no trace of gender. On the other hand, we find in one of the Salish dialects of the interior the occurrence of an exclusive and inclusive form of the pronoun, which is absent in all the other dialects of the same stock. We have no information on the history of American languages, and the study of dialects has not advanced far enough to permit us to draw far-reaching inferences in regard to this subject. It is therefore impossible, in the few cases here mentioned, to state whether the occurrence and non-occurrence of these categories are due to a loss of old forms in the one dialect or to a later differentiation in the other.

Although, therefore, an analytical grammar can not lay any claim to present a history of the development of grammatical categories, it is valuable as a presentation of the present state of grammatical development in each linguistic group. The results of our investigation must be supplemented at a later time by a thorough analysis and comparison of all the dialects of each linguistic stock.

Owing to the fundamental differences between different linguistic families, it has seemed advisable to develop the terminology of each independently of the others, and to seek for uniformity only in cases where it can be obtained without artificially stretching the definition of terms. It is planned to give a comparative discussion of the languages at the close of these volumes, when reference can be made to the published sketches.

So far as our present knowledge goes, the following linguistic families may be distinguished in North America north of Mexico:

1. Eskimo (arctic coast).
2. Athapascan (northwestern interior, Oregon, California, Southwest).
3. Tlingit (coast of southern Alaska).
4. Haida (Queen Charlotte islands, British Columbia).
5. Salishan (southern British Columbia and northern Washington).
6. Chemakum (west coast of Washington).
7. Wakashan (Vancouver island).
8. Algonquian (region south of Hudson Bay and eastern Woodlands).
9. Beothuk (Newfoundland).
10. Tsimshian (northern coast of British Columbia).
11. Siouan (northern plains west of Mississippi and North Carolina).
12. Iroquoian (lower Great Lakes and North Carolina).
13. Caddoan (southern part of plains west of Mississippi).
14. Muskhogean (southeastern United States).
15. Kiowa (middle Western plains).
16. Shoshonean (western plateaus of United States).

17. Kutenai (southeastern interior of British Columbia).
18. Pima (Arizona and Sonora).
19. Yuma (Arizona and lower California).
20. Chinook (lower Columbia river).
21. Yakona (Yaquina bay).
22. Kus (coast of central Oregon).
23. Takelma (Rogue river, Oregon).
24. Kalapuya (Willamette valley, Oregon).
25. Waiilaptuan (Cascade range east of Willamette, Ore.).
26. Klamath (southeastern interior of Oregon).
27. Sahaptin (interior of Oregon).
28. Quoratean (Klamath river).
29. Weitspekan (lower Klamath river).
30. Shasta (northeast interior of California).
31. Wishok (north coast of California).
32. Yana (eastern tributaries of upper Sacramento river, California).
33. Chimarico (head waters of Sacramento river, California).
34. Wintun (valley of Sacramento river).
35. Maidu (east of Sacramento river).
36. Yuki (north of Bay of San Francisco).
37. Pomo (coast north of Bay of San Francisco).
38. Washo (Lake Washoe, Nevada, and California).
39. Moquelumnan (east of lower Tulare river, California).
40. Yokuts (southern Tulare river, California).
41. Costanoan (south of Bay of San Francisco, California).
42. Esselenian (coast of southern California).
43. Salinan (coast of southern California).
44. Chumashan (coast of southern California).
45. Tanoan ⎫
46. Zuñi   ⎬ (Pueblos of New Mexico and Arizona).
47. Keres ⎭
48. Pakawan (from Cibolo creek, Texas, into the state of Coahuila, Mexico).
49. Karankawa (coast of Gulf of Mexico west of Atakapa).
50. Tonkawa (inland from preceding).
51. Atakapa (coast of Gulf of Mexico west of Chitimacha).
52. Chitimacha (coast of Gulf of Mexico west of Mississippi).
53. Tunica (coast of Gulf of Mexico west of Mississippi).
54. Yuchi (east Georgia).
55. Timuqua (Florida).

Indian Linguistic Families
of America North of Mexico

Indian Linguistic Families

By J. W. POWELL.

NOMENCLATURE OF LINGUISTIC FAMILIES.

The languages spoken by the pre-Columbian tribes of North America were many and diverse. Into the regions occupied by these tribes travelers, traders, and missionaries have penetrated in advance of civilization, and civilization itself has marched across the continent at a rapid rate. Under these conditions the languages of the various tribes have received much study. Many extensive works have been published, embracing grammars and dictionaries ; but a far greater number of minor vocabularies have been collected and very many have been published. In addition to these, the Bible, in whole or in part, and various religious books and school books, have been translated into Indian tongues to be used for purposes of instruction ; and newspapers have been published in the Indian languages. Altogether the literature of these languages and that relating to them are of vast extent.

While the materials seem thus to be abundant, the student of Indian languages finds the subject to be one requiring most thoughtful consideration, difficulties arising from the following conditions:

(1) A great number of linguistic stocks or families are discovered.

(2) The boundaries between the different stocks of languages are not immediately apparent, from the fact that many tribes of diverse stocks have had more or less association, and to some extent linguistic materials have been borrowed, and thus have passed out of the exclusive possession of cognate peoples.

(3) Where many peoples, each few in number, are thrown together, an intertribal language is developed. To a large extent this is gesture speech ; but to a limited extent useful and important words are adopted by various tribes, and out of this material an intertribal "jargon" is established. Travelers and all others who do not thoroughly study a language are far more likely to acquire this jargon speech than the real speech of the people ; and the tendency to base relationship upon such jargons has led to confusion.

83

(4) This tendency to the establishment of intertribal jargons was greatly accelerated on the advent of the white man, for thereby many tribes were pushed from their ancestral homes and tribes were mixed with tribes. As a result, new relations and new industries, especially of trade, were established, and the new associations of tribe with tribe and of the Indians with Europeans led very often to the development of quite elaborate jargon languages. All of these have a tendency to complicate the study of the Indian tongues by comparative methods.

The difficulties inherent in the study of languages, together with the imperfect material and the complicating conditions that have arisen by the spread of civilization over the country, combine to make the problem one not readily solved.

In view of the amount of material on hand, the comparative study of the languages of North America has been strangely neglected, though perhaps this is explained by reason of the difficulties which have been pointed out. And the attempts which have been made to classify them has given rise to much confusion, for the following reasons : First, later authors have not properly recognized the work of earlier laborers in the field. Second, the attempt has more frequently been made to establish an ethnic classification than a linguistic classification, and linguistic characteristics have been confused with biotic peculiarities, arts, habits, customs, and other human activities, so that radical differences of language have often been ignored and slight differences have been held to be of primary value.

The attempts at a classification of these languages and a corresponding classification of races have led to the development of a complex, mixed, and inconsistent synonymy, which must first be unraveled and a selection of standard names made therefrom according to fixed principles.

It is manifest that until proper rules are recognized by scholars the establishment of a determinate nomenclature is impossible. It will therefore be well to set forth the rules that have here been adopted, together with brief reasons for the same, with the hope that they will commend themselves to the judgment of other persons engaged in researches relating to the languages of North America.

A fixed nomenclature in biology has been found not only to be advantageous, but to be a prerequisite to progress in research, as the vast multiplicity of facts, still ever accumulating, would otherwise overwhelm the scholar. In philological classification fixity of nomenclature is of corresponding importance; and while the analogies between linguistic and biotic classification are quite limited, many of the principles of nomenclature which biologists have adopted having no application in philology, still in some important particulars the requirements of all scientific classifications are alike, and though many of the nomenclatural points met with in biology will not occur in philology, some of them do occur and may be governed by the same rules.

Perhaps an ideal nomenclature in biology may some time be established, as attempts have been made to establish such a system in chemistry; and possibly such an ideal system may eventually be established in philology. Be that as it may, the time has not yet come even for its suggestion. What is now needed is a rule of some kind leading scholars to use the same terms for the same things, and it would seem to matter little in the case of linguistic stocks what the nomenclature is, provided it becomes denotive and universal.

In treating of the languages of North America it has been suggested that the names adopted should be the names by which the people recognize themselves, but this is a rule of impossible application, for where the branches of a stock diverge very greatly no common name for the people can be found. Again, it has been suggested that names which are to go permanently into science should be simple and euphonic. This also is impossible of application, for simplicity and euphony are largely questions of personal taste, and he who has studied many languages loses speedily his idiosyncrasies of likes and dislikes and learns that words foreign to his vocabulary are not necessarily barbaric.

Biologists have decided that he who first distinctly characterizes and names a species or other group shall thereby cause the name thus used to become permanently affixed, but under certain conditions adapted to a growing science which is continually revising its classifications. This law of priority may well be adopted by philologists.

By the application of the law of priority it will occasionally happen that a name must be taken which is not wholly unobjectionable or which could be much improved. But if names may be modified for any reason, the extent of change that may be wrought in this manner is unlimited. and such modifications would ultimately become equivalent to the introduction of new names, and a fixed nomenclature would thereby be overthrown. The rule of priority has therefore been adopted.

Permanent biologic nomenclature dates from the time of Linnæus simply because this great naturalist established the binominal system and placed scientific classification upon a sound and enduring basis. As Linnæus is to be regarded as the founder of biologic classification, so Gallatin may be considered the founder of systematic philology relating to the North American Indians. Before his time much linguistic work had been accomplished, and scholars owe a lasting debt of gratitude to Barton, Adelung, Pickering, and others. But Gallatin's work marks an era in American linguistic science from the fact that he so thoroughly introduced comparative methods, and because he circumscribed the boundaries of many families, so that a large part of his work remains and is still to be considered sound. There is no safe resting place anterior to Galla-tin, because no scholar prior to his time had properly adopted com-parative methods of research, and because no scholar was privileged to work with so large a body of material. It must further be said of Gallatin that he had a very clear conception of the task he was performing, and brought to it both learning and wisdom. Gallatin's work has therefore been taken as the starting point, back of which we may not go in the historic consideration of the systematic phi-lology of North America. The point of departure therefore is the year 1836, when Gallatin's "Synopsis of Indian Tribes" appeared in vol. 2 of the Transactions of the American Antiquarian Society.

It is believed that a name should be simply a denotive word, and that no advantage can accrue from a descriptive or connotive title. It is therefore desirable to have the names as simple as possible, consistent with other and more important considerations. For this reason it has been found impracticable to recognize as family names designations based on several distinct terms, such as descriptive phrases, and words compounded from two or more geographic names. Such phrases and compound words have been rejected.

There are many linguistic families in North America, and in a number of them there are many tribes speaking diverse languages. It is important, therefore, that some form should be given to the family name by which it may be distinguished from the name of a single tribe or language. In many cases some one language within a stock has been taken as the type and its name given to the entire family; so that the name of a language and that of the stock to which it belongs are identical. This is inconvenient and leads to confusion. For such reasons it has been decided to give each family name the termination "an" or "ian."

Conforming to the principles thus enunciated, the following rules have been formulated:

I. The law of priority relating to the nomenclature of the sys-tematic philology of the North American tribes shall not extend to authors whose works are of date anterior to the year 1836.

II. The name originally given by the founder of a linguistic group to designate it as a family or stock of languages shall be permanently retained to the exclusion of all others.

III. No family name shall be recognized if composed of more than one word.

IV. A family name once established shall not be canceled in any subsequent division of the group, but shall be retained in a restricted sense for one of its constituent portions.

V. Family names shall be distinguished as such by the termina-tion "an" or "ian."

VI. No name shall be accepted for a linguistic family unless used to designate a tribe or group of tribes as a linguistic stock.

VII. No family name shall be accepted unless there is given the habitat of tribe or tribes to which it is applied.

VIII. The original orthography of a name shall be rigidly preserved except as provided for in rule III, and unless a typographical error is evident.

The terms " family " and " stock " are here applied interchangeably to a group of languages that are supposed to be cognate.

A single language is called a stock or family when it is not found to be cognate with any other language. Languages are said to be cognate when such relations between them are found that they are supposed to have descended from a common ancestral speech. The evidence of cognation is derived exclusively from the vocabulary. Grammatic similarities are not supposed to furnish evidence of cognation, but to be phenomena, in part relating to stage of culture and in part adventitious. It must be remembered that extreme peculiarities of grammar, like the vocal mutations of the Hebrew or the monosyllabic separation of the Chinese, have not been discovered among Indian tongues. It therefore becomes necessary in the classification of Indian languages into families to neglect grammatic structure, and to consider lexical elements only. But this statement must be clearly understood. It is postulated that in the growth of languages new words are formed by combination, and that these new words change by attrition to secure economy of utterance, and also by assimilation (analogy) for economy of thought. In the comparison of languages for the purposes of systematic philology it often becomes necessary to dismember compounded words for the purpose of comparing the more primitive forms thus obtained. The paradigmatic words considered in grammatic treatises may often be the very words which should be dissected to discover in their elements primary affinities. But the comparison is still lexic, not grammatic.

A lexic comparison is between vocal elements; a grammatic comparison is between grammatic methods, such, for example, as gender systems. The classes into which things are relegated by distinction of gender may be animate and inanimate, and the animate may subsequently be divided into male and female, and these two classes may ultimately absorb, in part at least, inanimate things. The growth of a system of genders may take another course. The animate and inanimate may be subdivided into the standing, the sitting, and the lying, or into the moving, the erect and the reclined; or, still further, the superposed classification may be based upon the supposed constitution of things, as the fleshy, the woody, the rocky, the earthy, the watery. Thus the number of genders may increase, while further on in the history of a language the genders may decrease so as almost to disappear.   All of these characteristics are in part adventitious, but to a large extent the gender is a phenomenon of growth, indicating the stage to which the language has attained. A proper case system may not have been established in a language by the fixing of case particles, or, having been established, it may change by the increase or diminution of the number of cases.   A tense system also has a beginning, a growth, and a decadence.   A mode system is variable in the various stages of the history of a language.   In like manner a pronominal system undergoes changes. Particles may be prefixed, infixed, or affixed in compounded words, and which one of these methods will finally prevail can be determined only in the later stage of growth.   All of these things are held to belong to the grammar of a language and to be grammatic methods, distinct from lexical elements.

With terms thus defined, languages are supposed to be cognate when fundamental similarities are discovered in their lexical elements. When the members of a family of languages are to be classed in subdivisions and the history of such languages investigated, grammatic characteristics become of primary importance.   The words of a language change by the methods described, but the fundamental elements or roots are more enduring.   Grammatic methods also change, perhaps even more rapidly than words, and the changes may go on to such an extent that primitive methods are entirely lost, there being no radical grammatic elements to be preserved. Grammatic structure is but a phase or accident of growth, and not a primordial element of language.   The roots of a language are its most permanent characteristics, and while the words which are formed from them may change so as to obscure their elements or in some cases even to lose them, it seems that they are never lost from all, but can be recovered in large part.   The grammatic structure or plan of a language is forever changing, and in this respect the language may become entirely transformed.

LITERATURE RELATING TO THE CLASSIFICATION OF INDIAN LANGUAGES.

While the literature relating to the languages of North America is very extensive, that which relates to their classification is much less extensive.   For the benefit of future students in this line it is thought best to present a concise account of such literature, or at least so much as has been consulted in the preparation of this paper.

1836. Gallatin (Albert).
A synopsis of the Indian tribes within the United States east of the Rocky Mountains, and in the British and Russian possessions in North America. In Transactions and Collections of the American Antiquarian Society (Archæologia Americana) Cambridge, 1836, vol. 2.

The larger part of the volume consists of Gallatin's paper.   A short chapter is devoted to general observations, including certain historical data, and the remainder to the discussion of linguistic material and the affinities of the various tribes mentioned. Vocabularies of many of the families are appended. Twenty-eight linguistic divisions are recognized in the general table of the tribes. Some of these divisions are purely geographic, such as the tribes of Salmon River, Queen Charlotte's Island, etc. Vocabularies from these localities were at hand, but of their linguistic relations the author was not sufficiently assured. Most of the linguistic families recognized by Gallatin were defined with much precision. Not all of his conclusions are to be accepted in the presence of the data now at hand, but usually they were sound, as is attested by the fact that they have constituted the basis for much classificatory work since his time.

The primary, or at least the ostensible, purpose of the colored map which accompanies Gallatin's paper was, as indicated by its title, to show the distribution of the tribes, and accordingly their names appear upon it, and not the names of the linguistic families. Nevertheless, it is practically a map of the linguistic families as determined by the author, and it is believed to be the first attempted for the area represented. Only eleven of the twenty-eight families named in this table appear, and these represent the families with which he was best acquainted. As was to be expected from the early period at which the map was constructed, much of the western part of the United States was left uncolored. Altogether the map illustrates well the state of knowledge of the time.

1840. Bancroft (George).
History of the colonization of the United States, Boston, 1840, vol. 3.

In Chapter XXII of this volume the author gives a brief synopsis of the Indian tribes east of the Mississippi, under a linguistic classification, and adds a brief account of the character and methods of Indian languages. A linguistic map of the region is incorporated, which in general corresponds with the one published by Gallatin in 1836. A notable addition to the Gallatin map is the inclusion of the Uchees in their proper locality. Though considered a distinct family by Gallatin, this tribe does not appear upon his map. Moreover, the Choctaws and Muskogees, which appear as separate families upon Gallatin's map (though believed by that author to belong to the same family), are united upon Bancroft's map under the term Mobilian.

The linguistic families treated of are, I. Algonquin, II. Sioux or Dahcota, III. Huron-Iroquois, IV. Catawba, V. Cherokee, VI. Uchee, VII. Natchez, VIII. Mobilian.

1841. Scouler (John).
Observations of the indigenous tribes of the northwest coast of America. In Journal of the Royal Geographical Society of London. London, 1841, vol. 11.

The chapter cited is short, but long enough to enable the author to construct a very curious classification of the tribes of which he treats. In his account Scouler is guided chiefly, to use his own words, "by considerations founded on their physical character, manners and customs, and on the affinities of their languages." As the linguistic considerations are mentioned last, so they appear to be the least weighty of his "considerations."

Scouler's definition of a family is very broad indeed, and in his "Northern Family," which is a branch of his "Insular Group," he includes such distinct linguistic stocks as "all the Indian tribes in the Russian territory," the Queen Charlotte Islanders, Koloshes, Ugalentzes, Atnas, Kolchans, Kenáïes, Tun Ghaase, Haidahs, and Chimmesyans. His Nootka-Columbian family is scarcely less incongruous, and it is evident that the classification indicated is only to a comparatively slight extent linguistic.

1846. Hale (Horatio).
United States exploring expedition, during the years 1838, 1839, 1840, 1841, 1842, under the command of Charles Wilkes, U. S. Navy, vol. 6, ethnography and philology. Philadelphia, 1846.

In addition to a large amount of ethnographic data derived from the Polynesian Islands, Micronesian Islands, Australia, etc., more than one-half of this important volume is devoted to philology, a large share relating to the tribes of northwestern America.

The vocabularies collected by Hale, and the conclusions derived by him from study of them, added much to the previous knowledge of the languages of these tribes. His conclusions and classification were in the main accepted by Gallatin in his linguistic writings of 1848.

1846. Latham (Robert Gordon).
Miscellaneous contributions to the ethnography of North America. In Proceedings of the Philological Society of London. London, 1846, vol. 2.

In this article, which was read before the Philological Society, January 24, 1845, a large number of North American languages are examined and their affinities discussed in support of the two following postulates made at the beginning of the paper: First, "No American language has an isolated position when compared with the other tongues en masse rather than with the language of any particular class;" second, "The affinities between the language of the New World, as determined by their *vocabularies*, is not less real than that inferred from the analogies of their *grammatical structure*." The author's conclusions are that both statements are substantiated by the evidence presented. The paper contains no new family names.

1847. Prichard (James Cowles).
Researches into the physical history of mankind (third edition), vol. 5, containing researches into the history of the Oceanic and of the American nations. London, 1847.

It was the purpose of this author, as avowed by himself, to determine whether the races of men are the cooffspring of a single stock or have descended respectively from several original families. Like other authors on this subject, his theory of what should constitute a race was not clearly defined. The scope of the inquiry required the consideration of a great number of subjects and led to the accumulation of a vast body of facts. In volume 5 the author treats of the American Indians, and in connection with the different tribes has something to say of their languages. No attempt at an original classification is made, and in the main the author follows Gallatin's classification and adopts his conclusions.

1848. Gallatin (Albert).

Hale's Indians of Northwest America, and vocabularies of North America, with an introduction. In Transactions of the American Ethnological Society, New York, 1848, vol. 2.

The introduction consists of a number of chapters, as follows: First, Geographical notices and Indian means of subsistence; second, Ancient semi-civilization of New Mexico, Rio Gila and its vicinity; third, Philology; fourth, Addenda and miscellaneous. In these are brought together much valuable information, and many important deductions are made which illustrate Mr. Gallatin's great acumen. The classification given is an amplification of that adopted in 1836, and contains changes and additions. The latter mainly result from a consideration of the material supplied by Mr. Hale, or are simply taken from his work.

The groups additional to those contained in the Archæologia Americana are:

1. Arrapahoes.	6. Palainih.
2. Jakon.	7. Sahaptin.
3. Kalapuya.	8. Selish (Tsihaili-Selish).
4. Kitunaha.	9. Saste.
5. Lutuami.	10. Waiilatpu.

1848. Latham (Robert Gordon).

On the languages of the Oregon Territory. In Journal of the Ethnological Society of London, Edinburgh, 1848, vol. 1.

This paper was read before the Ethnological Society on the 11th of December. The languages noticed are those that lie between "Russian America and New California," of which the author aims to give an exhaustive list. He discusses the value of the groups to which these languages have been assigned, viz, Athabascan and Nootka-Columbian, and finds that they have been given too high value, and that they are only equivalent to the primary subdivisions of *stocks*, like the Gothic, Celtic, and Classical, rather than to the stocks themselves. He further finds that the Athabascan, the Kolooch, the Nootka-Columbian, and the Cadiak groups are subordinate members of one large and important class—the Eskimo.

No new linguistic groups are presented.

1848. Latham (Robert Gordon).

On the ethnography of Russian America. In Journal of the Ethnological Society of London, Edinburgh, 1848, vol. 1.

This essay was read before the Ethnological Society February 19, 1845. Brief notices are given of the more important tribes, and the languages are classed in two groups, the Eskimaux and the Kolooch. Each of these groups is found to have affinities—

(1) With the Athabascan tongues, and perhaps equal affinities.

(2) Each has affinities with the Oregon languages, and each perhaps equally.

(3) Each has definite affinities with the languages of New California, and each perhaps equal ones.

(4) Each has miscellaneous affinities with all the other tongues of North and South America.

> 1848. Berghaus (Heinrich).
> Physikalischer Atlas oder Sammlung von Karten, auf denen die hauptsäch-
> lichsten erscheinungen der anorganischen und organischen Natur nach
> ihrer geographischen Verbreitung und Vertheilung bildlich dargestellt
> sind. Zweiter Band, Gotha, 1848.

This, the first edition of this well known atlas, contains, among other maps, an ethnographic map of North America, made in 1845. It is based, as is stated, upon material derived from Gallatin, Humboldt, Clavigero, Hervas, Vater, and others. So far as the eastern part of the United States is concerned it is largely a duplication of Gallatin's map of 1836, while in the western region a certain amount of new material is incorporated.

1852. In the edition of 1852 the ethnographic map bears date of 1851. Its eastern portion is substantially a copy of the earlier edition, but its western half is materially changed, chiefly in accordance with the knowledge supplied by Hall in 1848.

Map number 72 of the last edition of Berghaus by no means marks an advance upon the edition of 1852. Apparently the number of families is much reduced, but it is very difficult to interpret the meaning of the author, who has attempted on the same map to indicate linguistic divisions and tribal habitats with the result that confusion is made worse confounded.

> 1853. Gallatin (Albert).
> Classification of the Indian Languages; a letter inclosing a table of generic
> Indian Families of languages. In Information respecting the History,
> Condition, and Prospects of the Indian Tribes of the United States, by
> Henry R. Schoolcraft. Philadelphia, 1853, vol. 3.

This short paper by Gallatin consists of a letter addressed to W. Medill, Commissioner of Indian Affairs, requesting his cooperation in an endeavor to obtain vocabularies to assist in a more complete study of the grammar and structure of the languages of the Indians of North America. It is accompanied by a "Synopsis of Indian Tribes," giving the families and tribes so far as known. In the main the classification is a repetition of that of 1848, but it differs from that in a number of particulars. Two of the families of 1848 do not appear in this paper, viz, Arapaho and Kinai. Queen Charlotte Island, employed as a family name in 1848, is placed under the Wakash family, while the Skittagete language, upon which the name Queen Charlotte Island was based in 1848, is here given as a family designation for the language spoken at "Sitka, bet. 52 and 59 lat." The following families appear which are not contained in the list of 1848:

1. Cumanches.	5. Natchitoches.
2. Gros Ventres.	6. Pani, Towiacks.
3. Kaskaias.	7. Ugaljachmutzi.
4. Kiaways.	

1853. Gibbs (George).
Observations on some of the Indian dialects of northern California. In Information respecting the History, Condition, and Prospects of the Indian tribes of the United States, by Henry R. Schoolcraft. Philadelphia, 1853, vol. 3.

The "Observations" are introductory to a series of vocabularies collected in northern California, and treat of the method employed in collecting them and of the difficulties encountered. They also contain notes on the tribes speaking the several languages as well as on the area covered. There is comparatively little of a classificatory nature, though in one instance the name Quoratem is proposed as a proper one for the family "should it be held one."

1854. Latham (Robert Gordon).
On the languages of New California. In Proceedings of the Philological Society of London for 1852 and 1853. London, 1854, vol. 6.

Read before the Philological Society, May 13, 1853. A number of languages are examined in this paper for the purpose of determining the stocks to which they belong and the mutual affinities of the latter. Among the languages mentioned are the Saintskla, Umkwa, Lutuami, Paduca, Athabascan, Dieguno, and a number of the Mission languages.

1855. Lane (William Carr).
Letter on affinities of dialects in New Mexico. In Information respecting the History, Condition, and Prospects of the Indian tribes of the United States, by Henry R. Schoolcraft. Philadelphia, 1855, vol. 5.

The letter forms half a page of printed matter. The gist of the communication is in effect that the author has heard it said that the Indians of certain pueblos speak three different languages, which he has heard called, respectively, (1) Chu-cha-cas and Kes-whaw-hay; (2) E-nagh-magh; (3) Tay-waugh. This can hardly be called a classification, though the arrangement of the pueblos indicated by Lane is quoted at length by Keane in the Appendix to Stanford's Compendium.

1856. Latham (Robert Gordon).

On the languages of Northern, Western, and Central America. In Transactions of the Philological Society of London, for 1856. London [1857?].

This paper was read before the Philological Society May 9, 1856,
and is stated to be " a supplement to two well known contributions
to American philology by the late A. Gallatin."

So far as classification of North American languages goes, this is
perhaps the most important paper of Latham's, as in it a number
of new names are proposed for linguistic groups, such as Copeh for
the Sacramento River tribes, Ehnik for the Karok tribes, Mariposa
Group and Mendocino Group for the Yokut and Pomo tribes respectively, Moquelumne for the Mutsun, Pujuni for the Meidoo, Weitspek for the Eurocs.

1856. Turner (William Wadden).

Report upon the Indian tribes, by Lieut. A. W. Whipple, Thomas Ewbank,
esq., and Prof. William W. Turner, Washington, D. C., 1855. In Reports
of Explorations and Surveys to ascertain the most practicable and
economical route for a railroad from the Mississippi to the Pacific Ocean.
Washington, 1856, vol. 3. part 3.

Chapter V of the above report is headed " Vocabularies of North
American Languages," and is by Turner, as is stated in a foot-note.
Though the title page of Part III is dated 1855, the chapter by
Turner was not issued till 1856, the date of the full volume, as is
stated by Turner on page 84. The following are the vocabularies
given, with their arrangement in families:

I. Delaware.	Algonkin.	XI. Navajo.	Apache.
II. Shawnee.		XII. Pinal Leño.	
III. Choctaw.		XIII. Kiwomi.	Keres.
IV. Kichai.	Pawnee?	XIV. Cochitemi.	
V. Huéco.		XV. Acoma.	
VI. Caddo.		XVI. Zuñi.	
VII. Comanche.	Shoshonee.	XVII. Pima.	
VIII. Chemehuevi.		XVIII. Cuchan.	Yuma.
IX. Cahuillo.		XIX. Coco-Maricopa.	
X. Kioway.		XX. Mojave.	
		XXI. Diegeno.	

Several of the family names, viz, Keres, Kiowa, Yuma, and Zuñi,
have been adopted under the rules formulated above.

1858. Buschmann (Johann Carl Eduard).

Die Völker und Sprachen Neu-Mexiko's und der Westseite des britischen
Nordamerika's, dargestellt von Hrn. Buschmann. In Abhandlungen
(aus dem Jahre 1857) der königlichen Akademie der Wissenschaften zu
Berlin. Berlin, 1858.

This work contains a historic review of early discoveries in New
Mexico and of the tribes living therein, with such vocabularies as
were available at the time. On pages 315–414 the tribes of British
America, from about latitude 54° to 60°, are similarly treated, the
various discoveries being reviewed; also those on the North Pacific
coast. Much of the material should have been inserted in the

volume of 1859 (which was prepared in 1854), to which cross reference is frequently made, and to which it stands in the nature of a supplement.

> 1859. Buschmann (Johann Carl Eduard).
> Die Spuren der aztekischen Sprache im nördlichen Mexico und höheren amerikanischen Norden. Zugleich eine Musterung der Völker und Sprachen des nördlichen Mexico's und der Westseite Nordamerika's von Guadalaxara an bis zum Eismeer. In Abhandlungen aus dem Jahre 1854 der königlichen Akademie der Wissenschaften zu Berlin. Berlin, 1859.

The above, forming a second supplemental volume of the Transactions for 1854, is an extensive compilation of much previous literature treating of the Indian tribes from the Arctic Ocean southward to Guadalajara, and bears specially upon the Aztec language and its traces in the languages of the numerous tribes scattered along the Pacific Ocean and inland to the high plains. A large number of vocabularies and a vast amount of linguistic material are here brought together and arranged in a comprehensive manner to aid in the study attempted. In his classification of the tribes east of the Rocky Mountains, Buschmann largely followed Gallatin. His treatment of those not included in Gallatin's paper is in the main original. Many of the results obtained may have been considered bold at the time of publication, but recent philological investigations give evidence of the value of many of the author's conclusions.

> 1859. Kane (Paul).
> Wanderings of an artist among the Indians of North America from Canada to Vancouver's Island and Oregon through the Hudson's Bay Company's territory and back again. London, 1859.

The interesting account of the author's travels among the Indians, chiefly in the Northwest, and of their habits, is followed by a four-page supplement, giving the names, locations, and census of the tribes of the Northwest coast. They are classified by language into Chymseyan, including the Nass, Chymseyans, Skeena and Sabassas Indians, of whom twenty-one tribes are given; Ha-eelb-zuk or Ballabola, including the Milbank Sound Indians, with nine tribes; Klen-e-kate, including twenty tribes; Hai-dai, including the Kygargey and Queen Charlotte's Island Indians, nineteen tribes being enumerated; and Qua-colth, with twenty-nine tribes. No statement of the origin of these tables is given, and they reappear, with no explanation, in Schoolcraft's Indian Tribes, volume v, pp. 487–489.

In his Queen Charlotte Islands, 1870, Dawson publishes the part of this table relating to the Haida, with the statement that he received it from Dr. W. F. Tolmie. The census was made in 1836–'41 by the late Mr. John Work, who doubtless was the author of the more complete tables published by Kane and Schoolcraft.

1862. Latham (Robert Gordon).
Elements of comparative philology. London, 1862.

The object of this volume is, as the author states in his preface, "to lay before the reader the chief facts and the chief trains of reasoning in Comparative Philology." Among the great mass of material accumulated for the purpose a share is devoted to the languages of North America. The remarks under these are often taken verbatim from the author's earlier papers, to which reference has been made above, and the family names and classification set forth in them are substantially repeated.

1862. Hayden (Ferdinand Vandeveer).
Contributions to the ethnography and philology of the Indian tribes of the Missouri Valley. Philadelphia, 1862.

This is a valuable contribution to our knowledge of the Missouri River tribes, made at a time when the information concerning them was none too precise. The tribes treated of are classified as follows:

I. Knisteneaux, or Crees.	
II. Blackfeet.	Algonkin Group, A.
III. Shyennes.	
IV. Arapohos.	
V. Atsinas.	Arapoho Group, B.
VI. Pawnees.	
VII. Arikaras.	Pawnee Group, C.
VIII. Dakotas.	
IX. Assiniboins.	
X. Crows.	
XI. Minnitarees.	Dakota Group, D
XII. Mandans.	
XIII. Omahas.	
XIV. Iowas.	

1864. Orozco y Berra (Manuel).
Geografía de las Lenguas y Carta Etnográfica de México Precedidas de un ensayo de clasificacion de las mismas lenguas y de apuntes para las inmigraciones de las tribus. Mexico, 1864.

The work is divided into three parts. (1) Tentative classification of the languages of Mexico; (2) notes on the immigration of the tribes of Mexico; (3) geography of the languages of Mexico.

The author states that he has no knowledge whatever of the languages he treats of. All he attempts to do is to summarize the opinions of others. His authorities were (1) writers on native grammars; (2) missionaries; (3) persons who are reputed to be versed in such matters. He professes to have used his own judgment only when these authorities left him free to do so.

His stated method in compiling the ethnographic map was to place before him the map of a certain department, examine all his authorities bearing on that department, and to mark with a distinctive color all localities said to belong to a particular language. When this was done he drew a boundary line around the area of that language. Examination of the map shows that he has partly expressed on it the classification of languages as given in the first part of his text, and partly limited himself to indicating the geographic boundaries of languages, without, however, giving the boundaries of all the languages mentioned in his lists.

1865. Pimentel (Francisco).
Cuadro Descriptivo y Comparativo de las Lenguas Indígenas de México. México, 1865.

According to the introduction this work is divided into three parts: (1) descriptive; (2) comparative; (3) critical.

The author divides the treatment of each language into (1) its mechanism; (2) its dictionary; (3) its grammar. By "mechanism" he means pronunciation and composition; by "dictionary" he means the commonest or most notable words.

In the case of each language he states the localities where it is spoken, giving a short sketch of its history, the explanation of its etymology, and a list of such writers on that language as he has become acquainted with. Then follows: "mechanism, dictionary, and grammar." Next he enumerates its dialects if there are any, and compares specimens of them when he is able. He gives the Our Father when he can.

Volume I (1862) contains introduction and twelve languages. Volume II (1865) contains fourteen groups of languages, a vocabulary of the Opata language, and an appendix treating of the Comanche, the Coahuilteco, and various languages of upper California.

Volume III (announced in preface of Volume II) is to contain the "comparative part" (to be treated in the same "mixed" method as the "descriptive part"), and a scientific classification of all the languages spoken in Mexico.

In the "critical part" (apparently dispersed through the other two parts) the author intends to pass judgment on the merits of the languages of Mexico, to point out their good qualities and their defects.

1870. Dall (William Healey).
On the distribution of the native tribes of Alaska and the adjacent territory. In Proceedings of the American Association for the Advancement of Science. Cambridge, 1870, vol. 18.

In this important paper is presented much interesting information concerning the inhabitants of Alaska and adjacent territories. The natives are divided into two groups, the Indians of the interior, and the inhabitants of the coast, or Esquimaux. The latter are designated by the term Orarians, which are composed of three lesser groups, Eskimo, Aleutians, and Tuski. The Orarians are distinguished, first, by their language; second, by their distribution; third, by their habits; fourth, by their physical characteristics.

1870. Dall (William Healey).
Alaska and its Resources. Boston, 1870.

The classification followed is practically the same as is given in the author's article in the Proceedings of the American Association for the Advancement of Science.

1877.   Dall (William Healey).
Tribes of the extreme northwest.   In Contributions to North American Ethnology (published by United States Geographical and Geological Survey
  of the Rocky Mountain Region).   Washington, 1877, vol. 1.

This is an amplification of the paper published in the Proceedings
of the American Association, as above cited.   The author states
that "numerous additions and corrections, as well as personal observations of much before taken at second hand, have placed it in my
power to enlarge and improve my original arrangement."

In this paper the Orarians are divided into "two well marked
groups," the Innuit, comprising all the so-called Eskimo and Tuskis,
and the Aleuts.   The paper proper is followed by an appendix by
Gibbs and Dall, in which are presented a series of vocabularies
from the northwest, including dialects of the Tlinkit and Haida
nations, T'sim-si-ans, and others.

1877.   Gibbs (George).
Tribes of Western Washington and Northwestern Oregon.   In Contributions
  to North American Ethnology.   Washington, 1887, vol. 1.

This is a valuable article, and gives many interesting particulars
of the tribes of which it treats.   References are here and there
made to the languages of the several tribes, with, however, no
attempt at their classification.   A table follows the report, in which
is given by Dall, after Gibbs, a classification of the tribes mentioned
by Gibbs.   Five families are mentioned, viz: Nūtka, Sahaptin,
Tinneh, Selish, and T'sinūk.   The comparative vocabularies follow
Part II.

1877.   Powers (Stephen).
Tribes of California.   In Contributions to North American Ethnology.   Washington, 1877, vol. 3.

The extended paper on the Californian tribes which makes up the
bulk of this volume is the most important contribution to the subject ever made.   The author's unusual opportunities for personal
observation among these tribes were improved to the utmost and
the result is a comparatively full and comprehensive account of
their habits and character.

Here and there are allusions to the languages spoken, with reference to the families to which the tribes belong.   No formal classification is presented.

1877.   Powell (John Wesley).
Appendix.   Linguistics edited by J. W. Powell.   In Contributions to North
  American Ethnology.   Washington, 1877, vol. 3.

This appendix consists of a series of comparative vocabularies
collected by Powers, Gibbs and others, classified into linguistic
families, as follows:

Family.	Family.
1. Ká-rok.	8. Mūt'-sūn.
2. Yú-rok.	9. Santa Barbara.
3. Chim-a-rí-ko.	10. Yó-kuts.
4. Wish-osk.	11. Mai'-du.
5. Yú-ki.	12. A-cho-mâ'-wi.
6. Pómo.	13. Shaś-ta.
7. Win-tūn'.	

1877. Gatschet (Albert Samuel).
Indian languages of the Pacific States and Territories. In Magazine of American History. New York, 1877, vol. 1.

After some remarks concerning the nature of language and of the special characteristics of Indian languages, the author gives a synopsis of the languages of the Pacific region. The families mentioned are:

1. Shóshoni.	11. Pomo.	21. Yakon.
2. Yuma.	12. Wishosk.	22. Cayuse.
3. Pima.	13. Eurok.	23. Kalapuya.
4. Santa Barbara.	14. Weits-pek.	24. Chinook.
5. Mutsun.	15. Cahrok.	25. Sahaptin.
6. Yocut.	16. Tolewa.	26. Selish.
7. Meewoc.	17. Shasta.	27. Nootka.
8. Meidoo.	18. Pit River.	28. Kootenai.
9. Wintoon.	19. Klamath.	
10. Yuka.	20. Tinné.	

This is an important paper, and contains notices of several new stocks, derived from a study of the material furnished by Powers.

The author advocates the plan of using a system of nomenclature similar in nature to that employed in zoology in the case of generic and specific names, adding after the name of the tribe the family to which it belongs; thus: Warm Springs, Sahaptin.

1878. Powell (John Wesley).
The nationality of the Pueblos. In the Rocky Mountain Presbyterian. Denver, November, 1878.

This is a half-column article, the object of which is to assign the several Pueblos to their proper stocks. A paragraph is devoted to contradicting the popular belief that the Pueblos are in some way related to the Aztecs. No vocabularies are given or cited, though the classification is stated to be a linguistic one.

1878. Keane (Augustus H).
Appendix. Ethnography and philology of America. In Stanford's Compendium of Geography and Travel, edited and extended by H. W. Bates. London, 1878.

In the appendix are given, first, some of the more general characteristics and peculiarities of Indian languages, followed by a classification of all the tribes of North America, after which is given an alphabetical list of American tribes and languages, with their habitats and the stock to which they belong.

The classification is compiled from many sources, and although it contains many errors and inconsistencies, it affords on the whole a good general idea of prevalent views on the subject.

1880. Powell (John Wesley).
Puebio Indians. In the American Naturalist. Philadelphia, 1880, vol. 14.

This is a two-page article in which is set forth a classification of the Pueblo Indians from linguistic considerations. The Pueblos are divided into four families or stocks, viz:

1. Shínumo.	3. Kéran.
2. Zunian.	4. Téwan.

Under the several stocks is given a list of those who have collected vocabularies of these languages and a reference to their publication.

1880. Eells (Myron).
The Twana language of Washington Territory. In the American Antiquarian. Chicago, 1880–'81, vol. 3.

This is a brief article—two and a half pages—on the Twana, Clallam, and Chemakum Indians. The author finds, upon a comparison of vocabularies, that the Chemakum language has little in common with its neighbors.

1885. Dall (William Healey).
The native tribes of Alaska. In Proceedings of the American Association for the Advancement of Science, thirty-fourth meeting, held at Ann Arbor, Mich., August, 1885. Salem, 1886.

This paper is a timely contribution to the subject of the Alaska tribes, and carries it from the point at which the author left it in 1869 to date, briefly summarizing the several recent additions to knowledge. It ends with a geographical classification of the Innuit and Indian tribes of Alaska, with estimates of their numbers.

1885. Bancroft (Hubert Howe).
The works of Hubert Howe Bancroft, vol. 3: the native races, vol. 3, myths and languages. San Francisco, 1882.

In the chapter on that subject the languages are classified by divisions which appear to correspond to groups, families, tribes, and dialects.

The classification does not, however, follow any consistent plan, and is in parts unintelligible.

1882. Gatschet (Albert Samuel).
Indian languages of the Pacific States and Territories and of the Pueblos of New Mexico. In the Magazine of American History. New York, 1882, vol. 8.

This paper is in the nature of a supplement to a previous one in the same magazine above referred to. It enlarges further on several of the stocks there considered, and, as the title indicates, treats also of the Pueblo languages. The families mentioned are:

1. Chimariko.	6. Takilma.
2. Washo.	7. Rio Grande Pueblo.
3. Yákona.	8. Kera.
4. Sayúskla.	9. Zuñi.
5. Kúsa.	

1883. Hale (Horatio).
Indian migrations, as evidenced by language. In The American Antiquarian and Oriental Journal. Chicago, 1883, vol. 5.

In connection with the object of this paper—the study of Indian migrations—several linguistic stocks are mentioned, and the linguistic affinities of a number of tribes are given. The stocks mentioned are:

Huron-Cherokee.	Algonkin.
Dakota.	Chahta-Muskoki.

1885. Tolmie (W. Fraser) and Dawson (George M.)
Comparative vocabularies of the Indian tribes of British Columbia, with a map illustrating distribution (Geological and Natural History Survey of Canada). Montreal, 1884.

The vocabularies presented constitute an important contribution to linguistic science. They represent "one or more dialects of every Indian language spoken on the Pacific slope from the Columbia River north to the Tshilkat River, and beyond, in Alaska; and from the outermost sea-board to the main continental divide in the Rocky Mountains." A colored map shows the area occupied by each linguistic family.

LINGUISTIC MAP.

In 1836 Gallatin conferred a great boon upon linguistic students by classifying all the existing material relating to this subject. Even in the light of the knowledge of the present day his work is found to rest upon a sound basis. The material of Gallatin's time, however, was too scanty to permit of more than an outline of the subject. Later writers have contributed to the work, and the names of Latham, Turner, Prichard, Buschmann, Hale, Gatschet, and others are connected with important classificatory results.

The writer's interest in linguistic work and the inception of a plan for a linguistic classification of Indian languages date back about 20 years, to a time when he was engaged in explorations in the West. Being brought into contact with many tribes, it was possible to collect a large amount of original material. Subsequently, when the Bureau of Ethnology was organized, this store was largely increased through the labors of others. Since then a very large body of literature published in Indian languages has been accumulated, and a great number of vocabularies have been gathered by the Bureau assistants and by collaborators in various parts of the country. The results of a study of all this material, and of much historical data, which necessarily enters largely into work of this character, appear in the accompanying map.

The contributions to the subject during the last fifty years have been so important, and the additions to the material accessible to the student of Gallatin's time have been so large, that much of the reproach which deservedly attached to American scholars because of the neglect of American linguistics has been removed. The field is a vast one, however, and the workers are comparatively few. Moreover, opportunities for collecting linguistic material are growing fewer day by day, as tribes are consolidated upon reservations, as they become civilized, and as the older Indians, who alone are skilled in their language, die, leaving, it may be, only a few imperfect vocabularies as a basis for future study. History has bequeathed to us the names of many tribes, which became extinct in early colonial times, of whose language not a hint is left and whose linguistic relations must ever remain unknown.

It is vain to grieve over neglected opportunities unless their contemplation stimulates us to utilize those at hand. There are yet many gaps to be filled, even in so elementary a part of the study as the classification of the tribes by language. As to the detailed study of the different linguistic families, the mastery and analysis of the languages composing them, and their comparison with one another and with the languages of other families, only a beginning has been made.

After the above statement it is hardly necessary to add that the accompanying map does not purport to represent final results. On the contrary, it is to be regarded as tentative, setting forth in visible form the results of investigation up to the present time, as a guide and aid to future effort.

Each of the colors or patterns upon the map represents a distinct linguistic family, the total number of families contained in the whole area being fifty-eight. It is believed that the families of languages represented upon the map can not have sprung from a common source; they are as distinct from one another in their vocabularies and apparently in their origin as from the Aryan or the Scythian families. Unquestionably, future and more critical study will result in the fusion of some of these families. As the means for analysis and comparison accumulate, resemblances now hidden will be brought to light, and relationships hitherto unsuspected will be shown to exist. Such a result may be anticipated with the more certainty inasmuch as the present classification has been made upon a conservative plan. Where relationships between families are suspected, but can not be demonstrated by convincing evidence, it has been deemed wiser not to unite them, but to keep

them apart until more material shall have accumulated and proof
of a more convincing character shall have been brought forward.
While some of the families indicated on the map may in future be
united to other families, and the number thus be reduced, there
seems to be no ground for the belief that the total of the linguistic
families of this country will be materially diminished, at least under
the present methods of linguistic analysis, for there is little reason
to doubt that, as the result of investigation in the field, there will
be discovered tribes speaking languages not classifiable under any of
the present families; thus the decrease in the total by reason of consolidation may be compensated by a corresponding increase through
discovery. It may even be possible that some of the similarities
used in combining languages into families may, on further study,
prove to be adventitious, and the number may be increased thereby.
To which side the numerical balance will fall remains for the future
to decide.

As stated above, all the families occupy the same basis of dissimilarity from one another—i. e., none of them are related—and consequently no two of them are either more or less alike than any other
two, except in so far as mere coincidences and borrowed material
may be said to constitute likeness and relationship. Coincidences
in the nature of superficial word resemblances are common in all
languages of the world. No matter how widely separated geograph-
ically two families of languages may be, no matter how unlike their
vocabularies, how distinct their origin, some words may always be
found which appear upon superficial examination to indicate relationship. There is not a single Indian linguistic family, for instance,
which does not contain words similar in sound, and more rarely similar in both sound and meaning, to words in English, Chinese, Hebrew,
and other languages. Not only do such resemblances exist, but
they have been discovered and pointed out, not as mere adventitious
similarities, but as proof of genetic relationship. Borrowed linguistic material also appears in every family, tempting the unwary
investigator into making false analogies and drawing erroneous conclusions. Neither coincidences nor borrowed material, however, can
be properly regarded as evidence of cognation.

While occupying the same plane of genetic dissimilarity, the families are by no means alike as regards either the extent of territory occupied, the number of tribes grouped under them respectively, or the
number of languages and dialects of which they are composed.
Some of them cover wide areas, whose dimensions are stated in
terms of latitude and longitude rather than by miles. Others occupy
so little space that the colors representing them are hardly discern-
ible upon the map. Some of them contain but a single tribe; others
are represented by scores of tribes. In the case of a few, the term
"family" is commensurate with language, since there is but one

language and no dialects. In the case of others, their tribes spoke several languages, so distinct from one another as to be for the most part mutually unintelligible, and the languages shade into many dialects more or less diverse.

The map, designed primarily for the use of students who are engaged in investigating the Indians of the United States, was at first limited to this area; subsequently its scope was extended to include the whole of North America north of Mexico. Such an extension of its plan was, indeed, almost necessary, since a number of important families, largely represented in the United States, are yet more largely represented in the territory to the north, and no adequate conception of the size and relative importance of such families as the Algonquian, Siouan, Salishan, Athapascan, and others can be had without including extralimital territory.

To the south, also, it happens that several linguistic stocks extend beyond the boundaries of the United States. Three families are, indeed, mainly extralimital in their position, viz: Yuman, the great body of the tribes of which family inhabited the peninsula of Lower California; Piman, which has only a small representation in southern Arizona; and the Coahuiltecan, which intrudes into southwestern Texas. The Athapascan family is represented in Arizona and New Mexico by the well known Apache and Navajo, the former of whom have gained a strong foothold in northern Mexico, while the Tañoan, a Pueblo family of the upper Rio Grande, has established a few pueblos lower down the river in Mexico. For the purpose of necessary comparison, therefore, the map is made to include all of North America north of Mexico, the entire peninsula of Lower California, and so much of Mexico as is necessary to show the range of families common to that country and to the United States. It is left to a future occasion to attempt to indicate the linguistic relations of Mexico and Central America, for which, it may be remarked in passing, much material has been accumulated.

It is apparent that a single map can not be made to show the locations of the several linguistic families at different epochs; nor can a single map be made to represent the migrations of the tribes composing the linguistic families. In order to make a clear presentation of the latter subject, it would be necessary to prepare a series of maps showing the areas successively occupied by the several tribes as they were disrupted and driven from section to section under the pressure of other tribes or the vastly more potent force of European encroachment. Although the data necessary for a complete representation of tribal migration, even for the period subsequent to the advent of the European, does not exist, still a very large body of material bearing upon the subject is at hand, and exceedingly valuable results in this direction could be presented did not the amount of time and labor and the large expense attendant upon such a project forbid the attempt for the present.

The map undertakes to show the habitat of the linguistic families only, and this is for but a single period in their history, viz, at the time when the tribes composing them first became known to the European, or when they first appear on recorded history. As the dates when the different tribes became known vary, it follows as a matter of course that the periods represented by the colors in one portion of the map are not synchronous with those in other portions. Thus the data for the Columbia River tribes is derived chiefly from the account of the journey of Lewis and Clarke in 1803–'05, long before which period radical changes of location had taken place among the tribes of the eastern United States. Again, not only are the periods represented by the different sections of the map not synchronous, but only in the case of a few of the linguistic families, and these usually the smaller ones, is it possible to make the coloring synchronous for different sections of the same family. Thus our data for the location of some of the northern members of the Shoshonean family goes back to 1804, a date at which absolutely no knowledge had been gained of most of the southern members of the group, our first accounts of whom began about 1850. Again, our knowledge of the eastern Algonquian tribes dates back to about 1600, while no information was had concerning the Atsina, Blackfeet, Cheyenne, and the Arapaho, the westernmost members of the family, until two centuries later.

Notwithstanding these facts, an attempt to fix upon the areas formerly occupied by the several linguistic families, and of the pristine homes of many of the tribes composing them, is by no means hopeless. For instance, concerning the position of the western tribes during the period of early contact of our colonies and its agreement with their position later when they appear in history, it may be inferred that as a rule it was stationary, though positive evidence is lacking. When changes of tribal habitat actually took place they were rarely in the nature of extensive migration, by which a portion of a linguistic family was severed from the main body, but usually in the form of encroachment by a tribe or tribes upon neighboring territory, which resulted simply in the extension of the limits of one linguistic family at the expense of another, the defeated tribes being incorporated or confined within narrower limits. If the above inference be correct, the fact that different chronologic periods are represented upon the map is of comparatively little importance, since, if the Indian tribes were in the main sedentary, and not nomadic, the changes resulting in the course of one or two centuries would not make material differences. Exactly the opposite opinion, however, has been expressed by many writers, viz, that the North

American Indian tribes were nomadic. The picture presented by these writers is of a medley of ever-shifting tribes, to-day here, to-morrow there, occupying new territory and founding new homes—if nomads can be said to have homes—only to abandon them. Such a picture, however, is believed to convey an erroneous idea of the former condition of our Indian tribes. As the question has significance in the present connection it must be considered somewhat at length.

INDIAN TRIBES SEDENTARY.

In-the first place, the linguistic map, based as it is upon the earliest evidence obtainable, itself offers conclusive proof, not only that the Indian tribes were in the main sedentary at the time history first records their position, but that they had been sedentary for a very long period. In order that this may be made plain, it should be clearly understood, as stated above, that each of the colors or patterns upon the map indicates a distinct linguistic family. It will be noticed that the colors representing the several families are usually in single bodies, i. e., that they represent continuous areas, and that with some exceptions the same color is not scattered here and there over the map in small spots. Yet precisely this last state of things is what would be expected had the tribes representing the families been nomadic to a marked degree. If nomadic tribes occupied North America, instead of spreading out each from a common center, as the colors show that the tribes composing the several families actually did, they would have been dispersed here and there over the whole face of the country. That they are not so dispersed is considered proof that in the main they were sedentary. It has been stated above that more or less extensive migrations of some tribes over the country had taken place prior to European occupancy. This fact is disclosed by a glance at the present map. The great Athapascan family, for instance, occupying the larger part of British America, is known from linguistic evidence to have sent off colonies into Oregon (Wilopah, Tlatskanai, Coquille), California (Smith River tribes, Kenesti or Wailakki tribes, Hupa), and Arizona and New Mexico (Apache, Navajo). How long before European occupancy of this country these migrations took place can not be told, but in the case of most of them it was undoubtedly many years. By the test of language it is seen that the great Siouan family, which we have come to look upon as almost exclusively western, had one offshoot in Virginia (Tutelo), another in North and South Carolina (Catawba), and a third in Mississippi (Biloxi); and the Algonquian family, so important in the early history of this country, while occupying a nearly continuous area in the north and east, had yet secured a foothold, doubtless in very recent times, in Wyoming and Colorado. These and other similar facts sufficiently prove the power of individual tribes or gentes to sunder relations with the great body of their kindred and to remove to distant homes. Tested by linguistic evidence, such instances appear to be exceptional, and the fact remains that in the great majority of cases the tribes composing linguistic families occupy continuous areas, and hence are and have been practically sedentary. Nor is the bond of a common language, strong and enduring as that bond is usually thought to be, entirely sufficient to explain the phenomenon here pointed out. When small in number the linguistic tie would undoubtedly aid in binding together the members of a tribe; but as the people speaking a common language increase in number and come to have conflicting interests, the linguistic tie has often proved to be an insufficient bond of union. In the case of our Indian tribes feuds and internecine conflicts were common between members of the same linguistic family. In fact, it is probable that a very large number of the dialects into which Indian languages are split originated as the result of internecine strife. Factions, divided and separated from the parent body, by contact, intermarriage, and incorporation with foreign tribes, developed distinct dialects or languages.

But linguistic evidence alone need not be relied upon to prove that the North American Indian was not nomadic.

Corroborative proof of the sedentary character of our Indian tribes is to be found in the curious form of kinship system, with mother-rite as its chief factor, which prevails. This, as has been pointed out in another place, is not adapted to the necessities of nomadic tribes, which need to be governed by a patriarchal system, and, as well, to be possessed of flocks and herds.

There is also an abundance of historical evidence to show that, when first discovered by Europeans, the Indians of the eastern United States were found living in fixed habitations. This does not necessarily imply that the entire year was spent in one place. Agriculture not being practiced to an extent sufficient to supply the Indian with full subsistence, he was compelled to make occasional changes from his permanent home to the more or less distant waters and forests to procure supplies of food. When furnished with food and skins for clothing, the hunting parties returned to the village which constituted their true home. At longer periods, for several reasons—among which probably the chief were the hostility of stronger tribes, the failure of the fuel supply near the village, and the compulsion exercised by the ever lively superstitious fancies of the Indians—the villages were abandoned and new ones formed to constitute new homes, new focal points from which to set out on their annual hunts and to which to return when these were completed. The tribes of the eastern United States had fixed and definitely bounded habitats, and their wanderings were in the nature of temporary excursions to established points resorted to from time immemorial. As, however, they had not yet entered completely into the agricultural condition, to which they were fast progressing from the hunter state, they may be said to have been nomadic to a very limited extent. The method of life thus sketched was substantially the one which the Indians were found practicing throughout the eastern part of the United States, as also, though to a less degree, in the Pacific States. Upon the Pacific coast proper the tribes were even more sedentary than upon the Atlantic, as the mild climate and the great abundance and permanent supply of fish and shellfish left no cause for a seasonal change of abode.

When, however, the interior portions of the country were first visited by Europeans, a different state of affairs was found to prevail. There the acquisition of the horse and the possession of firearms had wrought very great changes in aboriginal habits. The acquisition of the former enabled the Indian of the treeless plains to travel distances with ease and celerity which before were practically impossible, and the possession of firearms stimulated tribal aggressiveness to the utmost pitch. Firearms were everywhere doubly effective in producing changes in tribal habitats, since the somewhat gradual introduction of trade placed these deadly weapons in the hands of some tribes, and of whole congeries of tribes, long before others could obtain them. Thus the general state of tribal equilibrium which had before prevailed was rudely disturbed. Tribal warfare, which hitherto had been attended with inconsiderable loss of life and slight territorial changes, was now made terribly destructive, and the territorial possessions of whole groups of tribes were augmented at the expense of those less fortunate. The horse made wanderers of many tribes which there is sufficient evidence to show were formerly nearly sedentary. Firearms enforced migration and caused wholesale changes in the habitats of tribes, which, in the natural order of events, it would have taken many centuries to produce. The changes resulting from these combined agencies, great as they were, are, however, slight in comparison with the tremendous effects of the wholesale occupancy of Indian territory by Europeans. As the acquisition of territory by the settlers went on, a wave of migration from east to west was inaugurated which affected tribes far remote from the point of disturbance, ever forcing them within narrower and narrower bounds, and, as time went on, producing greater and greater changes throughout the entire country.

So much of the radical change in tribal habitats as took place in the area remote from European settlements, mainly west of the Mississippi, is chiefly unrecorded, save imperfectly in Indian tradition, and is chiefly to be inferred from linguistic evidence and from the few facts in our possession. As, however, the most important of these changes occurred after, and as a result of, European occupancy, they are noted in history, and thus the map really gives a better idea of the pristine or prehistoric habitat of the tribes than at first might be thought possible.

Before speaking of the method of establishing the boundary lines between the linguistic families, as they appear upon the map, the nature of the Indian claim to land and the manner and extent of its occupation should be clearly set forth.

POPULATION.

As the question of the Indian population of the country has a direct bearing upon the extent to which the land was actually occupied, a few words on the subject will be introduced here, particularly as the area included in the linguistic map is so covered with color that it may convey a false impression of the density of the Indian population. As a result of an investigation of the subject of the early Indian population, Col. Mallery long ago arrived at the conclusion that their settlements were not numerous, and that the population, as compared with the enormous territory occupied, was extremely small.[1]

Careful examination since the publication of the above tends to corroborate the soundness of the conclusions there first formulated. The subject may be set forth as follows:

The sea shore, the borders of lakes, and the banks of rivers, where fish and shell-fish were to be obtained in large quantities, were naturally the Indians' chief resort, and at or near such places were to be found their permanent settlements. As the settlements and lines of travel of the early colonists were along the shore, the lakes and the rivers, early estimates of the Indian population were chiefly based upon the numbers congregated along these highways, it being generally assumed that away from the routes of travel a like population existed. Again, over-estimates of population resulted from the fact that the same body of Indians visited different points during the year, and not infrequently were counted two or three times; change of permanent village sites also tended to augment estimates of population.

For these and other reasons a greatly exaggerated idea of the Indian population was obtained, and the impressions so derived have been dissipated only in comparatively recent times.

As will be stated more fully later, the Indian was dependent to no small degree upon natural products for his food supply. Could it be affirmed that the North American Indians had increased to a point where they pressed upon the food supply, it would imply a very much larger population than we are justified in assuming from other considerations. But for various reasons the Malthusian law,

---

[1] Proc. Am. Ass. Adv. Science, 1877, vol. 26.

whether applicable elsewhere or not, can not be applied to the Indians of this country. Everywhere bountiful nature had provided an unfailing and practically inexhaustible food supply. The rivers teemed with fish and mollusks, and the forests with game, while upon all sides was an abundance of nutritious roots and seeds. All of these sources were known, and to a large extent they were drawn upon by the Indian, but the practical lesson of providing in the season of plenty for the season of scarcity had been but imperfectly learned, or, when learned, was but partially applied. Even when taught by dire experience the necessity of laying up adequate stores, it was the almost universal practice to waste great quantities of food by a constant succession of feasts, in the superstitious observances of which the stores were rapidly wasted and plenty soon gave way to scarcity and even to famine.

Curiously enough, the hospitality which is so marked a trait among our North American Indians had its source in a law, the invariable practice of which has had a marked effect in retarding the acquisition by the Indian of the virtue of providence. As is well known, the basis of the Indian social organization was the kinship system. By its provisions almost all property was possessed in common by the gens or clan. Food, the most important of all, was by no means left to be exclusively enjoyed by the individual or the family obtaining it.

For instance, the distribution of game among the families of a party was variously provided for in different tribes, but the practical effect of the several customs relating thereto was the sharing of the supply. The hungry Indian had but to ask to receive and this no matter how small the supply, or how dark the future prospect. It was not only his privilege to ask, it was his *right to demand.* Undoubtedly what was originally a right, conferred by kinship connections, ultimately assumed broader proportions, and finally passed into the exercise of an almost indiscriminate hospitality. By reason of this custom, the poor hunter was virtually placed upon equality with the expert one, the lazy with the industrious, the improvident with the more provident. Stories of Indian life abound with instances of individual families or parties being called upon by those less fortunate or provident to share their supplies.

The effect of such a system, admirable as it was in many particulars, practically placed a premium upon idleness. Under such communal rights and privileges a potent spur to industry and thrift is wanting.

There is an obverse side to this problem, which a long and intimate acquaintance with the Indians in their villages has forced upon the writer. The communal ownership of food and the great hospitality practiced by the Indian have had a very much greater influence upon his character than that indicated in the foregoing

remarks. The peculiar institutions prevailing in this respect gave
to each tribe or clan a profound interest in the skill, ability and
industry of each member. He was the most valuable person in the
community who supplied it with the most of its necessities. For
this reason the successful hunter or fisherman was always held in
high honor, and the woman who gathered great store of seeds,
fruits, or roots, or who cultivated a good corn-field, was one who
commanded the respect and received the highest approbation of the
people. The simple and rude ethics of a tribal people are very
important to them, the more so because of their communal institutions; and everywhere throughout the tribes of the United States
it is discovered that their rules of conduct were deeply implanted
in the minds of the people. An organized system of teaching is
always found, as it is the duty of certain officers of the clan to
instruct the young in all the industries necessary to their rude life,
and simple maxims of industry abound among the tribes and are
enforced in diverse and interesting ways. The power of the elder
men in the clan over its young members is always very great, and
the training of the youth is constant and rigid. Besides this, a
moral sentiment exists in favor of primitive virtues which is very
effective in molding character. This may be illustrated in two
ways.

Marriage among all Indian tribes is primarily by legal appoint-
ment, as the young woman receives a husband from some other
prescribed clan or clans, and the elders of the clan, with certain exceptions, control these marriages, and personal choice has little to do with
the affair. When marriages are proposed, the virtues and industry
of the candidates, and more than all, their ability to properly live
as married couples and to supply the clan or tribe with a due
amount of subsistence, are discussed long and earnestly, and the
young man or maiden who fails in this respect may fail in securing
an eligible and desirable match. And these motives are constantly
presented to the savage youth.

A simple democracy exists among these people, and they have a
variety of tribal offices to fill. In this way the men of the tribe are
graded, and they pass from grade to grade by a selection practically
made by the people. And this leads to a constant discussion of the
virtues and abilities of all the male members of the clan, from boy-
hood to old age. He is most successful in obtaining clan and tribal
promotion who is most useful to the clan and the tribe. In this
manner all of the ambitious are stimulated, and this incentive to
industry is very great.

When brought into close contact with the Indian, and into intimate acquaintance with his language, customs, and religious ideas,
there is a curious tendency observable in students to overlook
aboriginal vices and to exaggerate aboriginal virtues. It seems to

be forgotten that after all the Indian is a savage, with the characteristics of a savage, and he is exalted even above the civilized man.
The tendency is exactly the reverse of what it is in the case of those
who view the Indian at a distance and with no precise knowledge of
any of his characteristics. In the estimation of such persons the
Indian's vices greatly outweigh his virtues; his language is a gib-
berish, his methods of war cowardly, his ideas of religion utterly
puerile.

The above tendencies are accentuated in the attempt to estimate
the comparative worth and position of individual tribes. No being
is more patriotic than the Indian. He believes himself to be the
result of a special creation by a partial deity and holds that his is
the one favored race. The name by which the tribes distinguish
themselves from other tribes indicates the further conviction that,
as the Indian is above all created things, so in like manner each particular tribe is exalted above all others. "Men of men" is the literal
translation of one name; "the only men" of another, and so on
through the whole category. A long residence with any one tribe
frequently inoculates the student with the same patriotic spirit.
Bringing to his study of a particular tribe an inadequate conception
of Indian attainments and a low impression of their moral and intellectual plane, the constant recital of its virtues, the bravery and
prowess of its men in war, their generosity, the chaste conduct and
obedience of its women as contrasted with the opposite qualities of
all other tribes, speedily tends to partisanship. He discovers many
virtues and finds that the moral and intellectual attainments are
higher than he supposed; but these advantages he imagines to be
possessed solely, or at least to an unusual degree, by the tribe in
question. Other tribes are assigned much lower rank in the scale.

The above is peculiarly true of the student of language. He who
studies only one Indian language and learns its manifold curious
grammatic devices, its wealth of words, its capacity of expression,
is speedily convinced of its superiority to all other Indian tongues,
and not infrequently to all languages by whomsoever spoken.

If like admirable characteristics are asserted for other tongues he
is apt to view them but as derivatives from one original. Thus he
is led to overlook the great truth that the mind of man is everywhere
practically the same, and that the innumerable differences of its
products are indices merely of different stages of growth or are the
results of different conditions of environment. In its development
the human mind is limited by no boundaries of tribe or race.

Again, a long acquaintance with many tribes in their homes leads
to the belief that savage people do not lack industry so much as
wisdom. They are capable of performing, and often do perform,
great and continuous labor. The men and women alike toil from
day to day and from year to year, engaged in those tasks that are

presented with the recurring seasons. In civilization, hunting and fishing are often considered sports, but in savagery they are labors, and call for endurance, patience, and sagacity. And these are exercised to a reasonable degree among all savage peoples.

It is probable that the real difficulty of purchasing quantities of food from Indians has, in most cases, not been properly understood. Unless the alien is present at a time of great abundance, when there is more on hand or easily obtainable than sufficient to supply the wants of the people, food can not be bought of the Indians. This arises from the fact that the tribal tenure is communal, and to get food by purchase requires a treaty at which all the leading members of the tribe are present and give consent.

As an illustration of the improvidence of the Indians generally, the habits of the tribes along the Columbia River may be cited. The Columbia River has often been pointed to as the probable source of a great part of the Indian population of this country, because of the enormous supply of salmon furnished by it and its tributaries. If an abundant and readily obtained supply of food was all that was necessary to insure a large population, and if population always increased up to the limit of food supply, unquestionably the theory of repeated migratory waves of surplus population from the Columbia Valley would be plausible enough. It is only necessary, however, to turn to the accounts of the earlier explorers of this region, Lewis and Clarke, for example, to refute the idea, so far at least as the Columbia Valley is concerned, although a study of the many diverse languages spread over the United States would seem sufficiently to prove that the tribes speaking them could not have originated at a common center, unless, indeed, at a period anterior to the formation of organized language.

The Indians inhabiting the Columbia Valley were divided into many tribes, belonging to several distinct linguistic families. They all were in the same culture status, however, and differed in habits and arts only in minor particulars. All of them had recourse to the salmon of the Columbia for the main part of their subsistence, and all practiced similar crude methods of curing fish and storing it away for the winter. Without exception, judging from the accounts of the above mentioned and of more recent authors, all the tribes suffered periodically more or less from insufficient food supply, although, with the exercise of due forethought and economy, even with their rude methods of catching and curing salmon, enough might here have been cured annually to suffice for the wants of the Indian population of the entire Northwest for several years.

In their ascent of the river in spring, before the salmon run, it was only with great difficulty that Lewis and Clarke were able to provide themselves by purchase with enough food to keep themselves from starving. Several parties of Indians from the vicinity of the

Dalles, the best fishing station on the river, were met on their way down in quest of food, their supply of dried salmon having been entirely exhausted.

Nor is there anything in the accounts of any of the early visitors to the Columbia Valley to authorize the belief that the population there was a very large one. As was the case with all fish-stocked streams, the Columbia was resorted to in the fishing season by many tribes living at considerable distance from it; but there is no evidence tending to show that the settled population of its banks or of any part of its drainage basin was or ever had been by any means excessive.

The Dalles, as stated above, was the best fishing station on the river, and the settled population there may be taken as a fair index of that of other favorable locations. The Dalles was visited by Ross in July, 1811, and the following is his statement in regard to the population:

The main camp of the Indians is situated at the head of the narrows, and may contain, during the salmon season, 3,000 souls, or more; but the constant inhabitants of the place do not exceed 100 persons, and are called Wy-am-pams; the rest are all foreigners from different tribes throughout the country, who resort hither, not for the purpose of catching salmon, but chiefly for gambling and speculation.[1]

And as it was on the Columbia with its enormous supply of fish, so was it elsewhere in the United States.

Even the practice of agriculture, with its result of providing a more certain and bountiful food supply, seems not to have had the effect of materially augmenting the Indian population. At all events, it is in California and Oregon, a region where agriculture was scarcely practiced at all, that the most dense aboriginal population lived. There is no reason to believe that there ever existed within the limits of the region included in the map, with the possible exception of certain areas in California, a population equal to the natural food supply. On the contrary, there is every reason for believing that the population at the time of the discovery might have been many times more than what it actually was had a wise economy been practised.

The effect of wars in decimating the people has often been greatly exaggerated. Since the advent of the white man on the continent, wars have prevailed to a degree far beyond that existing at an earlier time. From the contest which necessarily arose between the native tribes and invading nations many wars resulted, and their history is well known. Again, tribes driven from their ancestral homes often retreated to lands previously occupied by other tribes, and intertribal wars resulted therefrom. The acquisition of firearms and horses, through the agency of white men, also had its influence, and when a commercial value was given to furs and skins, the Indian aban-

---

[1] Adventures on the Columbia River, 1849, p. 117.

doned agriculture to pursue hunting and traffic, and sought new fields for such enterprises, and many new contests arose from this cause. Altogether the character of the Indian since the discovery of Columbus has been greatly changed, and he has become far more warlike and predatory. Prior to that time, and far away in the wilderness beyond such influence since that time, Indian tribes seem to have lived together in comparative peace and to have settled their difficulties by treaty methods. A few of the tribes had distinct organizations for purposes of war; all recognized it to a greater or less extent in their tribal organization; but from such study as has been given the subject, and from the many facts collected from time to time relating to the intercourse existing between tribes, it appears that the Indians lived in comparative peace. Their accumulations were not so great as to be tempting, and their modes of warfare were not excessively destructive. Armed with clubs and spears and bows and arrows, war could be prosecuted only by hand-to-hand conflict, and depended largely upon individual prowess, while battle for plunder, tribute, and conquest was almost unknown. Such intertribal wars as occurred originated from other causes, such as infraction of rights relating to hunting grounds and fisheries, and still oftener prejudices growing out of their superstitions.

That which kept the Indian population down sprang from another source, which has sometimes been neglected. The Indians had no reasonable or efficacious system of medicine. They believed that diseases were caused by unseen evil beings and by witchcraft, and every cough, every toothache, every headache, every chill, every fever, every boil, and every wound, in fact, all their ailments, were attributed to such cause. Their so-called medicine practice was a horrible system of sorcery, and to such superstition human life was sacrificed on an enormous scale. The sufferers were given over to priest doctors to be tormented, bedeviled, and destroyed; and a universal and profound belief in witchcraft made them suspicious, and led to the killing of all suspected and obnoxious people, and engendered blood feuds on a gigantic scale. It may be safely said that while famine, pestilence, disease, and war may have killed many, superstition killed more; in fact, a natural death in a savage tent is a comparatively rare phenomenon; but death by sorcery, medicine, and blood feud arising from a belief in witchcraft is exceedingly common.

Scanty as was the population compared with the vast area teeming with natural products capable of supporting human life, it may be safely said that at the time of the discovery, and long prior thereto, practically the whole of the area included in the present map was claimed and to some extent occupied by Indian tribes; but the possession of land by the Indian by no means implies occupancy in the modern or civilized sense of the term. In the latter sense occupation means to a great extent individual control and ownership. Very different was it with the Indians. Individual ownership of land was, as a rule, a thing entirely foreign to the Indian mind, and quite unknown in the culture stage to which he belonged. All land, of whatever character or however utilized, was held in common by the tribe, or in a few instances by the clan. Apparently an exception to this broad statement is to be made in the case of the Haida of the northwest coast, who have been studied by Dawson. According to him[1] the land is divided among the different families and is held as strictly personal property, with hereditary rights or possessions descending from one generation to another. "The lands may be bartered or given away. The larger salmon streams are, however, often the property jointly of a number of families." The tendency in this case is toward personal right in land.

TRIBAL LAND.

For convenience of discussion, Indian tribal land may be divided into three classes: First, the land occupied by the villages; second, the land actually employed in agriculture; third, the land claimed by the tribe but not occupied, except as a hunting ground.

Village sites.—The amount of land taken up as village sites varied considerably in different parts of the country. It varied also in the same tribe at different times. As a rule, the North American Indians lived in communal houses of sufficient size to accommodate several families. In such cases the village consisted of a few large structures closely grouped together, so that it covered very little ground. When territory was occupied by warlike tribes, the construction of rude palisades around the villages and the necessities of defense generally tended to compel the grouping of houses, and the permanent village sites of even the more populous tribes covered only a very small area. In the case of confederated tribes and in the time of peace the tendency was for one or more families to establish more or less permanent settlements away from the main village, where a livelihood was more readily obtainable. Hence, in territory which had enjoyed a considerable interval of peace the settlements were in the nature of small agricultural communities, established at short distances from each other and extending in the aggregate over a considerable extent of country. In the case of populous tribes the villages were probably of the character of the Choctaw towns described by Adair.[2] "The barrier towns, which are next to the Muskohge and Chikkasah countries, are compactly settled for social defense, according to the general method of other savage nations; but the rest, both in the center and toward the Mississippi, are only scattered plantations, as best suits a separate easy

---

[1] Report on the Queen Charlotte Islands, 1878, p. 117.
[2] Hist. of Am. Ind., 1775, p. 282.

way of living. A stranger might be in the middle of one of their populous, extensive towns without seeing half a dozen houses in the direct course of his path." More closely grouped settlements are described by Wayne in American State Papers, 1793, in his account of an expedition down the Maumee Valley, where he states that "The margins of the Miamis of the Lake and the Au Glaize appear like one continuous village for a number of miles, nor have I ever beheld such immense fields of corn in any part of America from Canada to Florida." Such a chain of villages as this was probably highly exceptional; but even under such circumstances the village sites proper formed but a very small part of the total area occupied.

From the foregoing considerations it will be seen that the amount of land occupied as village sites under any circumstances was inconsiderable.

Agricultural land.—It is practically impossible to make an accurate estimate of the relative amount of land devoted to agricultural purposes by any one tribe or by any family of tribes. None of the factors which enter into the problem are known to us with sufficient accuracy to enable reliable estimates to be made of the amount of land tilled or of the products derived from the tillage; and only in few cases have we trustworthy estimates of the population of the tribe or tribes practicing agriculture. Only a rough approximation of the truth can be reached from the scanty data available and from a general knowledge of Indian methods of subsistence.

The practice of agriculture was chiefly limited to the region south of the St. Lawrence and east of the Mississippi. In this region it was far more general and its results were far more important than is commonly supposed. To the west of the Mississippi only comparatively small areas were occupied by agricultural tribes and these lay chiefly in New Mexico and Arizona and along the Arkansas, Platte, and Missouri Rivers. The rest of that region was tenanted by non-agricultural tribes—unless indeed the slight attention paid to the cultivation of tobacco by a few of the west coast tribes, notably the Haida, may be considered agriculture. Within the first mentioned area most of the tribes, perhaps all, practiced agriculture to a greater or less extent, though unquestionably the degree of reliance placed upon it as a means of support differed much with different tribes and localities.

Among many tribes agriculture was relied upon to supply an important—and perhaps in the case of a few tribes, the most important—part of the food supply. The accounts of some of the early explorers in the southern United States, where probably agriculture was more systematized than elsewhere, mention corn fields of great extent, and later knowledge of some northern tribes, as the Iroquois and some of the Ohio Valley tribes, shows that they also raised corn in great quantities.

The practice of agriculture to a point where it shall prove the main and constant supply of a people, however, implies a degree of sedentariness to which our Indians as a rule had not attained and an amount of steady labor without immediate return which was peculiarly irksome to them. Moreover, the imperfect methods pursued in clearing, planting, and cultivating sufficiently prove that the Indians, though agriculturists, were in the early stages of development as such—a fact also attested by the imperfect and one-sided division of labor between the sexes, the men as a rule taking but small share of the burdensome tasks of clearing land, planting, and harvesting.

It is certain that by no tribe of the United States was agriculture pursued to such an extent as to free its members from the practice of the hunter's or fisher's art. Admitting the most that can be claimed for the Indian as an agriculturist, it may be stated that, whether because of the small population or because of the crude manner in which his operations were carried on, the amount of land devoted to agriculture within the area in question was infinitesimally small as compared with the total. Upon a map colored to show only the village sites and agricultural land, the colors would appear in small spots, while by far the greater part of the map would remain uncolored.

Hunting claims.—The great body of the land within the area mapped which was occupied by agricultural tribes, and all the land outside it, was held as a common hunting ground, and the tribal claim to territory, independent of village sites and corn fields, amounted practically to little else than hunting claims. The community of possession in the tribe to the hunting ground was established and practically enforced by hunting laws, which dealt with the divisions of game among the village, or among the families of the hunters actually taking part in any particular hunt. As a rule, such natural landmarks as rivers, lakes, hills, and mountain chains served to mark with sufficient accuracy the territorial tribal limits. In California, and among the Haida and perhaps other tribes of the northwest coast, the value of certain hunting and fishing claims led to their definition by artificial boundaries, as by sticks or stones.[1]

Such precautions imply a large population, and in such regions as California the killing of game upon the land of adjoining tribes was rigidly prohibited and sternly punished.

As stated above, every part of the vast area included in the present map is to be regarded as belonging, according to Indian ideas of land title, to one or another of the Indian tribes. To determine the several tribal possessions and to indicate the proper boundary lines between individual tribes and linguistic families is a work of great

---

[1] Powers, Cont. N. A. Eth. 1877, vol. 3, p. 109; Dawson, Queen Charlotte Islands, 1880, p. 117.

difficulty. This is due more to the imperfection and scantiness of available data concerning tribal claims than to the absence of claimants or to any ambiguity in the minds of the Indians as to the boundaries of their several possessions.

Not only is precise data wanting respecting the limits of land actually held or claimed by many tribes, but there are other tribes, which disappeared early in the history of our country, the boundaries to whose habitat is to be determined only in the most general way. Concerning some of these, our information is so vague that the very linguistic family they belonged to is in doubt. In the case of probably no one family are the data sufficient in amount and accuracy to determine positively the exact areas definitely claimed or actually held by the tribes. Even in respect of the territory of many of the tribes of the eastern United States, much of whose land was ceded by actual treaty with the Government, doubt exists. The fixation of the boundary points, when these are specifically mentioned in the treaty, as was the rule, is often extremely difficult, owing to the frequent changes of geographic names and the consequent disagreement of present with ancient maps. Moreover, when the Indian's claim to his land had been admitted by Government, and the latter sought to acquire a title through voluntary cession by actual purchase, land assumed a value to the Indian never attaching to it before.

Under these circumstances, either under plea of immemorial occupancy or of possession by right of conquest, the land was often claimed, and the claims urged with more or less plausibility by several tribes, sometimes of the same linguistic family, sometimes of different families.

It was often found by the Government to be utterly impracticable to decide between conflicting claims, and not infrequently the only way out of the difficulty lay in admitting the claim of both parties, and in paying for the land twice or thrice. It was customary for a number of different tribes to take part in such treaties, and not infrequently several linguistic families were represented. It was the rule for each tribe, through its representatives, to cede its share of a certain territory, the natural boundaries of which as a whole are usually recorded with sufficient accuracy. The main purpose of the Government in treaty-making being to obtain possession of the land, comparatively little attention was bestowed to defining the exact areas occupied by the several tribes taking part in a treaty, except in so far as the matter was pressed upon attention by disputing claimants. Hence the territory claimed by each tribe taking part in the treaty is rarely described, and occasionally not all the tribes interested in the proposed cession are even mentioned categorically. The latter statement applies more particularly to the territory west of the Mississippi, the data for determining ownership to which is much less precise, and the doubt and confusion respecting tribal boundary lines correspondingly greater than in the country east of that river. Under the above circumstances, it will be readily understood that to determine tribal boundaries within accurately drawn lines is in the vast majority of cases quite impossible.

Imperfect and defective as the terms of the treaties frequently are as regards the definition of tribal boundaries, they are by far the most accurate and important of the means at our command for fixing boundary lines upon the present map. By their aid the territorial possessions of a considerable number of tribes have been determined with desirable precision, and such areas definitely established have served as checks upon the boundaries of other tribes, concerning the location and extent of whose possessions little is known.

For establishing the boundaries of such tribes as are not mentioned in treaties, and of those whose territorial possessions are not given with sufficient minuteness, early historical accounts are all important. Such accounts, of course, rarely indicate the territorial possessions of the tribes with great precision. In many cases, however, the sites of villages are accurately given. In others the source of information concerning a tribe is contained in a general statement of the occupancy of certain valleys or mountain ranges or areas at the heads of certain rivers, no limiting lines whatever being assigned. In others, still, the notice of a tribe is limited to a brief mention of the presence in a certain locality of hunting or war parties.

Data of this loose character would of course be worthless in an attempt to fix boundary lines in accordance with the ideas of the modern surveyor. The relative positions of the families and the relative size of the areas occupied by them, however, and not their exact boundaries, are the chief concern in a linguistic map, and for the purpose of establishing these, and, in a rough way, the boundaries of the territory held by the tribes composing them, these data are very important, and when compared with one another and corrected by more definite data, when such are at hand, they have usually been found to be sufficient for the purpose.

SUMMARY OF DEDUCTIONS.

In conclusion, the more important deductions derivable from the data upon which the linguistic map is based, or that are suggested by it, may be summarized as follows:

First, the North American Indian tribes, instead of speaking related dialects, originating in a single parent language, in reality speak many languages belonging to distinct families, which have no apparent unity of origin.

Second, the Indian population of North America was greatly exaggerated by early writers, and instead of being large was in reality small as compared with the vast territory occupied and the abundant food supply; and furthermore, the population had nowhere augmented sufficiently, except possibly in California, to press upon the food supply.

Third, although representing a small population, the numerous tribes had overspread North America and had possessed themselves of all the territory, which, in the case of a great majority of tribes, was owned in common by the tribe.

Fourth, prior to the advent of the European, the tribes were probably nearly in a state of equilibrium, and were in the main sedentary, and those tribes which can be said with propriety to have been nomadic became so only after the advent of the European, and largely as the direct result of the acquisition of the horse and the introduction of firearms.

Fifth, while agriculture was general among the tribes of the eastern United States, and while it was spreading among western tribes, its products were nowhere sufficient wholly to emancipate the Indian from the hunter state.

LINGUISTIC FAMILIES.

Within the area covered by the map there are recognized fifty-eight distinct linguistic families.

These are enumerated in alphabetical order and each is accompanied by a table of the synonyms of the family name, together with a brief statement of the geographical area occupied by each family, so far as it is known. A list of the principal tribes of each family also is given.

ADAIZAN FAMILY.

= Adaize, Gallatin in Trans. and Coll. Am. Antiq. Soc., II, 116, 306, 1836.   Latham in Proc. Philolog. Soc., Lond., II, 31–59, 1846.   Latham, Opuscula, 293, 1860. Gallatin in Trans. Am. Eth. Soc., II, xcix, 1848.   Gallatin in Schoolcraft Ind. Tribes, III, 402, 1853.   Latham, Elements Comp. Phil., 477, 1862 (referred to as one of the most isolated languages of N. A.).   Keane, App. to Stanford's Comp. (Cent. and So. Am.), 478, 1878 (or Adees).

= Adaizi, Prichard, Phys. Hist. Mankind, v, 406, 1847.

= Adaise, Gallatin in Trans. Am. Eth. Soc., II, pt. 1, 77, 1848.

= Adahi, Latham, Nat. Hist. Man, 342, 1850.   Latham in Trans. Philolog. Soc., Lond., 103, 1856.   Latham, Opuscula, 366, 368, 1860.   Latham, Elements Comp., Phil., 473, 477, 1862 (same as his Adaize above).

= Adaes, Buschmann, Spuren der aztekischen Sprache, 424, 1859.

= Adees, Keane, App. to Stanford's Comp. (Cent. and So. Am.) 478, 1878 (same as his Adaize).

= Adái, Gatschet, Creek Mig. Leg., 41, 1884.

Derivation: From a Caddo word hadai, sig. "brush wood."

This family was based upon the language spoken by a single tribe who, according to Dr. Sibley, lived about the year 1800 near the old

Spanish fort or mission of Adaize, "about 40 miles from Natchi-toches, below the Yattassees, on a lake called Lac Macdon, which communicates with the division of Red River that passes by Bayau Pierre." [1] A vocabulary of about two hundred and fifty words is all that remains to us of their language, which according to the collector, Dr. Sibley, "differs from all others, and is so difficult to speak or understand that no nation can speak ten words of it."

It was from an examination of Sibley's vocabulary that Gallatin reached the conclusion of the distinctness of this language from any other known, an opinion accepted by most later authorities. A recent comparison of this vocabulary by Mr. Gatschet, with several Caddoan dialects, has led to the discovery that a considerable percentage of the Adái words have a more or less remote affinity with Caddoan, and he regards it as a Caddoan dialect. The amount of material, however, necessary to establish its relationship to Caddoan is not at present forthcoming, and it may be doubted if it ever will be, as recent inquiry has failed to reveal the existence of a single member of the tribe, or of any individual of the tribes once surrounding the Adái who remembers a word of the language.

Mr. Gatschet found that some of the older Caddo in the Indian Territory remembered the Adái as one of the tribes formerly belonging to the Caddo Confederacy. More than this he was unable to learn from them.

Owing to their small numbers, their remoteness from lines of travel, and their unwarlike character the Adái have cut but a small figure in history, and accordingly the known facts regarding them are very meager. The first historical mention of them appears to be by Cabeça de Vaca, who in his "Naufragios," referring to his stay in Texas, about 1530, calls them Atayos. Mention is also made of them by several of the early French explorers of the Mississippi, as d'Iberville and Joutel.

The Mission of Adayes, so called from its proximity to the home of the tribe, was established in 1715. In 1792 there was a partial emigration of the Adái to the number of fourteen families to a site south of San Antonio de Bejar, southwest Texas, where apparently they amalgamated with the surrounding Indian population and were lost sight of. (From documents preserved at the City Hall, San Antonio, and examined by Mr. Gatschet in December, 1886.) The Adái who were left in their old homes numbered one hundred in 1802, according to Baudry de Lozieres. According to Sibley, in 1809 there were only "twenty men of them remaining, but more women." In 1820 Morse mentions only thirty survivors.

---

[1] Travels of Lewis and Clarke, London, 1809, p. 189.

ALGONQUIAN FAMILY.

>Algonkin-Lenape, Gallatin in Trans. Am. Antiq. Soc., II, 23, 305, 1836. Berghaus (1845), Physik. Atlas, map 17, 1848. Ibid, 1852.

> Algonquin, Bancroft, Hist. U. S., III, 237, 1840. Prichard Phys. Hist. Mankind, v, 381, 1847 (follows Gallatin).

> Algonkins, Gallatin in Trans. Am. Eth. Soc., II, pt. 1, xcix, 77, 1848. Gallatin in Schoolcraft Ind. Tribes, III, 401, 1853.

> Algonkin, Turner in Pac. R. R. Rept., III, pt. 3, 55, 1856 (gives Delaware and Shawnee vocabs.). Hayden, Cont. Eth. and Phil. Missouri Inds., 232, 1862 (treats only of Crees, Blackfeet, Shyennes). Hale in Am. Antiq., 112, April, 1883 (treated with reference to migration).

< Algonkin, Latham in Trans. Philolog. Soc., Lond., 1856 (adds to Gallatin's list of 1836 the Bethuck, Shyenne, Blackfoot, and Arrapaho). Latham, Opuscula, 327, 1860 (as in preceding). Latham, Elements Comp. Phil., 447, 1862.

< Algonquin, Keane, App. Stanford's Comp., (Cent. and S. Am.), 460, 465, 1878 (list includes the Maquas, an Iroquois tribe).

> Saskatschawiner, Berghaus, Physik. Atlas, map 17, 1848 (probably designates the Arapaho).

> Arapahoes, Berghaus, Physik. Atlas, map 17, 1852.

× Algonkin und Beothuk, Berghaus, Physik. Atlas, map 72, 1887.

Derivation: Contracted from Algomequin, an Algonkin word, signifying "those on the other side of the river," i. e., the St. Lawrence River.

ALGONQUIAN AREA.

The area formerly occupied by the Algonquian family was more extensive than that of any other linguistic stock in North America, their territory reaching from Labrador to the Rocky Mountains, and from Churchill River of Hudson Bay as far south at least as Pamlico Sound of North Carolina. In the eastern part of this territory was an area occupied by Iroquoian tribes, surrounded on almost all sides by their Algonquian neighbors. On the south the Algonquian tribes were bordered by those of Iroquoian and Siouan (Catawba) stock, on the southwest and west by the Muskhogean and Siouan tribes, and on the northwest by the Kitunahan and the great Athapascan families, while along the coast of Labrador and the eastern shore of Hudson Bay they came in contact with the Eskimo, who were gradually retreating before them to the north. In Newfoundland they encountered the Beothukan family, consisting of but a single tribe. A portion of the Shawnee at some early period had separated from the main body of the tribe in central Tennessee and pushed their way down to the Savannah River in South Carolina, where, known as Savannahs, they carried on destructive wars with the surrounding tribes until about the beginning of the eighteenth century they were finally driven out and joined the Delaware in the north. Soon afterwards the rest of the tribe was expelled by the Cherokee and Chicasa, who thenceforward claimed all the country stretching north to the Ohio River.

The Cheyenne and Arapaho, two allied tribes of this stock, had become separated from their kindred on the north and had forced their way through hostile tribes across the Missouri to the Black Hills country of South Dakota, and more recently into Wyoming and Colorado, thus forming the advance guard of the Algonquian stock in that direction, having the Siouan tribes behind them and those of the Shoshonean family in front.

PRINCIPAL ALGONQUIAN TRIBES.

Abnaki.	Menominee.	Ottawa.
Algonquin.	Miami.	Pamlico.
Arapaho.	Micmac.	Pennacook.
Cheyenne.	Mohegan.	Pequot.
Conoy.	Montagnais.	Piankishaw.
Cree.	Montauk.	Pottawotomi.
Delaware.	Munsee.	Powhatan.
Fox.	Nanticoke.	Sac.
Illinois.	Narraganset.	Shawnee.
Kickapoo.	Nauset.	Siksika.
Mahican.	Nipmuc.	Wampanoag.
Massachuset.	Ojibwa.	Wappinger.

Population.—The present number of the Algonquian stock is about 95,600, of whom about 60,000 are in Canada and the remainder in the United States. Below is given the population of the tribes officially recognized, compiled chiefly from the United States Indian Commissioner's report for 1889 and the Canadian Indian report for 1888. It is impossible to give exact figures, owing to the fact that in many instances two or more tribes are enumerated together, while many individuals are living with other tribes or amongst the whites:

Abnaki:
```
    "Oldtown Indians," Maine.................................   410
    Passamaquoddy Indians, Maine ..........................   215?
    Abenakis of St. Francis and Bécancour, Quebec.........   369
    "Amalecites" of Témiscouata and Viger, Quebec.........   198
    "Amalecites" of Madawaska, etc., New Brunswick........   682
                                                           ———— 1,874?
```
Algonquin:
```
    Of Renfrew, Golden Lake and Carleton, Ontario.........   797
    With Iroquois (total 131) at Gibson, Ontario..........    31?
    With Iroquois at Lake of Two Mountains, Quebec........    30
    Quebec Province.......................................  3,909
                                                           ———— 4,767?
```
Arapaho:
```
    Cheyenne and Arapaho Agency, Indian Territory.......... 1,272
    Shoshone Agency, Wyoming (Northern Arapaho)...........   885
    Carlisle school, Pennsylvania, and Lawrence school, Kansas....   55
                                                           ———— 2,212
```

Cheyenne:

Pine Ridge Agency, South Dakota (Northern Cheyenne)........ 517
Cheyenne and Arapaho Agency, Indian Territory.............. 2,091
Carlisle school, Pennsylvania, and Lawrence school, Kansas.... 153
Tongue River Agency, Montana (Northern Cheyenne).......... 865
————— 3,626

Cree:

With Salteau in Manitoba, etc., British America (treaties Nos..
1, 2, and 5; total, 6,066)................................... 3,066?
Plain and Wood Cree, treaty No. 6, Manitoba, etc.............. 5,790
Cree (with Salteau, etc.), treaty No. 4, Manitoba, etc 8,530
—————17,386?

Delaware, etc.:

Kiowa, Comanche, and Wichita Agency, Indian Territory..... . 95
Incorporated with Cherokee, Indian Territory .... 1,000?
Delaware with the Seneca in New York....................... 3
Hampton and Lawrence schools 3
Muncie in New York, principally with Onondaga and Seneca ... 36
Munsee with Stockbridge (total 133), Green Bay Agency, Wis.. . 23?
Munsee with Chippewa at Pottawatomie and Great Nemaha
Agency, Kansas (total 75) .... 37?
Munsee with Chippewa on the Thames, Ontario............... 131
"Moravians" of the Thames, Ontario.... 288
Delaware with Six Nations on Grand River, Ontario 134
————— 1,750?

Kickapoo:

Sac and Fox Agency, Indian Territory........................ 325
Pottawatomie and Great Nemaha Agency, Kansas............. 237
In Mexico .... 200?
————— 762?

Menominee:

Green Bay Agency, Wisconsin 1,311
Carlisle school 1
————— 1,312

Miami:

Quapaw Agency, Indian Territory........................ 67
Indiana, no agency .... 300?
Lawrence and Carlisle schools................................ 7
————— 374?

Micmac:

Restigouche, Maria, and Gaspé, Quebec....................... 732
In Nova Scotia 2,145
New Brunswick 912
Prince Edward Island.. 319
————— 4,108

Misisauga:

Alnwick, New Credit, etc., Ontario........................... 774

Monsoni, Maskegon, etc.:

Eastern Rupert's Land, British America...................... 4,016

Montagnais:

Betsiamits, Lake St. John, Grand Romaine, etc., Quebec...... 1,607
Seven Islands, Quebec 312
————— 1,919

Nascapee:

Lower St. Lawrence, Quebec.................................. 2,860

7 ETH——4

Ojibwa:

White Earth Agency, Minnesota	6,263
La Pointe Agency, Wisconsin	4,778
Mackinac Agency, Michigan (about one-third of 5,563 Ottawa and Chippewa)	1,854?
Mackinac Agency, Michigan (Chippewa alone)	1,351
Devil's Lake Agency, North Dakota (Turtle Mountain Chippewa)	1,340
Pottawatomie and Great Nemaha Agency, Kansas (one-half of 75 Chippewa and Muncie)	38?
Lawrence and Carlisle schools	15
"Ojibbewas" of Lake Superior and Lake Huron, Ontario	5,201
"Chippewas" of Sarnia, etc., Ontario	1,956
"Chippewas" with Munsees on Thames, Ontario	454
"Chippewas" with Pottawatomies on Walpole Island, Ontario	658
"Ojibbewas" with Ottawas (total 1,856) on Manitoulin and Cockburn Islands, Ontario	928?
"Salteaux" of treaty Nos. 3 and 4, etc., Manitoba, etc	4,092
"Chippewas" with Crees in Manitoba, etc., treaties Nos. 1, 2, and 5 (total Chippewa and Cree, 6,066)	3,000?
	————31,928?

Ottawa:

Quapaw Agency, Indian Territory	137
Mackinac Agency, Michigan (5,563 Ottawa and Chippewa)	3,709?
Lawrence and Carlisle schools	20
With "Ojibbewas" on Manitoulin and Cockburn Islands, Ontario	928
	———— 4,794?

Peoria, etc.:

Quapaw Agency, Indian Territory	160
Lawrence and Carlisle schools	5
	———— 165

Pottawatomie:

Sac and Fox Agency, Indian Territory	480
Pottawatomie and Great Nemaha Agency, Kansas	462
Mackinac Agency, Michigan	77
Prairie band, Wisconsin	280
Carlisle, Lawrence and Hampton schools	117
With Chippewa on Walpole Island, Ontario	166
	———— 1,582

Sac and Fox:

Sac and Fox Agency, Indian Territory	515
Sac and Fox Agency, Iowa	381
Pottawatomie and Great Nemaha Agency, Kansas	77
Lawrence, Hampton, and Carlisle schools	8
	———— 981

Shawnee:

Quapaw Agency, Indian Territory	79
Sac and Fox Agency, Indian Territory	640
Incorporated with Cherokee, Indian Territory	800?
Lawrence, Carlisle, and Hampton schools	40
	———— 1,559?

Siksika:

Blackfoot Agency, Montana. (Blackfoot, Blood, Piegan)	1,811
Blackfoot reserves in Alberta, British America (with Sarcee and Assiniboine)	4,932
	———— 6,743

ATHAPASCAN FAMILY.

> Athapascas, Gallatin in Trans. and Coll. Am. Antiq. Soc., II, 16, 305, 1836. Prichard, Phys. Hist. Mankind, v, 375, 1847. Gallatin in Trans. Am. Eth. Soc., II, pt. 1, xcix, 77, 1848. Berghaus (1845), Physik. Atlas, map 17, 1848. Ibid., 1852. Turner in "Literary World," 281, April 17, 1852 (refers Apache and Navajo to this family on linguistic evidence).

> Athapaccas, Gallatin in Schoolcraft, Ind. Tribes, III, 401, 1853. (Evident misprint.)

> Athapascan, Turner in Pac. R. R. Rep., III, pt. 3, 84, 1856. (Mere mention of family; Apaches and congeners belong to this family, as shown by him in "Literary World." Hoopah also asserted to be Athapascan.)

> Athabaskans, Latham, Nat. Hist. Man, 302, 1850. (Under Northern Athabaskans, includes Chippewyans Proper, Beaver Indians, Daho-dinnis, Strong Bows, Hare Indians, Dog-ribs, Yellow Knives, Carriers. Under Southern Athabaskans, includes (p. 308) Kwalioqwa, Tlatskanai, Umkwa.)

= Athabaskan, Latham in Trans. Philolog. Soc. Lond., 65, 96, 1856. Buschmann (1854), Der athapaskische Sprachstamm, 250, 1856 (Hoopahs, Apaches, and Navajoes included). Latham, Opuscula, 333, 1860. Latham, El. Comp. Phil., 388, 1862. Latham in Trans. Philolog. Soc. Lond., II, 31–50, 1846 (indicates the coalescence of Athabascan family with Esquimaux). Latham (1844), in Jour. Eth. Soc. Lond., I, 161, 1848 (Nagail and Taculli referred to Athabascan). Scouler (1846), in Jour. Eth. Soc. Lond., I, 230, 1848. Latham, Opuscula, 257, 259, 276, 1860. Keane, App. to Stanford's Comp. (Cent. and So. Am.), 460, 463, 1878.

> Kinai, Gallatin in Trans. and Coll. Am. Antiq. Soc., II, 14, 305, 1836 (Kinai and Ugaljachmutzi; considered to form a distinct family, though affirmed to have affinities with western Esquimaux and with Athapascas). Prichard, Phys. Hist. Mankind, v, 440–443, 1847 (follows Gallatin; also affirms a relationship to Aztec). Gallatin in Trans. Am. Eth. Soc., II, pt. 1, 77, 1848.

> Kenay, Latham in Proc. Philolog. Soc. Lond., II, 32–34, 1846. Latham, Opuscula, 275, 1860. Latham, Elements Comp. Phil., 389, 1862 (referred to Esquimaux stock).

> Kinætzi, Prichard, Phys. Hist. Mankind, v, 441, 1847 (same as his Kinai above).

> Kenai, Gallatin in Trans. Am. Eth. Soc., II. xcix, 1848 (see Kinai above). Buschmann, Spuren der aztek. Sprache, 695, 1856 (refers it to Athapaskan).

× Northern, Scouler in Jour. Roy. Geog. Soc. Lond., XI, 218, 1841. (Includes Atnas, Kolchans, and Kenáïes of present family.)

× Haidah, Scouler, ibid., 224 (same as his Northern family).

> Chepeyans, Prichard, Phys. Hist. Mankind, v, 375, 1847 (same as Athapascas above).

> Tahkali-Umkwa, Hale in U. S. Expl. Exp., VI, 198, 201, 569, 1846 ("a branch of the great Chippewyan, or Athapascan, stock;" includes Carriers, Qualioguas, Tlatskanies, Umguas). Gallatin, after Hale in Trans. Am. Eth. Soc., II, pt. 1, 9, 1848.

> Digothi, Berghaus (1845), Physik Atlas, map 17, 1848. Digothi, Loucheux, ibid. 1852.

> Lipans, Latham, Nat. Hist. Man, 349, 1850 (Lipans (Sipans) between Rio Arkansas and Rio Grande).

> Tototune, Latham, Nat. Hist. Man, 325, 1850 (seacoast south of the Saintskla).
> Ugaljachmutzi, Gallatin in Schoolcraft, Ind. Tribes, III, 402, 1853 ("perhaps Athapascas").
> Umkwa, Latham in Proc. Philolog. Soc. Lond., VI, 72, 1854 (a single tribe). Latham, Opuscula, 300, 1860.
> Tahlewah, Gibbs in Schoolcraft, Ind. Tribes, III, 422, 1853 (a single tribe). Latham in Trans. Philolog. Soc. Lond., 76, 1856 (a single tribe). Latham. Opuscula, 342, 1860.
> Tolewa, Gatschet in Mag. Am. Hist., 163, 1877 (vocab. from Smith River, Oregon; affirmed to be distinct from any neighboring tongue). Gatschet in Beach, Ind. Miscellany, 438, 1877.
> Hoo-pah, Gibbs in Schoolcraft, Ind. Tribes, III, 422, 1853 (tribe on Lower Trinity, California).
> Hoopa, Powers in Overland Monthly, 155, August, 1872.
> Hú-pâ, Powers in Cont. N. A. Eth., III, 72, 1877 (affirmed to be Athapascan).
= Tinneh, Dall in Proc. Am. Ass. A. S., XVIII, 269, 1869 (chiefly Alaskan tribes). Dall, Alaska and its Resources, 428, 1870. Dall in Cont. N. A. Eth., I, 24, 1877. Bancroft, Native Races, III, 562, 583, 603, 1882.
= Tinné. Gatschet in Mag. Am, Hist., 165, 1877 (special mention of Hoopa, Rogue River, Umpqua.) Gatschet in Beach, Ind. Misc., 440, 1877. Gatschet in Geog. Surv. W. 100th M., VII, 406, 1879. Tolmie and Dawson, Comp. Vocabs., 62, 1884. Berghaus, Physik. Atlas, map 72, 1887.
= Tinney, Keane, App. to Stanford's Comp. (Cent. and So. Am.), 460, 463, 1878.
× Klamath, Keane, App. to Stanford's Comp. (Cent. and So. Am.), 475, 1878; or Lutuami, (Lototens and Tolewahs of his list belong here.)

Derivation: From the lake of the same name; signifying, according to Lacombe, "place of hay and reeds."

As defined by Gallatin, the area occupied by this great family is included in a line drawn from the mouth of the Churchill or Missinippi River to its source; thence along the ridge which separates the north branch of the Saskatchewan from those of the Athapascas to the Rocky Mountains; and thence northwardly till within a hundred miles of the Pacific Ocean, in latitude 52° 30'.

The only tribe within the above area excepted by Gallatin as of probably a different stock was the Quarrelers or Loucheux, living at the mouth of Mackenzie River. This tribe, however, has since been ascertained to be Athapascan.

The Athapascan family thus occupied almost the whole of British Columbia and of Alaska, and was, with the exception of the Eskimo, by whom they were cut off on nearly all sides from the ocean, the most northern family in North America.

Since Gallatin's time the history of this family has been further elucidated by the discovery on the part of Hale and Turner that isolated branches of the stock have become established in Oregon, California, and along the southern border of the United States.

The boundaries of the Athapascan family, as now understood, are best given under three primary groups—Northern, Pacific, and Southern.

Northern group.—This includes all the Athapascan tribes of British North America and Alaska. In the former region the Athapascans occupy most of the western interior, being bounded on the north by the Arctic Eskimo, who inhabit a narrow strip of coast; on the east by the Eskimo of Hudson's Bay as far south as Churchill River, south of which river the country is occupied by Algonquian tribes. On the south the Athapascan tribes extended to the main ridge between the Athapasca and Saskatchewan Rivers, where they met Algonquian tribes; west of this area they were bounded on the south by Salishan tribes, the limits of whose territory on Fraser River and its tributaries appear on Tolmie and Dawson's map of 1884. On the west, in British Columbia, the Athapascan tribes nowhere reach the coast, being cut off by the Wakashan, Salishan, and Chimmesyan families.

The interior of Alaska is chiefly occupied by tribes of this family. Eskimo tribes have encroached somewhat upon the interior along the Yukon, Kuskokwim, Kowak, and Noatak Rivers, reaching on the Yukon to somewhat below Shageluk Island,[1] and on the Kuskokwim nearly or quite to Kolmakoff Redoubt.[2] Upon the two latter they reach quite to their heads.[3] A few Kutchin tribes are (or have been) north of the Porcupine and Yukon Rivers, but until recently it has not been known that they extended north beyond the Yukon and Romanzoff Mountains. Explorations of Lieutenant Stoney, in 1885, establish the fact that the region to the north of those mountains is occupied by Athapascan tribes, and the map is colored accordingly. Only in two places in Alaska do the Athapascan tribes reach the coast—the K'naia-khotana, on Cook's Inlet, and the Ahtena, of Copper River.

Pacific group.—Unlike the tribes of the Northern group, most of those of the Pacific group have removed from their priscan habitats since the advent of the white race. The Pacific group embraces the following: Kwalhioqua, formerly on Willopah River, Washington, near the Lower Chinook;[4] Owilapsh, formerly between Shoalwater Bay and the heads of the Chehalis River, Washington, the territory of these two tribes being practically continuous; Tlatscanai, formerly on a small stream on the northwest side of Wapatoo Island.[5] Gibbs was informed by an old Indian that this tribe "formerly owned the prairies on the Tsihalis at the mouth of the Skukumchuck, but, on the failure of game, left the country, crossed the Columbia River, and occupied the mountains to the

---

[1] Dall, Map Alaska, 1877.

[2] Fide Nelson in Dall's address, Am. Assoc. Adv. Sci., 1885, p. 13.

[3] Cruise of the *Corwin*, 1887.

[4] Gibbs in Pac. R. R. Rep. I, 1855, p. 428.

[5] Lewis and Clarke, Exp., 1814, vol. 2, p. 382.

south "—a statement of too uncertain character to be depended upon; the Athapascan tribes now on the Grande Ronde and Siletz Reservations, Oregon,[1] whose villages on and near the coast extended from Coquille River southward to the California line, including, among others, the Upper Coquille, Sixes, Euchre, Creek, Joshua, Tutu tûnnĕ, and other "Rogue River" or "Tou-touten bands," Chasta Costa, Galice Creek, Naltunne tûnnĕ and Chetco villages;[2] the Athapascan villages formerly on Smith River and tributaries, California;[3] those villages extending southward from Smith River along the California coast to the mouth of Klamath River;[4] the Hupâ villages or "clans" formerly on Lower Trinity River, California;[5] the Kenesti or Wailakki (2), located as follows: "They live along the western slope of the Shasta Mountains, from North Eel River, above Round Valley, to Hay Fork; along Eel and Mad Rivers, extending down the latter about to Low Gap; also on Dobbins and Larrabie Creeks;"[6] and Saiaz, who " formerly occupied the tongue of land jutting down between Eel River and Van Dusen's Fork."[7]

Southern group.—Includes the Navajo, Apache, and Lipan. Engineer José Cortez, one of the earliest authorities on these tribes, writing in 1799, defines the boundaries of the Lipan and Apache as extending north and south from 29° N. to 36° N., and east and west from 99° W. to 114° W.; in other words from central Texas nearly to the Colorado River in Arizona, where they met tribes of the Yuman stock. The Lipan occupied the eastern part of the above territory, extending in Texas from the Comanche country (about Red River) south to the Rio Grande.[8] More recently both Lipan and Apache have gradually moved southward into Mexico where they extend as far as Durango.[9]

The Navajo, since first known to history, have occupied the country on and south of the San Juan River in northern New Mexico and Arizona and extending into Colorado and Utah. They were surrounded on all sides by the cognate Apache except upon the north, where they meet Shoshonean tribes.

---

[1] Gatschet and Dorsey, MS., 1883–'84.

[2] Dorsey, MS., map, 1884, B. E.

[3] Hamilton, MS., Haynarger Vocab., B. E.; Powers, Contr. N. A. Ethn., 1877, vol. 3, p. 65.

[4] Dorsey, MS., map, 1884, B. E.

[5] Powers, Contr. N. A. Ethn., 1877, vol. 3, pp. 72, 73.

[6] Powers, Contr. N. A. Ethn., 1877, vol. 3, p. 114.

[7] Powers, Contr. N. A. Ethn., 1877, vol. 3, p. 122.

[8] Cortez in Pac. R. R. Rep., 1856, vol. 3, pt. 3, pp. 118, 119.

[9] Bartlett, Pers. Narr., 1854; Orozco y Berra, Geog., 1864.

PRINCIPAL TRIBES.

A. Northern group:

Ah-tena.	Kutchin.	Sluacus-tinneh.
Kaiyuh-khotana.	Montagnais.	Taculli.
Kcaltana.	Montagnards.	Tahl-tan (1).
K'naia-khotana.	Nagailer.	Unakhotana.
Koyukukhotana.	Slave.	

B. Pacific group:

Ătaăkût.	Kwalhioqua.	Taltûctun tûde (on
Chasta Costa.	Kwaʇami.	Galice Creek).
Chetco.	Micikqwûtme tûnnĕ.	Tcêmê (Joshuas).
Dakube tede (on Ap-	Mikono tûnnĕ.	Tcĕtlĕstcan tûnnĕ.
plegate Creek).	Naltunne tûnnĕ.	Terwar.
Euchre Creek.	Owilapsh.	Tlatscanai.
Hupâ.	Qwinctûnnetûn.	Tolowa.
Kălts'erea tûnnĕ.	Saiaz.	Tutu tûnnĕ.
Kenesti or Wailakki.		

C. Southern group):

Arivaipa.	Lipan.	Navajo.
Chiricahua.	Llanero.	Pinal Coyotero.
Coyotero.	Mescalero.	Tchĭkûn.
Faraone.	Mimbreño.	Tchishi.
Gileño.	Mogollon.	
Jicarilla.	Na-isha.	

Population.—The present number of the Athapascan family is about 32.899, of whom about 8,595, constituting the Northern group, are in Alaska and British North America, according to Dall, Dawson, and the Canadian Indian Report for 1888; about 895, comprising the Pacific group, are in Washington, Oregon, and California; and about 23,409, belonging to the Southern group, are in Arizona, New Mexico, Colorado, and Indian Territory. Besides these are the Lipan and some refugee Apache, who are in Mexico. These have not been included in the above enumeration, as there are no means of ascertaining their number.

Northern group.—This may be said to consist of the following:

Ah-tena (1877)		364?
Ai-yan (1888)...		250
Al-ta-tin (Sicannie) estimated (1888)....................................		500
of whom there are at Fort Halkett (1887)......................	73	
of whom there are at Fort Liard (1887).................	78	
Chippewyan, Yellow Knives, with a few Slave and Dog Rib at Fort Resolution		469
Dog Rib at Fort Norman..		133
Dog Rib, Slave, and Yellow Knives at Fort Rae........................		657
Hare at Fort Good Hope..		364

Hare at Fort Norman 103
Kai-yuh-kho-tána (1877), Koyukukhotána (1877), and Unakhotána (1877)... 2,000?
K'nai-a Khotána (1880)........ .... 250?
Kutchin and Bastard Loucheux at Fort Good Hope 95
Kutchin at Peel River and La Pierre's House............................ 337
Kutchin on the Yukon (six tribes) 842
Nahanie at Fort Good Hope 8
Nahanie at Fort Halkett (including Mauvais Monde, Bastard Na-
    hanie, and Mountain Indians)................................. 332
Nahanie at Fort Liard.. 38
Nahanie at Fort Norman...................................... 43
                                                                      ────── 421
Nahanie at Fort Simpson and Big Island (Hudson Bay Company's Terri-
    tory)................................. 87
Slave, Dog Rib, and Hare at Fort Simpson and Big Island (Hudson Bay
    Company's Territory)... 658
Slave at Fort Liard........... 281
Slave at Fort Norman.. 84
Tenán Kutchin (1877) .... 700?
                                                                      ──────
                                                                      8,595?

To the Pacific Group may be assigned the following:

Hupa Indians, on Hoopa Valley Reservation, California............. 468
Rogue River Indians at Grande Ronde Reservation, Oregon 47
Siletz Reservation, Oregon (about one-half the Indians thereon).......... 300?
Umpqua at Grande Ronde Reservation, Oregon 80
                                                                      ──────
                                                                      895?

Southern Group, consisting of Apache, Lipan, and Navajo:

Apache children at Carlisle, Pennsylvania........................ 142
Apache prisoners at Mount Vernon Barracks, Alabama............... . 356
Coyotero Apache (San Carlos Reservation) .... 733?
Jicarilla Apache (Southern Ute Reservation, Colorado) 808
Lipan with Tonkaway on Oakland Reserve, Indian Territory.............. 15?
Mescalero Apache (Mescalero Reservation, New Mexico)........ 513
Na-isha Apache (Kiowa, Comanche, and Wichita Reservation, Indian
    Territory).... 326
Navajo (most on Navajo Reservation, Arizona and New Mexico; 4 at Car-
    lisle, Pennsylvania)......... 17,208
San Carlos Apache (San Carlos Reservation, Arizona) .. .. 1,352?
White Mountain Apache (San Carlos Reservation, Arizona).... 36
White Mountain Apache (under military at Camp Apache, Arizona)..... 1,920
                                                                      ──────
                                                                      23,409?

ATTACAPAN FAMILY.

=Attacapas, Gallatin in Trans. and Coll. Am. Antiq. Soc., II, 116, 306, 1836. Galla-
    tin in Trans. Am. Eth. Soc., II, pt. 1, xcix, 77, 1848. Latham, Nat. Hist. Man,
    343, 1850 (includes Attacapas and Carankuas). Gallatin in Schoolcraft, Ind.
    Tribes, III, 402, 1853. Buschmann, Spuren der aztek. Sprache, 426, 1859.
=Attacapa, Latham in Proc. Philolog. Soc. Lond., II, 31–50, 1846. Prichard, Phys.
    Hist. Mankind, v, 406, 1847 (or " Men eaters"). Latham in Trans. Philolog.
    Soc. Lond., 105, 1856. Latham, Opuscula, 293, 1860.

=Attakapa, Latham in Trans. Philolog. Soc. Lond., 103, 1856. Latham, Opuscula, 366, 1860. Latham, El. Comp. Phil., 477, 1862 (referred to as one of the two most isolated languages of N. A.).

=Atákapa, Gatschet, Creek Mig. Leg., I, 45, 1884. Gatschet in Science, 414, Apr. 29, 1887.

Derivation: From a Choctaw word meaning "man-eater."

Little is known of the tribe, the language of which forms the basis of the present family. The sole knowledge possessed by Gallatin was derived from a vocabulary and some scanty information furnished by Dr. John Sibley, who collected his material in the year 1805. Gallatin states that the tribe was reduced to 50 men. According to Dr. Sibley the Attacapa language was spoken also by another tribe, the "Carankouas," who lived on the coast of Texas, and who conversed in their own language besides. In 1885 Mr. Gatschet visited the section formerly inhabited by the Attacapa and after much search discovered one man and two women at Lake Charles, Calcasieu Parish, Louisiana, and another woman living 10 miles to the south; he also heard of five other women then scattered in western Texas; these are thought to be the only survivors of the tribe. Mr. Gatschet collected some two thousand words and a considerable body of text. His vocabulary differs considerably from the one furnished by Dr. Sibley and published by Gallatin, and indicates that the language of the western branch of the tribe was dialectically distinct from that of their brethren farther to the east.

The above material seems to show that the Attacapa language is distinct from all others, except possibly the Chitimachan.

BEOTHUKAN FAMILY.

=Bethuck, Latham in Trans. Philolog. Soc. Lond., 58, 1856 (stated to be "Algonkin rather than aught else"). Latham, Opuscula, 327, 1860. Latham, El. Comp. Phil., 453, 1862.

=Beothuk, Gatschet in Proc. Am. Philosoph. Soc., 408, Oct., 1885. Gatschet, ibid., 411, July, 1886 (language affirmed to represent a distinct linguistic family). Gatschet, ibid., 1, Jan.–June, 1890.

Derivation: Beothuk signifies "Indian" or "red Indian."

The position of the language spoken by the aborigines of Newfoundland must be considered to be doubtful.

In 1846 Latham examined the material then accessible, and was led to the somewhat ambiguous statement that the language "was akin to those of the ordinary American Indians rather than to the Eskimo; further investigation showing that, of the ordinary American languages, it was Algonkin rather than aught else."

Since then Mr. Gatschet has been able to examine a much larger and more satisfactory body of material, and although neither in amount nor quality is the material sufficient to permit final and satisfactory deductions, yet so far as it goes it shows that the language is quite distinct from any of the Algonquian dialects, and in fact from any other American tongue.

GEOGRAPHIC DISTRIBUTION.

It seems highly probable that the whole of Newfoundland at the time of its discovery by Cabot in 1497 was inhabited by Beothuk Indians.

In 1534 Cartier met with Indians inhabiting the southeastern part of the island, who, very likely, were of this people, though the description is too vague to permit certain identification. A century later the southern portion of the island appears to have been abandoned by these Indians, whoever they were, on account of European settlements, and only the northern and eastern parts of the island were occupied by them. About the beginning of the eighteenth century western Newfoundland was colonized by the Micmac from Nova Scotia. As a consequence of the persistent warfare which followed the advent of the latter and which was also waged against the Beothuk by the Europeans, especially the French, the Beothuk rapidly wasted in numbers. Their main territory was soon confined to the neighborhood of the Exploits River. The tribe was finally lost sight of about 1827, having become extinct, or possibly the few survivors having crossed to the Labrador coast and joined the Nascapi with whom the tribe had always been on friendly terms.

Upon the map only the small portion of the island is given to the Beothuk which is known definitely to have been occupied by them, viz., the neighborhood of the Exploits River, though, as stated above, it seems probable that the entire island was once in their possession.

CADDOAN FAMILY.

>Caddoes, Gallatin in Trans. and Coll. Am. Antiq. Soc., II, 116, 306, 1836 (based on Caddoes alone). Prichard, Phys. Hist. Mankind, v, 406, 1847. Gallatin in Schoolcraft, Ind. Tribes, III, 402, 1853 [gives as languages Caddo, Red River, (Nandakoes, Tachies, Nabedaches)].

>Caddokies, Gallatin in Trans. and Coll. Am. Antiq. Soc., II, 116, 1836 (same as his Caddoes). Prichard, Phys. Hist. Mankind, v, 1847.

>Caddo, Latham in Trans. Philolog. Soc. Lond., II, 31-50, 1846 (indicates affinities with Iroquois, Muskoge, Catawba, Pawnee). Gallatin in Trans. Am. Eth. Soc., II, pt. 1, xcix, 77, 1848, (Caddo only). Berghaus (1845), Physik. Atlas, map 17, 1848 (Caddos, etc.). Ibid., 1852. Latham, Nat. Hist. Man, 338, 1850 (between the Mississippi and Sabine). Latham in Trans. Philolog. Soc., Lond., 101, 1856. Turner in Pac. R. R. Rep., III, pt. 3, 55, 70, 1856 (finds resemblances to Pawnee but keeps them separate). Buschmann, Spuren der aztek. Sprache, 426, 448, 1859. Latham, Opuscula, 290, 366, 1860.

>Caddo, Latham, Elements Comp. Phil., 470, 1862 (includes Pawni and Riccari).

>Pawnees, Gallatin in Trans. and Coll. Am. Antiq. Soc., II, 128, 306, 1836 (two nations: Pawnees proper and Ricaras or Black Pawnees). Prichard, Phys. Hist. Mankind, v, 408, 1847 (follows Gallatin). Gallatin in Trans. Am. Eth. Soc.,

II, pt. 1, xcix, 1848. Latham, Nat. Hist. Man, 344, 1850 (or Panis; includes Loup and Republican Pawnees). Gallatin in Schoolcraft, Ind. Tribes, III, 402, 1853 (gives as languages: Pawnees, Ricaras, Tawakeroes, Towekas, Wachos?). Hayden, Cont. Eth. and Phil. Missouri Indians, 232, 345, 1862 (includes Pawnees and Arikaras).

>Panis, Gallatin in Trans. and Coll. Am. Antiq. Soc., II, 117, 128, 1836 (of Red River of Texas: mention of villages; doubtfully indicated as of Pawnee family). Prichard, Phys. Hist. Mankind, v, 407, 1847 (supposed from name to be of same race with Pawnees of the Arkansa). Latham, Nat. Hist. Man, 344, 1850 (Pawnees or). Gallatin in Schoolcraft, Ind. Tribes, III, 402, 1853 (here kept separate from Pawnee family).

>Pawnies, Gallatin in Trans. Am. Eth. Soc., II, pt. 1, 77, 1848 (see Pawnee above).

>Pahnies, Berghaus (1845), Physik. Atlas, map 17, 1848. Ibid., 1852.

>Pawnee(?), Turner in Pac. R. R. Rep., III, pt. 3, 55, 65, 1856 (Kichai and Hueco vocabularies).

=Pawnee, Keane, App. to Stanford's Comp. (Cent. and So. Am.), 478, 1878 (gives four groups, viz: Pawnees proper; Arickarees; Wichitas; Caddoes).

=Pani, Gatschet, Creek Mig. Legend, I, 42, 1884. Berghaus, Physik. Atlas, map 72, 1887.

>Towiaches, Gallatin in Trans. and Coll. Am. Antiq. Soc., II, 116, 128, 1836 (same as Panis above). Prichard, Phys. Hist. Mankind, v, 407, 1847.

>Towiachs, Latham, Nat. Hist. Man, 349, 1850 (includes Towiach, Tawakenoes, Towecas?, Wacos).

>Towiacks, Gallatin in Schoolcraft, Ind. Tribes, III, 402, 1853.

>Natchitoches, Gallatin in Trans. and Coll. Am. Antiq. Soc., II, 116, 1836 (stated by Dr. Sibley to speak a language different from any other). Latham, Nat. Hist. Man, 342, 1850. Prichard, Phys. Hist. Mankind, v, 406, 1847 (after Gallatin). Gallatin in Schoolcraft, Ind. Tribes, III, 402, 1853 (a single tribe only).

>Aliche, Latham, Nat. Hist. Man, 349, 1850 (near Nacogdoches; not classified).

>Yatassees, Gallatin in Trans. and Coll. Am. Antiq. Soc., II, 116, 1836 (the single tribe; said by Dr. Sibley to be different from any other; referred to as a family).

>Riccarees, Latham, Nat. Hist. Man, 344, 1850 (kept distinct from Pawnee family).

>Washita, Latham in Trans. Philolog. Soc., Lond., 103, 1856. Buschmann, Spuren der aztek. Sprache, 441, 1859 (revokes previous opinion of its distinctness and refers it to Pawnee family).

>Witchitas, Buschmann, ibid., (same as his Washita).

Derivation: From the Caddo term ka'-ede, signifying "chief" (Gatschet).

The Pawnee and Caddo, now known to be of the same linguistic family, were supposed by Gallatin and by many later writers to be distinct, and accordingly both names appear in the Archæologia Americana as family designations. Both names are unobjectionable, but as the term Caddo has priority by a few pages preference is given to it.

Gallatin states "that the Caddoes formerly lived 300 miles up Red River but have now moved to a branch of Red River." He refers to the Nandakoes, the Inies or Tachies, and the Nabedaches as speaking dialects of the Caddo language.

Under Pawnee two tribes were included by Gallatin: The Pawnees proper and the Ricaras. The Pawnee tribes occupied the country on the Platte River adjoining the Loup Fork. The Ricara towns were on the upper Missouri in latitude 46° 30'.

The boundaries of the Caddoan family, as at present understood, can best be given under three primary groups, Northern, Middle, and Southern.

Northern group.—This comprises the Arikara or Ree, now confined to a small village (on Fort Berthold Reservation, North Dakota,) which they share with the Mandan and Hidatsa tribes of the Siouan family. The Arikara are the remains of ten different tribes of "Paneas," who had been driven from their country lower down the Missouri River (near the Ponka habitat in northern Nebraska) by the Dakota. In 1804 they were in three villages, nearer their present location.[1]

According to Omaha tradition, the Arikara were their allies when these two tribes and several others were east of the Mississippi River.[2] Fort Berthold Reservation, their present abode, is in the northwest corner of North Dakota.

Middle group.—This includes the four tribes or villages of Pawnee, the Grand, Republican, Tapage, and Skidi. Dunbar says: "The original hunting ground of the Pawnee extended from the Niobrara," in Nebraska, "south to the Arkansas, but no definite boundaries can be fixed." In modern times their villages have been on the Platte River west of Columbus, Nebraska. The Omaha and Oto were sometimes southeast of them near the mouth of the Platte, and the Comanche were northwest of them on the upper part of one of the branches of the Loup Fork.[3] The Pawnee were removed to Indian Territory in 1876. The Grand Pawnee and Tapage did not wander far from their habitat on the Platte. The Republican Pawnee separated from the Grand about the year 1796, and made a village on a "large northwardly branch of the Kansas River, to which they have given their name; afterwards they subdivided, and lived in different parts of the country on the waters of Kansas River. In 1805 they rejoined the Grand Pawnee." The Skidi (Panimaha, or Pawnee Loup), according to Omaha tradition,[4] formerly dwelt east of the Mississippi River, where they were the allies of the Arikara, Omaha, Ponka, etc. After their passage of the Missouri they were conquered by the Grand Pawnee, Tapage, and Republican tribes, with whom they have remained to this day. De L'Isle[5] gives twelve Panimaha villages on the Missouri River north of the Pani villages on the Kansas River.

Southern group.—This includes the Caddo, Wichita, Kichai, and other tribes or villages which were formerly in Texas, Louisiana, Arkansas, and Indian Territory.

---

[1] Lewis, Travels of Lewis and Clarke, 15, 1809.

[2] Dorsey in Am. Naturalist, March, 1886, p. 215.

[3] Dorsey, Omaha map of Nebraska.

[4] Dorsey in Am. Nat., March, 1886, p. 215.

[5] Carte de la Louisiane, 1718.

The Caddo and Kichai have undoubtedly been removed from their priscan habitats, but the Wichita, judging from the survival of local names (Washita River, Indian Territory, Wichita Falls, Texas) and the statement of La Harpe,[1] are now in or near one of their early abodes. Dr. Sibley[2] locates the Caddo habitat 35 miles west of the main branch of Red River, being 120 miles by land from Natchitoches, and they formerly lived 375 miles higher up. Cornell's Atlas (1870) places Caddo Lake in the northwest corner of Louisiana, in Caddo County. It also gives both Washita and Witchita as the name of a tributary of Red River of Louisiana. This duplication of names seems to show that the Wichita migrated from northwestern Louisiana and southwestern Arkansas to the Indian Territory. After comparing the statements of Dr. Sibley (as above) respecting the habitats of the Anadarko, Ioni, Nabadache, and Eyish with those of Schermerhorn respecting the Kädo hadatco,[3] of Le Page Du Pratz (1758) concerning the Natchitoches, of Tonti[4] and La Harpe[5] about the Yatasi, of La Harpe (as above) about the Wichita, and of Sibley concerning the Kichai, we are led to fix upon the following as the approximate boundaries of the habitat of the southern group of the Caddoan family: Beginning on the northwest with that part of Indian Territory now occupied by the Wichita, Chickasaw, and Kiowa and Comanche Reservations, and running along the southern border of the Choctaw Reservation to the Arkansas line; thence due east to the headwaters of Washita or Witchita River, Polk County, Arkansas; thence through Arkansas and Louisiana along the western bank of that river to its mouth; thence southwest through Louisiana striking the Sabine River near Salem and Belgrade; thence southwest through Texas to Tawakonay Creek, and along that stream to the Brazos River; thence following that stream to Palo Pinto, Texas; thence northwest to the mouth of the North Fork of Red River; and thence to the beginning.

PRINCIPAL TRIBES.

A. Pawnee.
> Grand Pawnee.
> Tappas.
> Republican Pawnee.
> Skidi.

B. Arikara.

C. Wichita.
> (Ki-¢i'-tcac, Omaha pronunciation of the name of a Pawnee tribe, Ki-dhi'-chash or Ki-ri'-chash).

---

[1] In 1719, *fide* Margry, VI. 289, " the Ousita village is on the southwest branch of the Arkansas River.

[2] 1805, in Lewis and Clarke, Discov., 1806, p. 66.

[3] Second Mass. Hist. Coll., vol. 2, 1814, p. 23.

[4] 1690, in French, Hist. Coll. La., vol. 1, p. 72.

[5] 1719, in Margry, vol. 6, p. 264.

D. Kichai.

E. Caddo (Kä'-do).

Population.—The present number of the Caddoan stock is 2,259, of whom 447 are on the Fort Berthold Reservation, North Dakota, and the rest in the Indian Territory, some on the Ponca, Pawnee, and Otoe Reservation, the others on the Kiowa, Comanche, and Wichita Reservation. Below is given the population of the tribes officially recognized, compiled chiefly from the Indian Report for 1889:

Arikara		448
Pawnee		824
Wichita	176	
Towakarehu	145	
Waco	64	
		385
Kichai		63
Caddo		539
Total		2,259

CHIMAKUAN FAMILY.

=Chimakum, Gibbs in Pac. R. R. Rep., I, 431, 1855 (family doubtful).

=Chemakum, Eells in Am. Antiquarian, 52, Oct., 1880 (considers language different from any of its neighbors).

<Puget Sound Group, Keane, App. Stanford's Comp. (Cent. and So. Am.), 474, 1878 (Chinakum included in this group).

<Nootka, Bancroft, Native Races, III, 564, 1882 (contains Chimakum).

Derivation unknown.

Concerning this language Gibbs, as above cited, states as follows:

The language of the Chimakum "differs materially from either that of the Clallams or the Nisqually, and is not understood by any of their neighbors. In fact, they seem to have maintained it a State secret. To what family it will ultimately be referred, cannot now be decided."

Eells also asserts the distinctness of this language from any of its neighbors. Neither of the above authors assigned the language family rank, and accordingly Mr. Gatschet, who has made a comparison of vocabularies and finds the language to be quite distinct from any other, gives it the above name.

The Chimakum are said to have been formerly one of the largest and most powerful tribes of Puget Sound. Their warlike habits early tended to diminish their numbers, and when visited by Gibbs in 1854 they counted only about seventy individuals. This small remnant occupied some fifteen small lodges on Port Townsend Bay. According to Gibbs "their territory seems to have embraced the shore from Port Townsend to Port Ludlow."[1] In 1884 there were, according to

---

[1] Dr. Boas was informed in 1889, by a surviving Chimakum woman and several Clallam, that the tribe was confined to the peninsula between Hood's Canal and Port Townsend.

Mr. Myron Eells, about twenty individuals left, most of whom are living near Port Townsend, Washington. Three or four live upon the Skokomish Reservation at the southern end of Hood's Canal.

The Quile-ute, of whom in 1889 there were 252 living on the Pacific south of Cape Flattery, belong to the family. The Hoh, a sub-tribe of the latter, number 71 and are under the Puyallup Agency.

PRINCIPAL TRIBES.

The following tribes are recognized:

Chimakum.   Quile-ute.

CHIMARIKAN FAMILY.

=Chim-a-ri′-ko, Powell in Cont. N. A. Eth., III, 474, 1877.   Gatschet in Mag. Am. Hist., 255, April, 1882 (stated to be a distinct family).

According to Powers, this family was represented, so far as known, by two tribes in California, one the Chi-mál-a-kwe, living on New River, a branch of the Trinity, the other the Chimariko, residing upon the Trinity itself from Burnt Ranch up to the mouth of North Fork, California. The two tribes are said to have been as numerous formerly as the Hupa, by whom they were overcome and nearly exterminated. Upon the arrival of the Americans only twenty-five of the Chimalakwe were left. In 1875 Powers collected a Chimariko vocabulary of about two hundred words from a woman, supposed to be one of the last three women of that tribe. In 1889 Mr. Curtin, while in Hoopa Valley, found a Chimariko man seventy or more years old, who is believed to be one of the two living survivors of the tribe. Mr. Curtin obtained a good vocabulary and much valuable information relative to the former habitat and history of the tribe. Although a study of these vocabularies reveals a number of words having correspondences with the Kulanapan (Pomo) equivalents, yet the greater number show no affinities with the dialects of the latter family, or indeed with any other. The family is therefore classed as distinct.

PRINCIPAL TRIBES.

Chimariko.   Chimalakwe.

CHIMMESYAN FAMILY.

=Chimmesyan, Latham in Jour. Eth. Soc. Lond., I, 154, 1848 (between 53° 30′ and 55° 30′ N. L.). Latham, Opuscula, 250, 1860.

Chemmesyan, Latham, Nat. Hist. Man, 300, 1850 (includes Naaskok, Chemmesyan, Kitshatlah, Kethumish). Latham in Trans. Philolog. Soc. Lond., 72, 1856. Latham, Opuscula, 339, 1860. Latham, Elements Comp. Phil., 401, 1862.

=Chymseyans, Kane, Wanderings of an Artist, app., 1859 (a census of tribes of N. W. coast classified by languages).

=Chimsyans, Schoolcraft, Ind. Tribes, V. 487, 1855 (gives Kane's list but with many orthographical changes). Dall in Proc. Am. Ass., 269, 1869 (published in 1870).

Dall in Cont. N. A. Eth., I, 36, 39, 40, 1877 (probably distinct from T'linkets).
Bancroft, Native Races, III, 564, 607, 1882.

=Tshimsian, Tolmie and Dawson, Comp. Vocabs., 14–25, 1884.

=Tsimpsi-an', Dall in Proc. Am. Ass., 379, 1885 (mere mention of family).

×Northern, Scouler in Jour. Roy. Geog. Soc. Lond., XI, 220, 1841 (includes Chimmesyans).

×Haidah, Scouler in Jour. Roy. Geog. Soc. Lond., XI, 220, 1841 (same as his Northern family).

<Naas, Gallatin in Trans. Am. Eth. Soc., II, pt. 1, c, 1848 (including Chimmesyan).
Berghaus (1851), Physik. Atlas, map 17, 1852.

<Naass, Gallatin in Trans. Am. Eth. Soc., II, pt. 1, 77, 1848. Gallatin in Schoolcraft,
Ind. Tribes, III, 402, 1853.

=Nasse, Dall in Cont. N. A. Eth., I, 36, 40, 1877 (or Chimsyan).

<Nass, Bancroft, Nat. Races, III, 564, 606, 1882 (includes Nass and Sebassa Indians
of this family, also Hailtza).

=Hydahs, Keane, App. to Stanford's Comp. (Cent. and So. Am.), 473, 1878 (includes
Tsimsheeans, Nass, Skeenas, Sebasses of present family).

Derivation: From the Chimsian ts'em, "on;" kcian, "main river:"
"On the main (Skeena) river."

This name appears in a paper of Latham's published in 1848. To
it is referred a vocabulary of Tolmie's. The area where it is spoken
is said by Latham to be 50° 30′ and 55° 30′. The name has become
established by long usage, and it is chiefly on this account that it
has been given preference over the Naas of Gallatin of the same
year. The latter name was given by Gallatin to a group of languages now known to be not related, viz, Hailstla, Haceltzuk
Billechola, and Chimeysan. Billechola belongs under Salishan, a
family name of Gallatin's of 1836.

Were it necessary to take Naas as a family name it would best
apply to Chimsian, it being the name of a dialect and village of
Chimsian Indians, while it has no pertinency whatever to Hailstla
and Haceltzuk, which are closely related and belong to a family
quite distinct from the Chimmesyan. As stated above, however,
the term Naas is rejected in favor of Chimmesyan of the same date.

For the boundaries of this family the linguistic map published
by Tolmie and Dawson, in 1884, is followed.

PRINCIPAL TRIBES.

Following is a list of the Chimmesyan tribes, according to Boas:[1]

A. Nasqa':
    Nasqa'.
    Gyitksa'n.
B. Tsimshian proper:
    Ts'emsia'n.

Gyits'umrä'lon.
Gyits'ala'ser.
Gyitqā'tla.
Gyitg·ā'ata.
Gyidesdzo'.

Population.—The Canadian Indian Report for 1888 records a total
for all the tribes of this family of 5,000. In the fall of 1887 about
1,000 of these Indians, in charge of Mr. William Duncan, removed

[1] B. A. A. S. Fifth Rep. of Committee on NW. Tribes of Canada. Newcastle-
upon-Tyne meeting, 1889, pp. 8–9.

to Annette Island, about 60 miles north of the southern boundary of Alaska, near Port Chester, where they have founded a new settlement called New Metlakahtla. Here houses have been erected, day and industrial schools established, and the Indians are understood to be making remarkable progress in civilization.

CHINOOKAN FAMILY.

>Chinooks, Gallatin in Trans. and Coll. Am. Antiq. Soc., II, 134, 306, 1836 (a single tribe at mouth of Columbia).

=Chinooks, Hale in U. S. Expl. Expd., VI, 198, 1846. Gallatin, after Hale, in Trans. Am. Eth. Soc., II, pt. 1, 15, 1848 (or Tsinuk).

=Tshinuk, Hale in U. S. Expl. Expd., VI, 562, 569, 1846 (contains Watlala or Upper Chinook, including Watlala, Nihaloitih, or Echeloots; and Tshinuk, including Tshinuk, Tlatsap, Wakaikam).

=Tsinuk, Gallatin, after Hale, in Trans. Am. Eth. Soc., II, pt. 1, 15, 1848. Berghaus (1851), Physik. Atlas, map 17, 1852.

>Cheenook, Latham in Jour. Eth. Soc. Lond., I, 236, 1848. Latham, Opuscula, 253, 1860.

>Chinuk, Latham, Nat. Hist. Man, 317, 1850 (same as Tshinúk; includes Chinúks proper, Klatsops, Kathlamut, Wakáikam, Watlala, Nihaloitih). Latham in Trans. Philolog. Soc. Lond., 73, 1856 (mere mention of family name). Latham, Opuscula, 340, 1860. Buschmann, Spuren der aztek. Sprache, 616–619, 1859.

=Tschinuk, Berghaus (1851), Physik. Atlas, map 17, 1852. Latham in Trans. Philolog. Soc. Lond., 73, 1856 (mere mention of family name). Latham, Opuscula, 340, 1860. Latham, El. Comp. Phil., 402, 1862 (cites a short vocabulary of Watlala).

=Tshinook, Gallatin in Schoolcraft, Ind. Tribes, III, 402, 1853 (Chinooks, Clatsops, and Watlala). Tolmie and Dawson, Comp. Vocabs. Brit. Col., 51, 61, 1884.

>Tshinuk, Buschmann, Spuren der aztek. Sprache, 616, 1859 (same as his Chinuk).

=T'sinúk, Dall, after Gibbs, in Cont. N. A. Eth., I, 241, 1877 (mere mention of family).

=Chinook, Gatschet in Mag. Am. Hist., 167, 1877 (names and gives habitats of tribes). Gatschet in Beach, Ind. Misc., 442, 1877.

<Chinooks, Keane, App. to Stanford's Comp. (Cent. and So. Am.), 474, 1878 (includes Skilloots, Watlalas, Lower Chinooks, Wakiakums, Cathlamets, Clatsops, Calapooyas, Clackamas, Killamooks, Yamkally, Chimook Jargon; of these Calapooyas and Yamkally are Kalapooian, Killamooks are Salishan).

>Chinook, Bancroft, Nat. Races, III, 565, 626–628, 1882 (enumerates Chinook, Wakiakum, Cathlamet, Clatsop, Multnomah, Skilloot, Watlala).

×Nootka-Columbian, Scouler in Jour. Roy. Geog. Soc. Lond., XI, 224, 1841 (includes Cheenooks, and Cathlascons of present family).

×Southern, Scouler, ibid., 224 (same as his Nootka-Columbian family above).

The vocabulary of the Chinook tribe, upon which the family name was based, was derived from the mouth of the Columbia. As now understood the family embraces a number of tribes, speaking allied languages, whose former homes extended from the mouth of the river for some 200 miles, or to The Dalles. According to Lewis and Clarke, our best authorities on the pristine home of this family, most of their villages were on the banks of the river, chiefly upon the northern bank, though they probably claimed the land upon either bank for several miles back.

Their villages also extended on the Pacific coast north nearly to the northern extreme of Shoalwater Bay, and to the south to about Tillamook Head, some 20 miles from the mouth of the Columbia.

PRINCIPAL TRIBES.

Lower Chinook:	Cathlapotle.	Echeloot.
Chinook.	Chilluckquittequaw.	Multnoma.
Clatsop.	Clackama.	Wahkiacum.
Upper Chinook:	Cooniac.	Wasco.
Cathlamet.		

Population.—There are two hundred and eighty-eight Wasco on the Warm Springs Reservation, Oregon, and one hundred and fifty on the Yakama Reservation, Washington. On the Grande Ronde Reservation, Oregon, there are fifty-nine Clackama. From information derived from Indians by Mr. Thomas Priestly, United States Indian Agent at Yakama, it is learned that there still remain three or four families of "regular Chinook Indians," probably belonging to one of the down-river tribes, about 6 miles above the mouth of the Columbia. Two of these speak the Chinook proper, and three have an imperfect command of Clatsop. There are eight or ten families, probably also of one of the lower river tribes, living near Freeport, Washington.

Some of the Watlala, or Upper Chinook, live near the Cascades, about 55 miles below The Dalles. There thus remain probably between five and six hundred of the Indians of this family.

CHITIMACHAN FAMILY.

= Chitimachas, Gallatin in Trans. and Coll. Am. Antiq. Soc., II, 114, 117, 1836.   Prichard, Phys. Hist. Mankind, v, 407, 1847.

= Chetimachas, Gallatin in Trans. and Coll. Am. Antiq. Soc., II, 306, 1836.   Gallatin in Trans. Am. Eth. Soc., II, pt. 1, xcix, 1848.   Latham, Nat. Hist. Man, 341, 1850.   Gallatin in Schoolcraft, Ind. Tribes, III, 402, 1853.

= Chetimacha, Latham in Proc. Philolog. Soc. Lond., II, 31–50, 1846.   Latham, Opuscula, 293, 1860.

= Chetemachas, Gallatin in Trans. Am. Eth. Soc., II, pt. 1, 77, 1848 (same as Chitimachas).

= Shetimasha, Gatschet, Creek Mig. Legend, I, 44, 1884.   Gatschet in Science, 414, April 29, 1887.

Derivation: From Choctaw words tchúti, "cooking vessels," másha, "they possess," (Gatschet).

This family was based upon the language of the tribe of the same name, "formerly living in the vicinity of Lake Barataria, and still existing (1836) in lower Louisiana."

Du Pratz asserted that the Taensa and Chitimacha were kindred tribes of the Na'htchi. A vocabulary of the Shetimasha, however, revealed to Gallatin no traces of such affinity. He considered both to represent distinct families, a conclusion subsequent investigations have sustained.

In 1881 Mr. Gatschet visited the remnants of this tribe in Louisiana. He found about fifty individuals, a portion of whom lived on Grand River, but the larger part in Charenton, St. Mary's Parish. The tribal organization was abandoned in 1879 on the death of their chief.

CHUMASHAN FAMILY.

> Santa Barbara, Latham in Trans. Philolog. Soc., Lond., 85, 1856 (includes Santa Barbara, Santa Inez, San Luis Obispo languages). Buschmann, Spuren der aztek. Sprache, 531, 535, 538, 602, 1859. Latham, Opuscula, 351, 1860. Powell in Cont. N. A. Eth., III, 550, 567, 1877 (Kasuá, Santa Inez, Id. of Santa Cruz, Santa Barbara). Gatschet in U. S. Geog. Surv. W. 100th M., VII, 419, 1879 (cites La Purisima, Santa Inez, Santa Barbara, Kasuá, Mugu, Santa Cruz Id.).

× Santa Barbara, Gatschet in Mag. Am. Hist., 156, 1877 (Santa Inez, Santa Barbara, Santa Cruz Id., San Luis Obispo, San Antonio).

Derivation: From Chumash, the name of the Santa Rosa Islanders.

The several dialects of this family have long been known under the group or family name, "Santa Barbara," which seems first to have been used in a comprehensive sense by Latham in 1856, who included under it three languages, viz: Santa Barbara, Santa Inez, and San Luis Obispo. The term has no special pertinence as a family designation, except from the fact that the Santa Barbara Mission, around which one of the dialects of the family was spoken, is perhaps more widely known than any of the others. Nevertheless, as it is the family name first applied to the group and has, moreover, passed into current use its claim to recognition would not be questioned were it not a compound name. Under the rule adopted the latter fact necessitates its rejection. As a suitable substitute the term Chumashan is here adopted. Chumash is the name of the Santa Rosa Islanders, who spoke a dialect of this stock, and is a term widely known among the Indians of this family.

The Indians of this family lived in villages, the villages as a whole apparently having no political connection, and hence there appears to have been no appellation in use among them to designate themselves as a whole people.

Dialects of this language were spoken at the Missions of San Buenaventura, Santa Barbara, Santa Iñez, Purísima, and San Luis Obispo. Kindred dialects were spoken also upon the Islands of Santa Rosa and Santa Cruz, and also, probably, upon such other of the Santa Barbara Islands as formerly were permanently inhabited.

These dialects collectively form a remarkably homogeneous family, all of them, with the exception of the San Luis Obispo, being closely related and containing very many words in common. Vocabularies representing six dialects of the language are in possession of the Bureau of Ethnology.

The inland limits of this family can not be exactly defined, although a list of more than one hundred villages with their sites, obtained by Mr. Henshaw in 1884, shows that the tribes were essentially maritime and were closely confined to the coast.

Population.—In 1884 Mr. Henshaw visited the several counties formerly inhabited by the populous tribes of this family and discovered that about forty men, women, and children survived. The adults still speak their old language when conversing with each other, though on other occasions they use Spanish. The largest settlement is at San Buenaventura, where perhaps 20 individuals live near the outskirts of the town.

COAHUILTECAN FAMILY.

= Coahuilteco, Orozco y Berra, Geografía de las Lenguas de México, map, 1864.
= Tejano ó Coahuilteco, Pimentel, Cuadro Descriptivo y Comparativo de las Lenguas Indígenas de México, II, 409, 1865. (A preliminary notice with example from the language derived from Garcia's Manual, 1760.)

Derivation: From the name of the Mexican State Coahuila.

This family appears to have included numerous tribes in southwestern Texas and in Mexico. They are chiefly known through the record of the Rev. Father Bartolomé Garcia (Manual para administrar, etc.), published in 1760. In the preface to the "Manual" he enumerates the tribes and sets forth some phonetic and grammatic differences between the dialects.

On page 63 of his Geografía de las Lenguas de México, 1864, Orozco y Berra gives a list of the languages of Mexico and includes Coahuilteco, indicating it as the language of Coahuila, Nuevo Leon, and Tamaulipas. He does not, however, indicate its extension into Texas. It would thus seem that he intended the name as a general designation for the language of all the cognate tribes.

Upon his colored ethnographic map, also, Orozco y Berra designates the Mexican portion of the area formerly occupied by the tribes of this family Coahuilteco.[1] In his statement that the language and tribes are extinct this author was mistaken, as a few Indians still survive who speak one of the dialects of this family, and in 1886 Mr. Gatschet collected vocabularies of two tribes, the Comecrudo and Cotoname, who live on the Rio Grande, at Las Prietas, State of Tamaulipas. Of the Comecrudo some twenty-five still remain, of whom seven speak the language.

The Cotoname are practically extinct, although Mr. Gatschet obtained one hundred and twenty-five words from a man said to be of this blood. Besides the above, Mr. Gatschet obtained information of the existence of two women of the Pinto or Pakawá tribe who live at La Volsa, near Reynosa, Tamaulipas, on the Rio Grande, and who are said to speak their own language.

---

[1] Geografía de las Lenguas de México, map, 1864.

PRINCIPAL TRIBES.

Alasapa.	Miakan.	Pastancoya.
Cachopostate.	Orejone.	Patacale.
Casa chiquita.	Pacuáche.	Pausane.
Chayopine.	Pajalate.	Payseya.
Comecrudo.	Pakawá.	Sanipao.
Cotoname.	Pamaque.	Tâcame.
Mano de perro.	Pampopa.	Venado.
Mescal.		

COPEHAN FAMILY.

> Cop-eh, Gibbs in Schoolcraft, Ind. Tribes, III, 421, 1853 (mentioned as a dialect).

= Copeh, Latham in Trans. Philolog. Soc., Lond., 79, 1856 (of Upper Sacramento; cites vocabs. from Gallatin and Schoolcraft). Latham, Opuscula, 345, 1860. Latham, El. Comp. Phil., 412, 1862.

= Wintoons, Powers in Overland Monthly, 530, June, 1874 (Upper Sacramento and Upper Trinity). Gatschet in Mag. Am. Hist., 160, 1877 (defines habitat and names tribes). Gatschet in Beach, Ind. Miscellany, 434, 1877.

= Win-tún, Powell in Cont. N. A. Eth., III, 518–534, 1877 (vocabularies of Wintun, Sacramento River, Trinity Indians). Gatschet in U. S. Geog. Surv. W. 100th M., VII, 418, 1879 (defines area occupied by family).

× Klamath, Keane, App. to Stanford's Comp. (Cent. and So. Am.), 475, 1878 (cited as including Copahs, Patawats, Wintoons). Bancroft, Nat. Races, III, 565, 1882 (contains Copah).

> Napa, Keane, ibid., 476, 524, 1878 (includes Myacomas, Calayomanes, Caymus, Ulucas, Suscols). Bancroft, Nat. Races, III, 567, 1882 (includes Napa, Myacoma, Calayomane, Caymus, Uluca, Suscol).

This name was proposed by Latham with evident hesitation. He says of it: "How far this will eventually turn out to be a convenient name for the group (or how far the group itself will be real), is uncertain." Under it he places two vocabularies, one from the Upper Sacramento and the other from Mag Redings in Shasta County. The head of Putos Creek is given as headquarters for the language. Recent investigations have served to fully confirm the validity of the family.

GEOGRAPHIC DISTRIBUTION.

The territory of the Copehan family is bounded on the north by Mount Shasta and the territory of the Sastean and Lutuamian families, on the east by the territory of the Palaihnihan, Yanan, and Pujunan families, and on the south by the bays of San Pablo and Suisun and the lower waters of the Sacramento.

The eastern boundary of the territory begins about 5 miles east of Mount Shasta, crosses Pit River a little east of Squaw Creek, and reaches to within 10 miles of the eastern bank of the Sacramento at Redding. From Redding to Chico Creek the boundary is about 10 miles east of the Sacramento. From Chico downward the Pujunan family encroaches till at the mouth of Feather River it occupies

the eastern bank of the Sacramento. The western boundary of the
Copehan family begins at the northernmost point of San Pablo Bay,
trends to the northwest in a somewhat irregular line till it reaches
John's Peak, from which point it follows the Coast Range to the
upper waters of Cottonwood Creek, whence it deflects to the west,
crossing the headwaters of the Trinity and ending at the southern
boundary of the Sastean family.

PRINCIPAL TRIBES.

A. Patwin:	Napa.	B. Wintu:
Chenposel.	Olelato.	Daupom.
Guilito.	Olposel.	Nomlaki.
Korusi.	Suisun.	Nommuk.
Liwaito.	Todetabi.	Norelmuk.
Lolsel.	Topaidisel.	Normuk.
Makhelchel.	Waikosel.	Waikenmuk.
Malaka.	Wailaksel.	Wailaki.

COSTANOAN FAMILY.

= Costano, Latham in Trans. Philolog. Soc. Lond., 82,1856 (includes the Ahwastes,
   Olhones or Costanos, Romonans, Tulomos, Altatmos). Latham, Opuscula, 348,
   1860.
< Mutsun, Gatschet in Mag. Am. Hist., 157, 1877 (includes Ahwastes, Olhones, Al-
   tahmos, Romonans, Tulomos). Powell in Cont. N. A. Eth., III, 535, 1877 (includes
   under this family vocabs. of Costano, Mŭtsūn, Santa Clara, Santa Cruz).

Derivation: From the Spanish costano, "coast-men."

Under this group name Latham included five tribes, given above,
which were under the supervision of the Mission Dolores. He
gives a few words of the Romonan language, comparing it with
Tshokoyem which he finds to differ markedly. He finally expresses
the opinion that, notwithstanding the resemblance of a few words,
notably personal pronouns, to Tshokoyem of the Moquelumnan
group, the affinities of the dialects of the Costano are with the
Salinas group, with which, however, he does not unite it but prefers to keep it by itself. Later, in 1877, Mr. Gatschet,[1] under the
family name Mutsun, united the Costano dialects with the ones
classified by Latham under Moquelumnan. This arrangement was
followed by Powell in his classification of vocabularies.[2] More
recent comparison of all the published material by Mr. Curtin, of
the Bureau, revealed very decided and apparently radical differences between the two groups of dialects. In 1888 Mr. H. W.
Henshaw visited the coast to the north and south of San Francisco,
and obtained a considerable body of linguistic material for further
comparison. The result seems fully to justify the separation of the
two groups as distinct families.

---

[1] Mag. Am. Hist., 1877, p. 157.   [2] Cont. N. A. Eth., 1877, vol. 3, p. 535.

The territory of the Costanoan family extends from the Golden Gate to a point near the southern end of Monterey Bay. On the south it is bounded from Monterey Bay to the mountains by the Esselenian territory. On the east side of the mountains it extends to the southern end of Salinas Valley. On the east it is bounded by a somewhat irregular line running from the southern end of Salinas Valley to Gilroy Hot Springs and the upper waters of Conestimba Creek, and northward from the latter points by the San Joaquin River to its mouth. The northern boundary is formed by Suisun Bay, Carquinez Straits, San Pablo and San Francisco Bays, and the Golden Gate.

Population.—The surviving Indians of the once populous tribes of this family are now scattered over several counties and probably do not number, all told, over thirty individuals, as was ascertained by Mr. Henshaw in 1888. Most of these are to be found near the towns of Santa Cruz and Monterey. Only the older individuals speak the language.

ESKIMAUAN FAMILY.

> Eskimaux, Gallatin in Trans. and Coll. Am. Antiq. Soc., II, 9, 305, 1836. Gallatin in Trans. Am. Eth. Soc., II, pt. 1, xcix, 77, 1848. Gallatin in Schoolcraft, Ind. Tribes, III, 401, 1853.

= Eskimo, Berghaus (1845), Physik. Atlas, map 17, 1848. Ibid., 1852. Latham, Nat. Hist. Man, 288, 1850 (general remarks on origin and habitat). Buschmann, Spuren der aztek. Sprache, 689, 1859. Latham, El. Comp. Phil., 385, 1862. Bancroft, Nat. Races, III, 562, 574, 1882.

> Esquimaux, Prichard, Phys. Hist. Mankind, v, 367-371, 1847 (follows Gallatin). Latham in Jour. Eth. Soc. Lond., I, 182-191, 1848. Latham, Opuscula, 266-274, 1860.

> Eskimo, Dall in Proc. Am. Ass., 266, 1869 (treats of Alaskan Eskimo and Tuski only). Berghaus, Physik. Atlas, map 72, 1887 (excludes the Aleutian).

> Eskimos, Keane, App. Stanford's Comp. (Cent. and So. Am.), 460, 1878 (excludes Aleutian).

> Ounángan, Veniamínoff, Zapíski ob ostrovaχ Unaláshkinskago otdailo, II, 1, 1840 (Aleutians only).

>Ūnŭġŭn, Dall in Cont. N. A. Eth., I, 22, 1877 (Aleuts a division of his Orarian group).

> Unangan, Berghaus, Physik. Atlas, map 72, 1887.

× Northern, Scouler in Jour. Roy. Geog. Soc. Lond., XI, 218, 1841 (includes Ugalentzes of present family).

× Haidah, Scouler, ibid., 224, 1841 (same as his Northern family).

> Ugaljachmutzi, Gallatin in Schoolcraft, Ind. Tribes, III, 402, 1853 (lat. 60°, between Prince Williams Sound and Mount St. Elias, perhaps Athapascas). Aleuten, Holmberg, Ethnog. Skizzen d. Völker Russ. Am., 1855.

> Aleutians, Dall in Proc. Am. Ass., 266, 1869. Dall, Alaska and Resources, 374. 1870 (in both places a division of his Orarian family).

> Aleuts, Keane, App. Stanford's Comp. (Cent. and So. Am.), 460, 1878 (consist of Unalaskans of mainland and of Fox and Shumagin Ids., with Akkhas of rest of Aleutian Arch.).

> Aleut, Bancroft, Nat. Races, III. 562, 1882 (two dialects, Unalaska and Atkha).

> Konjagen, Holmberg, Ethnograph. Skizzen Völker Russ. Am., 1855 (Island of Koniag or Kadiak).

= Orarians, Dall in Proc. Am. Ass., 265, 1869 (group name; includes Innuit, Aleutians, Tuski). Dall, Alaska and Resources, 374, 1870. Dall in Cont. N. A. Eth., I, 8, 9, 1877.

× Tinneh, Dall in Proc. Am. Ass., 269, 1869 (includes " Ugalensé ").

> Innūit, Dall in Cont. N. A. Eth., I, 9, 1877 (" Major group " of Orarians: treats of Alaska Innuit only). Berghaus, Physik. Atlas, map 72, 1887 (excludes the Aleutians).

Derivation: From an Algonkin word eskimantik, "eaters of raw flesh."

GEOGRAPHIC DISTRIBUTION.

The geographic boundaries of this family were set forth by Gallatin in 1836 with considerable precision, and require comparatively little revision and correction.

In the linear extent of country occupied, the Eskimauan is the most remarkable of the North American linguistic families. It extends coastwise from eastern Greenland to western Alaska and to the extremity of the Aleutian Islands, a distance of considerably more than 5,000 miles. The winter or permanent villages are usually situated on the coast and are frequently at considerable distances from one another, the intervening areas being usually visited in summer for hunting and fishing purposes. The interior is also visited by the Eskimo for the purpose of hunting reindeer and other animals, though they rarely penetrate farther than 50 miles. A narrow strip along the coast, perhaps 30 miles wide, will probably, on the average, represent Eskimo occupancy.

Except upon the Aleutian Islands, the dialects spoken over this vast area are very similar, the unity of dialect thus observable being in marked contrast to the tendency to change exhibited in other linguistic families of North America.

How far north the east coast of Greenland is inhabited by Eskimo is not at present known. In 1823 Capt. Clavering met with two families of Eskimo north of 74° 30'. Recent explorations (1884–'85) by Capt. Holm, of the Danish Navy, along the southeast coast reveal the presence of Eskimo between 65° and 66° north latitude. These Eskimo profess entire ignorance of any inhabitants north of themselves, which may be taken as proof that if there are fiords farther up the coast which are inhabited there has been no intercommunication in recent times at least between these tribes and those to the south. It seems probable that more or less isolated colonies of Eskimo do actually exist along the east coast of Greenland far to the north.

Along the west coast of Greenland, Eskimo occupancy extends to about 74°. This division is separated by a considerable interval of uninhabited coast from the Etah Eskimo who occupy the coast from Smith Sound to Cape York, their most northerly village being in

78° 18'. For our knowledge of these interesting people we are chiefly indebted to Ross and Bessels.

In Grinnell Land, Gen. Greely found indications of permanent Eskimo habitations near Fort Conger, lat. 81° 44'.

On the coast of Labrador the Eskimo reach as far south as Hamilton Inlet, about 55° 30'. Not long since they extended to the Straits of Belle Isle, 50° 30'.

On the east coast of Hudson Bay the Eskimo reach at present nearly to James Bay. According to Dobbs[1] in 1744 they extended as far south as east Maine River, or about 52°. The name Notaway (Eskimo) River at the southern end of the bay indicates a former Eskimo extension to that point.

According to Boas and Bessels the most northern Eskimo of the middle group north of Hudson Bay reside on the southern extremity of Ellesmere Land around Jones Sound. Evidences of former occupation of Prince Patrick, Melville, and other of the northern Arctic islands are not lacking, but for some unknown cause, probably a failure of food supply, the Eskimo have migrated thence and the islands are no longer inhabited. In the western part of the central region the coast appears to be uninhabited from the Coppermine River to Cape Bathurst. To the west of the Mackenzie, Herschel Island marks the limit of permanent occupancy by the Mackenzie Eskimo, there being no permanent villages between that island and the settlements at Point Barrow.

The intervening strip of coast is, however, undoubtedly hunted over more or less in summer. The Point Barrow Eskimo do not penetrate far into the interior, but farther to the south the Eskimo reach to the headwaters of the Nunatog and Koyuk Rivers. Only visiting the coast for trading purposes, they occupy an anomalous position among Eskimo.

Eskimo occupancy of the rest of the Alaska coast is practically continuous throughout its whole extent as far to the south and east as the Atna or Copper River, where begin the domains of the Koluschan family. Only in two places do the Indians of the Athapascan family intrude upon Eskimo territory, about Cook's Inlet, and at the mouth of Copper River.

Owing to the labors of Dall, Petroff, Nelson, Turner, Murdoch, and others we are now pretty well informed as to the distribution of the Eskimo in Alaska.

Nothing is said by Gallatin of the Aleutian Islanders and they were probably not considered by him to be Eskimauan. They are now known to belong to this family, though the Aleutian dialects are unintelligible to the Eskimo proper. Their distribution has been entirely changed since the advent of the Russians and the introduction

---

[1] Dobbs (Arthur). An account of the Countries adjoining to Hudson's Bay. London, 1744.

of the fur trade, and at present they occupy only a very small portion of the islands. Formerly they were much more numerous than at present and extended throughout the chain.

The Eskimauan family is represented in northeast Asia by the Yuit of the Chukchi peninsula, who are to be distinguished from the sedentary Chukchi or the Tuski of authors, the latter being of Asiatic origin. According to Dall the former are comparatively recent arrivals from the American continent, and, like their brethren of America, are confined exclusively to the coast.

PRINCIPAL TRIBES AND VILLAGES.

Greenland group—East Greenland villages :

Akorninak.	Kemisak.	Sermiligak.
Aluik.	Kikkertarsoak.	Sermilik.
Anarnitsok.	Kinarbik.	Taterat.
Angmagsalik.	Maneetsuk.	Umanak.
Igdlolnarsuk.	Narsuk.	Umerik.
Ivimiut.	Okkiosorbik.	

West coast villages :

Akbat.	Karsuit.	Tessuisak.

Labrador group:

Itivimiut.	Suqinimiut.	Taqagmiut.
Kiguaqtagmiut.		

Middle Group :

Aggomiut.	Kangormiut.	Pilingmiut.
Ahaknanelet.	Kinnepatu.	Sagdlirmiut.
Aivillirmiut.	Kramalit.	Sikosuilarmiut.
Akudliarmiut.	Nageuktormiut.	Sinimiut.
Akudnirmiut.	Netchillirmiut.	Ugjulirmiut.
Amitormiut.	Nugumiut.	Ukusiksalingmiut.
Iglulingmiut.	Okomiut.	

Alaska group :

Chiglit.	Kittegareut.	Nushagagmiut.
Chugachigmiut.	Kopagmiut.	Nuwungmiut.
Ikogmiut.	Kuagmiut.	Oglemiut.
Imahklimiut.	Kuskwogmiut.	Selawigmiut.
Inguhklimiut.	Magemiut.	Shiwokugmiut.
Kaialigmiut.	Mahlemiut.	Ukivokgmiut.
Kangmaligmiut.	Nunatogmiut.	Unaligmiut.
Kaviagmiut.	Nunivagmiut.	

Aleutian group :

Atka.	Unalashka.

Asiatic group :

Yuit.

Population.—Only a rough approximation of the population of the Eskimo can be given, since of some of the divisions next to nothing is known. Dall compiles the following estimates of the Alaskan Eskimo from the most reliable figures up to 1885: Of the Northwestern Innuit 3,100 (?), including the Kopagmiut, Kangmaligmiut, Nuwukmiut, Nunatogmiut, Kuagmiut, the Inguhklimiut of Little Diomede Island 40 (?), Shiwokugmiut of St. Lawrence Island 150 (?), the Western Innuit 14,500 (?), the Aleutian Islanders (Unungun) 2,200 (?); total of the Alaskan Innuit, about 20,000.

The Central or Baffin Land Eskimo are estimated by Boas to number about 1,100.[1]

From figures given by Rink, Packard, and others, the total number of Labrador Eskimo is believed to be about 2,000.

According to Holm (1884-'85) there are about 550 Eskimo on the east coast of Greenland. On the west coast the mission Eskimo numbered 10,122 in 1886, while the northern Greenland Eskimo, the Arctic Highlanders of Ross, number about 200.

Thus throughout the Arctic regions generally there is a total of about 34,000.

ESSELENIAN FAMILY.

< Salinas, Latham in Trans. Philolog. Soc. Lond., 85, 1856 (includes Gioloco?, Ruslen, Soledad, Eslen, Carmel, San Antonio, and San Miguel, cited as including Eslen). Latham, Opuscula, 350, 1860.

As afterwards mentioned under the Salinan family, the present family was included by Latham in the heterogeneous group called by him Salinas. For reasons there given the term Salinan was restricted to the San Antonio and San Miguel languages, leaving the present family without a name. It is called Esselenian, from the name of the single tribe Esselen, of which it is composed.

Its history is a curious and interesting one. Apparently the first mention of the tribe and language is to be found in the Voyage de la Pérouse, Paris, 1797, page 288, where Lamanon (1786) states that the language of the Ecclemachs (Esselen) differs "absolutely from all those of their neighbors." He gives a vocabulary of twenty-two words and by way of comparison a list of the ten numerals of the Achastlians (Costanoan family). It was a study of the former short vocabulary, published by Taylor in the California Farmer, October 24, 1862, that first led to the supposition of the distinctness of this language.

A few years later the Esselen people came under the observation of Galiano,[2] who mentions the Eslen and Runsien as two distinct nations, and notes a variety of differences in usages and customs which are of no great weight. It is of interest to note, however, that this author also appears to have observed essential differences

---

[1] Sixth Ann. Rep. Bu. Eth., 426, 1888.
[2] Relacion del viage hecho por las Goletas Sutil y Mexicana en el año de 1792. Madrid, 1802, p. 172.

in the languages of the two peoples, concerning which he says: "The same difference as in usage and custom is observed in the languages of the two nations, as will be perceived from the following comparison with which we will conclude this chapter."

Galiano supplies Esselen and Runsien vocabularies of thirty-one words, most of which agree with the earlier vocabulary of Lamanon. These were published by Taylor in the California Farmer under date of April 20, 1860.

In the fall of 1888 Mr. H. W. Henshaw visited the vicinity of Monterey with the hope of discovering survivors of these Indians. Two women were found in the Salinas Valley to the south who claimed to be of Esselen blood, but neither of them was able to recall any of the language, both having learned in early life to speak the Runsien language in place of their own. An old woman was found in the Carmelo Valley near Monterey and an old man living near the town of Cayucos, who, though of Runsien birth, remembered considerable of the language of their neighbors with whom they were connected by marriage. From them a vocabulary of one hundred and ten words and sixty-eight phrases and short sentences were obtained. These serve to establish the general correctness of the short lists of words collected so long ago by Lamanon and Galiano, and they also prove beyond reasonable doubt that the Esselen language forms a family by itself and has no connection with any other known.

The tribe or tribes composing this family occupied a narrow strip of the California coast from Monterey Bay south to the vicinity of the Santa Lucia Mountain, a distance of about 50 miles.

IROQUOIAN FAMILY.

> Iroquois, Gallatin in Trans. Am. Antiq. Soc., II, 21, 23, 305, 1836 (excludes Cherokee). Prichard, Phys. Hist. Mankind, v, 381, 1847 (follows Gallatin). Gallatin in Trans. Am. Eth. Soc., II, pt. 1, xcix, 77, 1848 (as in 1836). Gallatin in Schoolcraft, Ind. Tribes, III, 401, 1853. Latham in Trans. Philolog. Soc. Lond., 58, 1856. Latham, Opuscula, 327, 1860. Latham, Elements Comp. Phil., 463, 1862.

> Irokesen, Berghaus (1845), Physik. Atlas, map 17, 1848. Ibid., 1852.

× Irokesen, Berghaus, Physik. Atlas, map 72, 1887 (includes Kataba and said to be derived from Dakota).

> Huron-Iroquois, Bancroft, Hist. U. S., III, 243, 1840.

> Wyandot-Iroquois, Keane, App. Stanford's Comp. (Cent. and So. Am.), 460, 468, 1878.

> Cherokees, Gallatin in Am. Antiq. Soc., II, 89, 306, 1836 (kept apart from Iroquois though probable affinity asserted). Bancroft, Hist. U. S., III, 246, 1840. Prichard, Phys. Hist. Mankind, v, 401, 1847. Gallatin in Trans. Am. Eth. Soc., II, pt. 1, xcix, 77, 1848. Latham in Trans. Philolog. Soc. Lond., 58, 1856 (a separate group perhaps to be classed with Iroquois and Sioux). Gallatin in Schoolcraft, Ind. Tribes, III, 401, 1853. Latham, Opuscula, 327, 1860. Keane, App. Stanford's Comp. (Cent. and So. Am.), 460, 472, 1878 (same as Chelekees or Tsalagi — "apparently entirely distinct from all other American tongues").

> Tschirokies, Berghaus (1845), Physik. Atlas, map 17, 1848.

> Chelekees, Keane, App. Stanford's Comp. (Cent. and So. Am.), 472, 1878 (or Cherokees).

> Cheroki, Gatschet, Creek Mig. Legend, I, 24, 1884. Gatschet in Science, 413, April 29, 1887.

= Huron-Cherokee, Hale in Am. Antiq., 20, Jan., 1883 (proposed as a family name instead of Huron-Iroquois; relationship to Iroquois affirmed).

Derivation: French adaptation of the Iroquois word hiro, used to conclude a speech, and koué, an exclamation (Charlevoix). Hale gives as possible derivations ierokwa, the indeterminate form of the verb to smoke, signifying "they who smoke;" also the Cayuga form of bear, iakwai.[1] Mr. Hewitt[2] suggests the Algonkin words irin, true, or real; ako, snake; with the French termination ois, the word becomes Irinakois.

With reference to this family it is of interest to note that as early as 1798 Barton[3] compared the Cheroki language with that of the Iroquois and stated his belief that there was a connection between them. Gallatin, in the Archæologia Americana, refers to the opinion expressed by Barton, and although he states that he is inclined to agree with that author, yet he does not formally refer Cheroki to that family, concluding that "We have not a sufficient knowledge of the grammar, and generally of the language of the Five Nations, or of the Wyandots, to decide that question."[4]

Mr. Hale was the first to give formal expression to his belief in the affinity of the Cheroki to Iroquois.[5] Recently extensive Cheroki vocabularies have come into possession of the Bureau of Ethnology, and a careful comparison of them with ample Iroquois material has been made by Mr. Hewitt. The result is convincing proof of the relationship of the two languages as affirmed by Barton so long ago.

GEOGRAPHIC DISTRIBUTION.

Unlike most linguistic stocks, the Iroquoian tribes did not occupy a continuous area, but when first known to Europeans were settled in three distinct regions, separated from each other by tribes of other lineage. The northern group was surrounded by tribes of Algonquian stock, while the more southern groups bordered upon the Catawba and Maskoki.

A tradition of the Iroquois points to the St. Lawrence region as the early home of the Iroquoian tribes, whence they gradually moved down to the southwest along the shores of the Great Lakes.

When Cartier, in 1534, first explored the bays and inlets of the Gulf of St. Lawrence he met a Huron-Iroquoian people on the shores of the Bay of Gaspé, who also visited the northern coast of the gulf. In the following year when he sailed up the St. Lawrence River he

---

[1] Iroquois Book of Rites, 1883, app., p. 173.

[2] American Anthropologist, 1888, vol. 1, p. 188.

[3] New Views of the Origin of the Tribes and Nations of America. Phila., 1798.

[4] Trans. Am. Antiq. Soc., 1836, vol. 2, p. 92.

[5] Am. Antiq., 1883, vol. 5, p. 20.

found the banks of the river from Quebec to Montreal occupied by an Iroquoian people. From statements of Champlain and other early explorers it seems probable that the Wyandot once occupied the country along the northern shore of Lake Ontario.

The Conestoga, and perhaps some allied tribes, occupied the country about the Lower Susquehanna, in Pennsylvania and Maryland, and have commonly been regarded as an isolated body, but it seems probable that their territory was contiguous to that of the Five Nations on the north before the Delaware began their westward movement.

As the Cherokee were the principal tribe on the borders of the southern colonies and occupied the leading place in all the treaty negotiations, they came to be considered as the owners of a large territory to which they had no real claim. Their first sale, in 1721, embraced a tract in South Carolina, between the Congaree and the South Fork of the Edisto,[1] but about one-half of this tract, forming the present Lexington County, belonging to the Congaree.[2] In 1755 they sold a second tract above the first and extending across South Carolina from the Savannah to the Catawba (or Wateree),[3] but all of this tract east of Broad River belonged to other tribes. The lower part, between the Congaree and the Wateree, had been sold 20 years before, and in the upper part the Broad River was acknowledged as the western Catawba boundary.[4] In 1770 they sold a tract, principally in Virginia and West Virginia, bounded east by the Great Kanawha,[5] but the Iroquois claimed by conquest all of this tract northwest of the main ridge of the Alleghany and Cumberland Mountains, and extending at least to the Kentucky River,[6] and two years previously they had made a treaty with Sir William Johnson by which they were recognized as the owners of all between Cumberland Mountains and the Ohio down to the Tennessee.[7] The Cumberland River basin was the only part of this tract to which the Cherokee had any real title, having driven out the former occupants, the Shawnee, about 1721.[8] The Cherokee had no villages north of the Tennessee (this probably includes the Holston as its upper part), and at a conference at Albany the Cherokee delegates presented to the Iroquois the skin of a deer, which they said belonged to the Iroquois, as the animal had been killed north of the Tennessee.[9] In 1805, 1806, and 1817 they sold several tracts, mainly in

---

[1] Cession No. 1, on Royce's Cherokee map, 1884.
[2] Howe in Schoolcraft, Ind. Tribes, 1854, vol. 4, p. 163.
[3] Cession 2, on Royce's Cherokee map, 1884.
[4] Howe in Schoolcraft, Ind. Tribes, 1854, vol. 4, pp. 155–159.
[5] Cession 4, on Royce's Cherokee map, 1884.
[6] Sir William Johnson in Parkman's Conspiracy of Pontiac, app.
[7] Bancroft, Hist. U. S.
[8] Ramsey, Annals of Tennessee, 1853.
[9] Ramsey, Annals of Tennessee, 1853.

middle Tennessee, north of the Tennessee River and extending to the Cumberland River watershed, but this territory was claimed and had been occupied by the Chickasaw, and at one conference the Cherokee admitted their claim.[1] The adjacent tract in northern Alabama and Georgia, on the headwaters of the Coosa, was not permanently occupied by the Cherokee until they began to move westward, about 1770.

The whole region of West Virginia, Kentucky, and the Cumberland River region of Tennessee was claimed by the Iroquois and Cherokee, but the Iroquois never occupied any of it and the Cherokee could not be said to occupy any beyond the Cumberland Mountains. The Cumberland River was originally held by the Shawnee, and the rest was occupied, so far as it was occupied at all, by the Shawnee, Delaware, and occasionally by the Wyandot and Mingo (Iroquoian), who made regular excursions southward across the Ohio every year to hunt and to make salt at the licks. Most of the temporary camps or villages in Kentucky and West Virginia were built by the Shawnee and Delaware. The Shawnee and Delaware were the principal barrier to the settlement of Kentucky and West Virginia for a period of 20 years, while in all that time neither the Cherokee nor the Iroquois offered any resistance or checked the opposition of the Ohio tribes.

The Cherokee bounds in Virginia should be extended along the mountain region as far at least as the James River, as they claim to have lived at the Peaks of Otter,[2] and seem to be identical with the Rickohockan or Rechahecrian of the early Virginia writers, who lived in the mountains beyond the Monacan, and in 1656 ravaged the lowland country as far as the site of Richmond and defeated the English and the Powhatan Indians in a pitched battle at that place.[3]

The language of the Tuscarora, formerly of northeastern North Carolina, connect them directly with the northern Iroquois. The Chowanoc and Nottoway and other cognate tribes adjoining the Tuscarora may have been offshoots from that tribe.

PRINCIPAL TRIBES.

Cayuga.	Neuter.	Seneca.
Cherokee.	Nottoway.	Tionontate.
Conestoga.	Oneida.	Tuscarora.
Erie.	Onondaga.	Wyandot.
Mohawk.		

Population.—The present number of the Iroquoian stock is about 43,000, of whom over 34,000 (including the Cherokees) are in the United States while nearly 9,000 are in Canada. Below is given the population of the different tribes, compiled chiefly from the

[1] Blount (1792) in Am. State Papers, 1832, vol. 4, p. 326.

[2] Schoolcraft, Notes on Iroquois, 1847.

[3] Bancroft, Hist. U. S.

Canadian Indian Report for 1888, and the United States Census Bulletin for 1890:

Cherokee:

Cherokee and Choctaw Nations, Indian Territory (exclusive of adopted Indians, negroes, and whites)	25,557
Eastern Band, Qualla Reservation, Cheowah, etc., North Carolina (exclusive of those practically white)	1,500 ?
Lawrence school, Kansas	6
	27,063 ?

Caughnawaga:

Caughnawaga, Quebec	1,673

Cayuga:

Grand River, Ontario	972?
With Seneca, Quapaw Agency, Indian Territory (total 255)	128?
Cattaraugus Reserve, New York	165
Other Reserves in New York	36
	1,301 ?

" Iroquois ":

Of Lake of Two Mountains, Quebec, mainly Mohawk (with Algonquin)	345
With Algonquin at Gibson, Ontario (total 131)	31 ?
	376 ?

Mohawk:

Quinte Bay, Ontario	1,050
Grand River, Ontario	1,302
Tonawanda, Onondaga, and Cattaraugus Reserves, New York	6
	2,358

Oneida:

Oneida and other Reserves, New York	295
Green Bay Agency, Wisconsin ("including homeless Indians")	1,716
Carlisle and Hampton schools	104
Thames River, Ontario	778
Grand River, Ontario	236
	3,129

Onondaga:

Onondaga Reserve, New York	380
Allegany Reserve, New York	77
Cattaraugus Reserve, New York	38
Tuscarora (41) and Tonawanda (4) Reserves, New York	45
Carlisle and Hampton schools	4
Grand River, Ontario	346
	890

Seneca:

With Cayuga, Quapaw Agency, Indian Territory (total 255)	127 ?
Allegany Reserve, New York	862
Cattaraugus Reserve, New York	1,318
Tonawanda Reserve, New York	517
Tuscarora and Onondaga Reserves, New York	12
Lawrence, Hampton, and Carlisle schools	13
Grand River, Ontario	206
	3,055?

St. Regis:

    St. Regis Reserve, New York...... 1,053

    Onondaga and other Reserves, New York.......................... 17

    St. Regis Reserve, Quebec............. 1,179

                                                        2,249

Tuscarora:

    Tuscarora Reserve, New York 398

    Cattaraugus and Tonawanda Reserves, New York................... 6

    Grand River, Ontario 329

                                                        733

Wyandot:

    Quapaw Agency, Indian Territory 288

    Lawrence, Hampton, and Carlisle schools.......................... 18

    " Hurons " of Lorette, Quebec..................................... 279

    " Wyandots " of Anderdon, Ontario.............................. 98

                                                        683

The Iroquois of St. Regis, Caughnawaga, Lake of Two Mountains (Oka), and Gibson speak a dialect mainly Mohawk and Oneida, but are a mixture of all the tribes of the original Five Nations.

KALAPOOIAN FAMILY.

= Kalapooiah, Scouler in Jour. Roy. Geog. Soc. Lond., XI, 225, 1841 (includes Kalapooiah and Yamkallie; thinks the Umpqua and Cathlascon languages are related). Buschmann, Spuren der aztek. Sprache, 599, 617, 1859, (follows Scouler).

= Kalapuya, Hale in U.S. Expl. Exp., VI, 217, 564, 1846 (of Willamet Valley above Falls). Gallatin in Trans. Am. Eth. Soc., I, pt. 1, c, 17, 77, 1848. Berghaus (1851), Physik. Atlas, map 17, 1852. Gallatin in Schoolcraft, Ind. Tribes, III, 402, 1853. Latham in Trans. Philolog. Soc. Lond., 73, 1856. Buschmann, Spuren der aztek. Sprache, 617, 1859. Latham, Opuscula, 340, 1860. Gatschet in Mag. Am. Hist., 167, 1877. Gatschet in Beach, Ind. Misc., 442, 1877.

> Calapooya, Bancroft, Nat. Races. III, 565, 629, 1882.

× Chinooks, Keane, App. Stanford's Comp. (Cent. and So. Am.), 474, 1878 (includes Calapooyas and Yamkally).

> Yamkally, Bancroft, Nat. Races, III, 565, 630, 1882 (bears a certain relationship to Calapooya).

Under this family name Scouler places two tribes, the Kalapooiah, inhabiting " the fertile Willamat plains " and the Yamkallie, who live " more in the interior, to ards the sources of the Willamat River." Scouler adds that the Umpqua " appear to belong to this Family, although their language is rather more remote from the Kalapooiah than the Yamkallie is." The Umpqua language is now placed under the Athapascan family. Scouler also asserts the intimate relationship of the Cathlascon tribes to the Kalapooiah family. They are now classed as Chinookan.

The tribes of the Kalapooian family inhabited the valley of Willamette River, Oregon, above the falls, and extended well up to the headwaters of that stream. They appear not to have reached the Columbia River, being cut off by tribes of the Chinookan family, and consequently were not met by Lewis and Clarke, whose statements of their habitat were derived solely from natives.

PRINCIPAL TRIBES

Ahántchuyuk   Calapooya.   Yámil.
(Pudding River   Chelamela.   Yonkalla (Ayankēld).
Indians).   Lákmiut.
Atfálati.   Santiam.

Population.—So far as known the surviving Indians of this family are all at the Grande Ronde Agency, Oregon.

The following is a census for 1890:

Atfálati	28	Santiam	27
Calapooya	22	Yámil	30
Lákmiut	29	Yonkalla	7
Mary's River	28		—
		Total	171

KARANKAWAN FAMILY.

= Karánkawa, Gatschet in Globus, XLIX, No. 8, 123, 1886 (vocabulary of 25 terms; distinguished as a family provisionally). Gatschet in Science, 414, April 9, 1887.

The Karankawa formerly dwelt upon the Texan coast, according to Sibley, upon an island or peninsula in the Bay of St. Bernard (Matagorda Bay). In 1804 this author, upon hearsay evidence, stated their number to be 500 men.[1] In several places in the paper cited it is explicitly stated that the Karankawa spoke the Attakapa language; the Attakapa was a coast tribe living to the east of them. In 1884 Mr. Gatschet found a Tonkawe at Fort Griffin, Texas, who claimed to have formerly lived among the Karankawa. From him a vocabulary of twenty-five terms was obtained, which was all of the language he remembered.

The vocabulary is unsatisfactory, not only because of its meagerness, but because most of the terms are unimportant for comparison. Nevertheless, such as it is, it represents all of the language that is extant. Judged by this vocabulary the language seems to be distinct not only from the Attakapa but from all others. Unsatisfactory as the linguistic evidence is, it appears to be safer to class the language provisionally as a distinct family upon the strength of it than to accept Sibley's statement of its identity with Attakapa, especially as we know nothing of the extent of his information or whether indeed his statement was based upon a personal knowledge of the language.

---

[1] Am. State Papers, 1832, vol. 4, p. 722.

A careful search has been made with the hope of finding a few survivors of this family, but thus far not a single descendant of the tribe has been discovered and it is probable that not one is now living.

KERESAN FAMILY.

> Keres, Turner in Pac. R. R. Rep., III, pt. 3, 55, 86–90, 1856 (includes Kiwomi, Cochitemi, Acoma).

= Kera, Powell in Rocky Mt. Presbyterian, Nov., 1878 (includes San Felipe, Santo Domingo, Cóchiti, Santa Aña, Cia, Acoma, Laguna, Povate, Hasatch, Mogino). Gatschet in U. S. Geog. Surv. W. 100th M., VII, 417, 1879. Gatschet in Mag. Am. Hist. 259, 1882.

= Kéran, Powell in Am. Nat., 604, Aug., 1880 (enumerates pueblos and gives linguistic literature).

= Queres, Keane, App. Stanford's Comp. (Cent. and So. Am.), 479, 1878.

= Chu-cha-cas, Lane in Schoolcraft, Ind. Tribes, v, 689, 1855 (includes Laguna, Acoma, Santo Domingo, San Felipe, Santa Ana, Cochite, Sille).

= Chu-cha-chas, Keane, App. Stanford's Comp. (Cent. and So. Am.), 479, 1878 (misprint; follows Lane).

= Kes-whaw-hay, Lane in Schoolcraft, Ind. Tribes, v, 689, 1855 (same as Chu-cha-cas above). Keane, App. Stanford's Comp. (Cent. and So. Am.), 479, 1878 (follows Lane).

Derivation unknown. The name is pronounced with an explosive initial sound, and Ad. F. Bandelier spells it Qq'uêres, Quéra, Quéris.

Under this name Turner, as above quoted, includes the vocabularies of Kiwomi, Cochitemi, and Acoma.

The full list of pueblos of Keresan stock is given below. They are situated in New Mexico on the upper Rio Grande, on several of its small western affluents, and on the Jemez and San José, which also are tributaries of the Rio Grande.

VILLAGES.

Acoma.	Pueblito.[1]	Santo Domingo.
Acomita.[1]	Punyeestye.	Seemunah.
Cochití.	Punyekia.	Sia.
Hasatch.	Pusityitcho.	Wapuchuseamma.
Laguna.	San Felipe.	Ziamma.
Paguate.	Santa Ana.	

Population.—According to the census of 1890 the total population of the villages of the family is 3,560, distributed as follows:

Acoma[2]	566	San Felipe	554
Cochiti	268	Santo Domingo	670
Laguna[3]	1,143	Sia	106
Santa Ana	253		

[1] Summer pueblos only.

[2] Includes Acomita and Pueblito.

[3] Includes Hasatch, Paguate, Punyeestye, Punyekia, Pusityitcho, Seemunah, Wapuchuseamma, and Ziamma.

KIOWAN FAMILY.

= Kiaways, Gallatin in Schoolcraft, Ind. Tribes, III, 402, 1853 (on upper waters Arkansas).

= Kioway, Turner in Pac. R. R. Rep., III, pt. 3, 55, 80, 1856 (based on the Kioway (Caígua) tribe only). Buschmann, Spuren der aztek. Sprache, 432, 433, 1859. Latham, El. Comp. Phil., 444, 1862 ("more Paduca than aught else").

= Káyowē, Gatschet in Am. Antiq., 280, Oct., 1882 (gives phonetics of).

Derivation: From the Kiowa word Kó-i, plural Kó-igu, meaning "Káyowē man." The Comanche term káyowē means "rat."

The author who first formally separated this family appears to have been Turner. Gallatin mentions the tribe and remarks that owing to the loss of Dr. Say's vocabularies "we only know that both the Kiowas and Kaskaias languages were harsh, guttural, and extremely difficult."[1] Turner, upon the strength of a vocabulary furnished by Lieut. Whipple, dissents from the opinion expressed by Pike and others to the effect that the language is of the same stock as the Comanche, and, while admitting that its relationship to Camanche is greater than to any other family, thinks that the likeness is merely the result of long intercommunication. His opinion that it is entirely distinct from any other language has been indorsed by Buschmann and other authorities. The family is represented by the Kiowa tribe.

So intimately associated with the Comanches have the Kiowa been since known to history that it is not easy to determine their pristine home. By the Medicine Creek treaty of October 18, 1867, they and the Comanches were assigned their present reservation in the Indian Territory, both resigning all claims to other territory, especially their claims and rights in and to the country north of the Cimarron River and west of the eastern boundary of New Mexico.

The terms of the cession might be taken to indicate a joint ownership of territory, but it is more likely that the Kiowa territory adjoined the Comanche on the northwest. In fact Pope[2] definitely locates the Kiowa in the valley of the Upper Arkansas, and of its tributary, the Purgatory (Las Animas) River. This is in substantial accord with the statements of other writers of about the same period. Schermerhorn (1812) places the Kiowa on the heads of the Arkansas and Platte. Earlier still they appear upon the headwaters of the Platte, which is the region assigned them upon the map.[3] This region was occupied later by the Cheyenne and Arapaho of Algonquian stock.

Population.—According to the United States census for 1890 there are 1,140 Kiowa on the Kiowa, Comanche, and Wichita Reservation, Indian Territory.

---

[1] Trans. and Coll. Am. Antiq. Soc., 1836, vol. II, p. 133.

[2] Pac. R. R. Rep., 1855, vol. 2, pt. 3, p. 16.

[3] Pike, Exp. to sources of the Mississippi, App., 1810, pt. 3, p. 9.

KITUNAHAN FAMILY.

= Kitunaha, Hale in U. S. Expl. Exp., VI, 204, 535, 1846 (between the forks of the Columbia). Gallatin in Trans. Am. Eth. Soc., II, pt. 1, c, 10, 77, 1848 (Flatbow). Berghaus (1851), Physik. Atlas, map 17, 1852. Latham in Trans. Philolog. Soc. Lond., 70, 1856. Latham, Opuscula, 338, 1860. Latham, El. Comp. Phil., 395, 1862 (between 52° and 48° N. L., west of main ridge of Rocky Mountains). Gatschet in Mag. Am. Hist., 170, 1877 (on Kootenay River).

= Coutanies, Hale in U. S. Expl. Exp., VI, 204, 1846 (=Kitunaha).

= Kútanis, Latham, Nat. Hist. Man., 316, 1850 (Kitunaha).

= Kituanaha, Gallatin in Schoolcraft, Ind. Tribes, III, 402, 1853 (Coutaria or Flatbows, north of lat. 49°).

= Kootanies, Buschmann, Spuren der aztek. Sprache, 661, 1859.

= Kutani, Latham, El. Comp. Phil., 395, 1862 (or Kitunaha).

= Cootanie, Latham, El. Comp. Phil., 395, 1862 (synonymous with Kitunaha).

= Kootenai, Gatschet in Mag. Am. Hist., 170, 1877 (defines area occupied). Gatschet in Beach, Ind. Misc., 446, 1877. Bancroft, Nat. Races, III, 565, 1882.

= Kootenuha, Tolmie and Dawson, Comp. Vocabs., 79–87, 1884 (vocabulary of Upper Kootenuha).

= Flatbow, Hale in U. S. Expl. Exp., VI, 204, 1846 (= Kitunaha). Gallatin in Trans. Am. Eth. Soc., II, pt. 1, 10, 77, 1848 (after Hale). Buschmann, Spuren der aztek. Sprache, 661, 1859. Latham, El. Comp. Phil., 395, 1862 (or Kitunaha). Gatschet in Mag. Am. Hist., 170, 1877.

= Flachbogen. Berghaus (1851), Physik. Atlas, map 17, 1852.

× Shushwaps, Keane, App. Stanford's Comp. (Cent. and So. Am.), 460, 474, 1878 (includes Kootenais (Flatbows or Skalzi).

This family was based upon a tribe variously termed Kitunaha, Kutenay, Cootenai, or Flatbow, living on the Kootenay River, a branch of the Columbia in Oregon.

Mr. Gatschet thinks it is probable that there are two dialects of the language spoken respectively in the extreme northern and southern portions of the territory occupied, but the vocabularies at hand are not sufficient to definitely settle the question.

The area occupied by the Kitunahan tribes is inclosed between the northern fork of the Columbia River, extending on the south along the Cootenay River. By far the greater part of the territory occupied by these tribes is in British Columbia.

TRIBES.

The principal divisions or tribes are Cootenai, or Upper Cootenai; Akoklako, or Lower Cootenai; Klanoh-Klatklam, or Flathead Cootenai; Yaketahnoklatakmakanay, or Tobacco Plains Cootenai.

Population.—There are about 425 Cootenai at Flathead Agency, Montana, and 539 at Kootenay Agency, British Columbia; total, 964.

KOLUSCHAN FAMILY.

= Koluschen, Gallatin in Trans. and Coll. Am. Antiq. Soc., II, 14, 1836 (islands and adjacent coast from 60° to 55° N. L.).

= Koulischen, Gallatin in Trans. and Coll. Am. Antiq. Soc., II, 306, 1836. Gallatin in Trans. Am. Eth. Soc., II, pt. 1, c, 77, 1848, (Koulischen and Sitka languages)· Gallatin in Schoolcraft, Ind. Tribes, III, 402, 1853 (Sitka, bet. 52° and 59° lat.).

< Kolooch, Latham in Trans. Philolog. Soc. Lond., II, 31–50, 1846 (tends to merge
    Kolooch into Esquimaux). Latham in Jour. Eth. Soc. Lond., I, 163, 1848 (com-
    pared with Eskimo language.). Latham, Opuscula, 259, 276, 1860.
= Koluschians, Prichard, Phys. Hist. Mankind, V, 433, 1847 (follows Gallatin).
    Scouler (1846) in Jour. Eth. Soc. Lond., I, 231, 1848.
< Kolúch, Latham, Nat. Hist. Man, 294, 1850 (more likely forms a subdivision of Es-
    kimo than a separate class; includes Kenay of Cook's Inlet, Atna of Copper
    River, Koltshani, Ugalents, Sitkans, Tungaas, Inkhuluklait, Magimut, Inkalit;
    Digothi and Nehanni are classed as "doubtful Kolúches").
= Koloschen, Berghaus (1845), Physik. Atlas, map 17, 1848. Ibid., 1852. Buschmann,
    Spuren der aztek. Sprache, 680, 1859. Berghaus, Physik. Atlas, map 72, 1887.
= Kolush, Latham, El. Comp. Phil., 401, 1862 (mere mention of family with short
    vocabulary).
= Kaloshians, Dall in Proc. Am. Ass., 375, 1885 (gives tribes and population).
× Northern, Scouler in Jour. Roy. Geog. Soc. Lond., XI, 218, 1841 (includes Koloshes
    and Tun Ghasse).
× Haidah, Scouler, ibid, 219, 1841 (same as his Northern).
= Klen-ee-kate, Schoolcraft, Ind. Tribes, V, 489, 1855.
= Klen-e-kate, Kane, Wanderings of an Artist, app., 1859 (a census of N. W. coast
    tribes classified by language).
= Thlinkithen, Holmberg in Finland Soc., 284, 1856 (fide Buschmann, 676, 1859).
= Thl'nkets, Dall in Proc. Am. Ass., 268, 269, 1869 (divided into Sitka-kwan, Stahkin-
    kwan, "Yakutats").
= T'linkets, Dall in Cont. N. A. Eth., I, 36, 1877 (divided into Yăk'ūtăts, Chilkăht'-
    kwăn, Sitka-kwan, Stākhin'-kwān, Kygāh'ni).
= Thlinkeet, Keane, App. Stanford's Comp. (Cent. and So. Am.), 460, 462, 1878 (from
    Mount St. Elias to Nass River; includes Ugalenzes, Yakutats, Chilkats, Hoodnids,
    Hoodsinoos, Takoos, Auks, Kakas, Stikines, Eeliknûs, Tungass, Sitkas). Ban-
    croft, Nat. Races, III, 562, 579, 1882.
= Thlinkit, Tolmie and Dawson, Comp. Vocabs., 14, 1884 (vocab. of Skutkwan Sept;
    also map showing distribution of family). Berghaus, Physik. Atlas, map 72, 1887.
= Tlinkit, Dall in Proc. Am. Ass., 375, 1885 (enumerates tribes and gives population).

Derivation: From the Aleut word kolosh, or more properly, kaluga,
meaning "dish," the allusion being to the dish-shaped lip ornaments.

This family was based by Gallatin upon the Koluschen tribe (the
Tshinkitani of Marchand), "who inhabit the islands and the adjacent coast from the sixtieth to the fifty-fifth degree of north latitude."

In the Koluschan family, Gallatin observes that the remote analogies to the Mexican tongue to be found in several of the northern
tribes, as the Kinai, are more marked than in any other.

The boundaries of this family as given by Gallatin are substantially in accordance with our present knowledge of the subject.
The southern boundary is somewhat indeterminate owing to the
fact, ascertained by the census agents in 1880, that the Haida tribes
extend somewhat farther north than was formerly supposed and
occupy the southeast half of Prince of Wales Island. About latitude 56°, or the mouth of Portland Canal, indicates the southern
limit of the family, and 60°, or near the mouth of Atna River, the
northern limit. Until recently they have been supposed to be exclu-

sively an insular and coast people, but Mr. Dawson has made the interesting discovery[1] that the Tagish, a tribe living inland on the headwaters of the Lewis River, who have hitherto been supposed to be of Athapascan extraction, belong to the Koluschan family. This tribe, therefore, has crossed the coast range of mountains, which for the most part limits the extension of this people inland and confines them to a narrow coast strip, and have gained a permanent foothold in the interior, where they share the habits of the neighboring Athapascan tribes.

TRIBES.

Auk.	Hunah.	Tagish.
Chilcat.	Kek.	Taku.
Hanega.	Sitka.	Tongas.
Hoodsunu.	Stahkin.	Yakutat.

Population.—The following figures are from the census of 1880.[2] The total population of the tribes of this family, exclusive of the Tagish, is 6,437, distributed as follows:

Auk	640	Kek	568
Chilcat	988	Sitka	721
Hanega (including Kouyon and Klanak)	587	Stahkin	317
		Taku	269
Hoodsunu	666	Tongas	273
Hunah	908	Yakutat	500

KULANAPAN FAMILY.

✕ Kula-napo, Gibbs in Schoolcraft, Ind. Tribes, III, 421, 1853 (the name of one of the Clear Lake bands).

> Mendocino (?), Latham in Trans. Philolog. Soc. Lond., 77, 1856 (name suggested for Choweshak, Batemdaikai, Kulanapo, Yukai, Khwaklamayu languages). Latham, Opuscula, 343, 1860. Latham, El. Comp. Phil., 410, 1862 (as above).

> Pomo, Powers in Overland Monthly, IX, 498, Dec., 1872 (general description of habitat and of family). Powers in Cont. N. A. Eth., III, 146, 1877. Powell, ibid., 491 (vocabularies of Gal-li-no-mé-ro, Yo-kai'-a, Ba-tem-da-kaii, Chau-i-shek, Yu-kai, Ku-la-na-po, H'hana, Venaambakaiia, Ka'-bi-na-pek, Chwachamaju). Gatschet in Mag. Am. Hist., 16, 1877 (gives habitat and enumerates tribes of family). Gatschet in Beach, Ind. Misc., 436, 1877. Keane, App. Stanford's Comp. (Cent. and So. Am.), 476, 1878 (includes Castel Pomos, Ki, Cahto, Choam, Chadela, Matomey Ki, Usal or Calamet, Shebalne Pomos, Gallinomeros, Sanels, Socoas, Lamas, Comachos).

< Pomo, Bancroft, Nat. Races, III, 566, 1882 (includes Ukiah, Gallinomero, Masallamagoon, Gualala, Matole, Kulanapo, Sanél, Yonios, Choweshak, Batemdakaie, Chocuyem, Olamentke, Kainamare, Chwachamaju. Of these, Chocuyem and Olamentke are Moquelumnan).

The name applied to this family was first employed by Gibbs in 1853, as above cited. He states that it is the "name of one of the

---

[1] Annual Report of the Geological Survey of Canada, 1887.

[2] Petroff, Report on the Population, Industries, and Resources of Alaska, 1884, p. 33.

Clear Lake bands," adding that "the language is spoken by all the tribes occupying the large valley." The distinctness of the language is now generally admitted.

GEOGRAPHIC DISTRIBUTION.

The main territory of the Kulanapan family is bounded on the west by the Pacific Ocean, on the east by the Yukian and Copehan territories, on the north by the watershed of the Russian River, and on the south by a line drawn from Bodega Head to the southwest corner of the Yukian territory, near Santa Rosa, Sonoma County, California. Several tribes of this family, viz, the Kastel Pomo, Kai Pomo, and Kato Pomo, are located in the valley between the South Fork of Eel River and the main river, and on the headwaters of the South Fork, extending thence in a narrow strip to the ocean. In this situation they were entirely cut off from the main body by the intrusive Yuki tribes, and pressed upon from the north by the warlike Wailakki, who are said to have imposed their language and many of their customs upon them and as well doubtless to have extensively intermarried with them.

TRIBES.

Balló Kaì Pomo, "Oat Valley People."
Batemdikáyi.
Búldam Pomo (Rio Grande or Big River).
Chawishek.
Choam Chadila Pomo (Capello).
Chwachamajù.
Dápishul Pomo (Redwood Cañon).
Eastern People (Clear Lake about Lakeport).
Erío (mouth of Russian River).
Erússi (Fort Ross).
Gallinoméro (Russian River Valley below Cloverdale and in Dry
    Creek Valley).
Gualála (northwest corner of Sonoma County).
Kabinapek (western part of Clear Lake basin).
Kaimé (above Healdsburgh).
Kai Pomo (between Eel River and South Fork).
Kastel Pomo (between Eel River and South Fork).
Kato Pomo, "Lake People."
Komácho (Anderson and Rancheria Valleys).
Kulá Kai Pomo (Sherwood Valley).
Kulanapo.
Láma (Russian River Valley).
Misálamagūn or Musakakūn (above Healdsburgh).
Mitoám Kai Pomo, "Wooded Valley People" (Little Lake).
Poam Pomo.

Senel (Russian River Valley).
Shódo Kaí Pomo (Coyote Valley).
Síako (Russian River Valley).
Sokóa (Russian River Valley).
Yokáya Pomo, "Lower Valley People" (Ukiah City).
Yusâl (or Kámalel) Pomo, "Ocean People" (on coast and
along Yusal Creek).

KUSAN FAMILY.

= Kúsa, Gatschet in Mag. Am. Hist., 257, 1882.

Derivation: Milhau, in a manuscript letter to Gibbs (Bureau of
Ethnology), states that "Coos in the Rogue River dialect is said to
mean lake, lagoon or inland bay."

The "Kaus or Kwokwoos" tribe is merely mentioned by Hale as
living on a river of the same name between the Umqua and the Clamet.[1] Lewis and Clarke[2] also mention them in the same location as
the Cookkoo-oose. The tribe was referred to also under the name
Kaus by Latham,[3] who did not attempt its classification, having in
fact no material for the purpose.

Mr. Gatschet, as above, distinguishes the language as forming a
distinct stock. It is spoken on the coast of middle Oregon, on Coos
River and Bay, and at the mouth of Coquille River, Oregon.

TRIBES.

Anasitch.	Mulluk or Lower Coquille.
Melukitz.	Nacu?.

Population.—Most of the survivors of this family are gathered
upon the Siletz Reservation, Oregon, but their number can not be
stated as the agency returns are not given by tribes.

LUTUAMIAN FAMILY.

= Lutuami, Hale in U.S. Expl. Exp.,VI, 199, 569, 1846 (headwaters Klamath River and
lake). Gallatin in Trans. Am. Eth. Soc., II, pt. 1, c, 17, 77, 1848 (follows Hale).
Latham, Nat. Hist. Man, 325, 1850 (headwaters Clamet River). Berghaus(1851),
Physik. Atlas, map 17, 1852. Latham in Proc. Philolog. Soc. Lond., VI, 82, 1854.
Latham in Trans. Philolog. Soc. Lond., 74, 1856. Latham, Opuscula, 300, 310, 1860.
Latham, El. Comp. Phil., 407, 1862.

= Luturim, Gallatin in Schoolcraft, Ind. Tribes, III, 402, 1853 (misprint for Lutuami;
based on Clamets language).

= Lutumani, Latham, Opuscula, 341, 1860 (misprint for Lutuami).

= Tlamatl, Hale in U.S. Expl. Exp., VI, 218, 569, 1846 (alternative of Lutuami). Berghaus (1851), Physik. Atlas, map 17, 1852.

= Clamets, Hale in U.S. Expl. Exp., VI, 218, 569, 1846 (alternative of Lutuami).

[1] U. S. Expl. Exp., 1846, vol. 6, p, 221.   [3] Nat. Hist. Man, 1850, p. 325.
[2] Allen Ed., 1814, vol. 2, p. 118.

= Klamath, Gatschet in Mag. Am. Hist., 164, 1877. Gatschet in Beach. Ind. Misc., 439, 1877. Gatschet in Am. Antiq., 81–84, 1878 (general remarks upon family).

< Klamath, Keane, App. Stanford's Comp. (Cent. and So. Am.), 460, 475, 1878 (a geographic group rather than a linguistic family; includes, in addition to the Klamath proper or Lutuami, the Yacons, Modocs, Copahs, Shastas, Palaiks, Wintoons, Eurocs, Cahrocs, Lototens, Weeyots, Wishosks, Wallies, Tolewahs, Patawats, Yukas, "and others between Eel River and Humboldt Bay." The list thus includes several distinct families). Bancroft, Nat. Races, III, 565, 640, 1882 (includes Lutuami or Klamath, Modoc and Copah, the latter belonging to the Copehan family).

= Klamath Indians of Southwestern Oregon, Gatschet in Cont, N. A. Eth., II, pt. 1, xxxiii, 1890.

Derivation: From a Pit River word meaning "lake."

The tribes of this family appear from time immemorial to have occupied Little and Upper Klamath Lakes, Klamath Marsh, and Sprague River, Oregon. Some of the Modoc have been removed to the Indian Territory, where 84 now reside; others are in Sprague River Valley.

The language is a homogeneous one and, according to Mr. Gatschet who has made a special study of it, has no real dialects, the two divisions of the family, Klamath and Modoc, speaking an almost identical language.

The Klamaths' own name is É-ukshikni, "Klamath Lake people." The Modoc are termed by the Klamath Módokni, "Southern people."

TRIBES.

Klamath.   Modoc.

Population.—There were 769 Klamath and Modoc on the Klamaht Reservation in 1889. Since then they have slightly decreased.

MARIPOSAN FAMILY.

> Mariposa, Latham in Trans. Philolog. Soc. Lond., 84, 1856 (Coconoons language, Mariposa County). Latham, Opuscula, 350, 1860. Latham, El. Comp. Philology, 416, 1862 (Coconoons of Mercede River).

= Yo'-kuts, Powers in Cont. N. A. Eth., III, 369, 1877. Powell, ibid., 570 (vocabularies of Yo'-kuts, Wi'-chi-kik, Tin'-lin-neh, King's River, Coconoons, Calaveras County).

= Yocut, Gatschet in Mag. Am. Hist., 158, 1877 (mentions Taches, Chewenee, Watooga, Chookchancies, Coconoons and others). Gatschet in Beach, Ind. Misc., 432, 1877.

Derivation: A Spanish word meaning "butterfly," applied to a county in California and subsequently taken for the family name.

Latham mentions the remnants of three distinct bands of the Coconoon, each with its own language, in the north of Mariposa County. These are classed together under the above name. More recently the tribes speaking languages allied to the Coconūn have been treated of under the family name Yokut. As, however, the stock was established by Latham on a sound basis, his name is here restored.

The territory of the Mariposan family is quite irregular in outline. On the north it is bounded by the Fresno River up to the point of its junction with the San Joaquin ; thence by a line running to the northeast corner of the Salinan territory in San Benito County, California; on the west by a line running from San Benito to Mount Pinos. From the middle of the western shore of Tulare Lake to the ridge at Mount Pinos on the south, the Mariposan area is merely a narrow strip in and along the foothills. Occupying one-half of the western and all the southern shore of Tulare Lake, and bounded on the north by a line running from the southeast corner of Tulare Lake due east to the first great spur of the Sierra Nevada range is the territory of the intrusive Shoshoni. On the east the secondary range of the Sierra Nevada forms the Mariposan boundary.

In addition to the above a small strip of territory on the eastern bank of the San Joaquin is occupied by the Cholovone division of the Mariposan family, between the Tuolumne and the point where the San Joaquin turns to the west before entering Suisun Bay.

TRIBES.

Ayapaì (Tule River).
Chainímaini (lower King's River.)
Chukaímina (Squaw Valley).
Chŭk'chansi (San Joaquin River above Millerton).
Chunut (Kaweah River at the lake).
Coconūn' (Merced River).
Ititcha (King's River).
Kassovo (Day Creek).
Kau-í-a (Kaweah River ; foothills).
Kiawétni (Tule River at Porterville).
Mayáyu (Tule River, south fork).
Notoánaiti (on the lake).
Ochíngita (Tule River).
Pitkachì (extinct ; San Joaquin River below Millerton).
Pohállin Tinleh (near Kern lake).
Sawákhtu (Tule River, south fork).
Táchi (Kingston).
Télumni (Kaweah River below Visalia).
Tínlinneh (Fort Tejon).
Tisèchu (upper King's River).
Wíchikik (King's River).
Wikchúmni (Kaweah River ; foothills).
Wíksachi (upper Kaweah Valley).
Yúkol (Kaweah River plains).

Population.—There are 145 of the Indians of this family now attached to the Mission Agency, California.

MOQUELUMNAN FAMILY.

> Tcho-ko-yem, Gibbs in Schoolcraft, Ind. Tribes, III. 421, 1853 (mentioned as a band and dialect).

> Moquelumne, Latham in Trans. Philolog. Soc. Lond., 81, 1856 (includes Hale's Talatui, Tuolumne from Schoolcraft, Mumaltachi, Mullateco, Apangasi, Lapappu, Siyante or Typoxi, Hawhaw's band of Aplaches, San Rafael vocabulary, Tshokoyem vobabulary, Cocouyem and Yonkiousme Paternosters, Olamentke of Kostromitonov, Paternosters for Mission de Santa Clara and the Vallee de los Tulares of Mofras, Paternoster of the Langue Guiloco de la Mission de San Francisco). Latham, Opuscula, 347, 1860. Latham, El. Comp. Phil., 414, 1862 (same as above).

= Meewoc, Powers in Overland Monthly, 322, April, 1873 (general account of family with allusions to language). Gatschet in Mag. Am. Hist., 159, 1877 (gives habitat and bands of family). Gatschet in Beach, Ind. Misc., 433, 1877.

= Mi-wok, Powers in Cont. N. A. Eth., III, 246, 1877 (nearly as above).

< Mutsun, Powell in Cont. N. A. Eth., III, 535, 1877 (vocabs. of Mi'-wok, Tuolumne, Costano, Tcho-ko-yem, Mūtsūn, Santa Clara, Santa Cruz, Chum-te'-ya, Kawéya, San Raphael Mission, Talatui, Olamentke). Gatschet in Mag. Am. Hist., 157, 1877 (gives habitat and members of family). Gatschet, in Beach, Ind. Misc., 430, 1877.

× Runsiens, Keane, App. Stanford's Comp. (Cent. and So. Am.), 476, 1878 (includes Olhones, Eslenes, Santa Cruz, San Miguel, Lopillamillos, Mipacmacs, Kulanapos, Yolos, Suisunes, Talluches, Chowclas, Waches, Talches, Poowells).

Derivation: From the river and hill of same name in Calaveras County, California; according to Powers the Meewoc name for the river is Wakalumitoh.

The Talatui mentioned by Hale[1] as on the Kassima (Cosumnes) River belong to the above family. Though this author clearly distinguished the language from any others with which he was acquainted, he nowhere expressed the opinion that it is entitled to family rank or gave it a family name. Talatui is mentioned as a tribe from which he obtained an incomplete vocabulary.

It was not until 1856 that the distinctness of the linguistic family was fully set forth by Latham. Under the head of Moquelumne, this author gathers several vocabularies representing different languages and dialects of the same stock. These are the Talatui of Hale, the Tuolumne from Schoolcraft, the Sonoma dialects as represented by the Tshokoyem vocabulary, the Chocuyem and Youkiousme paternosters, and the Olamentke of Kostromitonov in Bäer's Beiträge. He also places here provisionally the paternosters from the Mission de Santa Clara and the Vallee de los Tulares of Mofras; also the language Guiloco de la Mission de San Francisco. The Costano containing the five tribes of the Mission of Dolores, viz., the Ahwastes, Olhones or Costanos of the coast, Romonans, Tulomos and the Altahmos seemed to Latham to differ from the Moquelumnan language. Concerning them he states "upon the whole, however, the affinities seem to run in the direction of the languages of the next

---

[1] U. S. Expl. Exp., 1846, vol. 6, pp. 630, 633.

group, especially in that of the Ruslen. He adds: "Nevertheless, for the present I place the Costano by itself, as a transitional form of speech to the languages spoken north, east, and south of the Bay of San Francisco." Recent investigation by Messrs. Curtin and Henshaw have confirmed the soundness of Latham's views and, as stated under head of the Costanoan family, the two groups of languages are considered to be distinct.

GEOGRAPHIC DISTRIBUTION.

The Moquelumnan family occupies the territory bounded on the north by the Cosumne River, on the south by the Fresno River, on the east by the Sierra Nevada, and on the west by the San Joaquin River, with the exception of a strip on the east bank occupied by the Cholovone. A part of this family occupies also a territory bounded on the south by San Francisco Bay and the western half of San Pablo Bay; on the west by the Pacific Ocean from the Golden Gate to Bodega Head; on the north by a line running from Bodega Head to the Yukian territory northeast of Santa Rosa, and on the east by a line running from the Yukian territory to the northernmost point of San Pablo Bay.

PRINCIPAL TRIBES.

Miwok division:

Awani.	Lopolatimne.	Seroushamne.
Chauchila.	Machemni.	Talatui.
Chumidok.	Mokelumni.	Tamoleka.
Chumtiwa.	Newichumni.	Tumidok.
Chumuch.	Olowidok.	Tumun.
Chumwit.	Olowit.	Walakumni.
Hettitoya.	Olowiya.	Yuloni.
Kani.	Sakaiakumni.	

Olamentke division:

Bollanos.	Nicassias.	Sonomi.
Chokuyem.	Numpali.	Tamal.
Guimen.	Olamentke.	Tulare.
Likatuit.	Olumpali.	Utchium.

Population.—Comparatively few of the Indians of this family survive, and these are mostly scattered in the mountains and away from the routes of travel. As they were never gathered on reservations, an accurate census has not been taken.

In the detached area north of San Francisco Bay, chiefly in Marin County, formerly inhabited by the Indians of this family, almost none remain. There are said to be none living about the mission of San Rafael, and Mr. Henshaw, in 1888, succeeded in locating only six at Tomales Bay, where, however, he obtained a very good vocabulary from a woman.

MUSKHOGEAN FAMILY.

>Muskhogee, Gallatin in Trans. and Coll. Am. Antiq. Soc., II, 94, 306, 1836 (based upon Muskhogees, Hitchittees, Seminoles). Prichard, Phys. Hist. Mankind, v, 402, 1847 (includes Muskhogees, Seminoles, Hitchittees).

>Muskhogies, Berghaus (1845), Physik. Atlas, map 17, 1848. Ibid., 1852.

>Muscogee, Keane, App. Stanford's Comp. (Cent. and So. Am.), 460, 471, 1878 (includes Muscogees proper, Seminoles, Choctaws, Chickasaws, Hitchittees, Coosadas or Coosas, Alibamons, Apalaches).

=Maskoki, Gatschet, Creek Mig. Legend, I, 50, 1884 (general account of family; four branches, Maskoki, Apalachian, Alibamu, Chahta). Berghaus, Physik. Atlas, map 72, 1887.

>Choctaw Muskhogee, Gallatin in Trans. and Coll. Am. Antiq. Soc., II, 119, 1836.

>Chocta-Muskhog, Gallatin in Trans. Am. Eth. Soc., II, pt. 1, xcix, 77, 1848. Gallatin in Schoolcraft, Ind. Tribes. III, 401, 1853.

=Chata-Muskoki, Hale in Am. Antiq., 108, April, 1883 (considered with reference to migration).

>Chahtas, Gallatin in Trans. and Coll. Am. Antiq. Soc., II, 100, 306, 1836 (or Choctaws).

>Chahtahs, Prichard, Phys. Hist. Mankind, v, 403, 1847 (or Choktahs or Flatheads).

>Tschahtas, Berghaus (1845), Physik. Atlas, map 17, 1848. Ibid., 1852.

>Choctah, Latham, Nat. Hist. Man, 337, 1850 (includes Choctahs, Muscogulges, Muskohges). Latham in Trans. Phil. Soc. Lond., 103, 1856. Latham, Opuscula, 366, 1860.

>Mobilian, Bancroft, Hist. U. S., 249, 1840.

>Flat-heads, Prichard, Phys. Hist. Mankind, v, 403, 1847 (Chahtahs or Choktahs).

>Coshattas, Latham, Nat. Hist. Man, 349, 1850 (not classified).

>Humas, Latham, Nat. Hist. Man, 341, 1850 (east of Mississippi above New Orleans).

Derivation: From the name of the principal tribe of the Creek Confederacy.

In the Muskhogee family Gallatin includes the Muskhogees proper, who lived on the Coosa and Tallapoosa Rivers; the Hitchittees, living on the Chattahoochee and Flint Rivers; and the Seminoles of the peninsula of Florida. It was his opinion, formed by a comparison of vocabularies, that the Choctaws and Chickasaws should also be classed under this family. In fact, he called[1] the family Choctaw Muskhogee. In deference, however, to established usage, the two tribes were kept separate in his table and upon the colored map. In 1848 he appears to be fully convinced of the soundness of the view doubtfully expressed in 1836, and calls the family the Chocta-Muskhog.

GEOGRAPHIC DISTRIBUTION.

The area occupied by this family was very extensive. It may be described in a general way as extending from the Savannah River and the Atlantic west to the Mississippi, and from the Gulf of Mexico north to the Tennessee River. All of this territory was held by Muskhogean tribes except the small areas occupied by the Yuchi, Nä'htchi, and some small settlements of Shawni.

---

[1] On p. 119, Archæologia Americana.

Upon the northeast Muskhogean limits are indeterminate. The Creek claimed only to the Savannah River; but upon its lower course the Yamasi are believed to have extended east of that river in the sixteenth to the eighteenth century.[1] The territorial line between the Muskhogean family and the Catawba tribe in South Carolina can only be conjectured.

It seems probable that the whole peninsula of Florida was at one time held by tribes of Timuquanan connection; but from 1702 to 1708, when the Apalachi were driven out, the tribes of northern Florida also were forced away by the English. After that time the Seminole and the Yamasi were the only Indians that held possession of the Floridian peninsula.

PRINCIPAL TRIBES.

Alibamu.	Choctaw.	Seminole.
Apalachi.	Creek or Maskoki proper.	Yamacraw.
Chicasa.	Koasáti.	Yamasi.

Population.—There is an Alibamu town on Deep Creek, Indian Territory, an affluent of the Canadian, Indian Territory. Most of the inhabitants are of this tribe. There are Alibamu about 20 miles south of Alexandria, Louisiana, and over one hundred in Polk County, Texas.

So far as known only three women of the Apalachi survived in 1886, and they lived at the Alibamu town above referred to. The United States Census bulletin for 1890 gives the total number of pure-blood Choctaw at 9,996, these being principally at Union Agency, Indian Territory. Of the Chicasa there are 3,464 at the same agency; Creek 9,291; Seminole 2,539; of the latter there are still about 200 left in southern Florida.

There are four families of Koasáti, about twenty-five individuals, near the town of Shepherd, San Jacinto County, Texas. Of the Yamasi none are known to survive.

NATCHESAN FAMILY.

>Natches, Gallatin in Trans. and Coll. Am. Antiq. Soc., II, 95, 306, 1836 (Natches only). Prichard, Phys. Hist. Mankind, V, 402, 403, 1847.

>Natsches, Berghaus (1845), Physik. Atlas, map 17, 1848. Ibid., 1852.

>Natchez, Bancroft, Hist. U. S., 248, 1840. Gallatin in Trans. Am. Eth. Soc., II, pt. 1, xcix, 77, 1848 (Natchez only). Latham, Nat. Hist. Man, 340, 1850 (tends to include Taensas, Pascagoulas, Colapissas, Biluxi in same family). Gallatin in Schoolcraft, Ind. Tribes, III, 401, 1853 (Natchez only). Keane. App. Stanford's Comp. (Cent. and So. Am.), 460, 473, 1878 (suggests that it may include the Utchees).

>Naktche, Gatschet, Creek Mig. Legend, I, 34, 1884. Gatschet in Science, 414, April 29, 1887.

---

[1]Gatschet, Creek Mig. Legend, 1884, vol. 1, p. 62.

>Taensa, Gatschet in The Nation, 382, May 4, 1882. Gatschet in Am. Antiq., IV, 238, 1882. Gatschet, Creek Mig. Legend, I, 33, 1884. Gatschet in Science, 414, April 29, 1887 (Taensas only).

The Na'htchi, according to Gallatin, a residue of the well-known nation of that name, came from the banks of the Mississippi, and joined the Creek less than one hundred years ago.[1] The seashore from Mobile to the Mississippi was then inhabited by several small tribes, of which the Na'htchi was the principal.

Before 1730 the tribe lived in the vicinity of Natchez, Miss., along St. Catherine Creek. After their dispersion by the French in 1730 most of the remainder joined the Chicasa and afterwards the Upper Creek. They are now in Creek and Cherokee Nations, Indian Territory.

The linguistic relations of the language spoken by the Taensa tribe have long been in doubt, and it is probable that they will ever remain so. As no vocabulary or text of this language was known to be in existence, the "Grammaire et vocabulaire de la langue Taensa, avec textes traduits et commentés par J.-D. Haumonté, Parisot, L. Adam," published in Paris in 1882, was received by American linguistic students with peculiar interest. Upon the strength of the linguistic material embodied in the above Mr. Gatschet (loc. cit.) was led to affirm the complete linguistic isolation of the language.

Grave doubts of the authenticity of the grammar and vocabulary have, however, more recently been brought forward.[2] The text contains internal evidences of the fraudulent character, if not of the whole, at least of a large part of the material. So palpable and gross are these that until the character of the whole can better be understood by the inspection of the original manuscript, alleged to be in Spanish, by a competent expert it will be far safer to reject both the vocabulary and grammar. By so doing we are left without any linguistic evidence whatever of the relations of the Taensa language.

D'Iberville, it is true, supplies us with the names of seven Taensa towns which were given by a Taensa Indian who accompanied him; but most of these, according to Mr. Gatschet, were given in the Chicasa trade jargon or, as termed by the French, the "Mobilian trade jargon," which is at least a very natural supposition. Under these circumstances we can, perhaps, do no better than rely upon the statements of several of the old writers who appear to be unanimous in regarding the language of the Taensa as of Na'htchi connection. Du Pratz's statement to that effect is weakened from the fact that the statement also includes the Shetimasha, the language of which is known from a vocabulary to be totally distinct not only from the Na'htchi but from any other. To supplement Du Pratz's testimony, such as it is, we have the statements of M. de Montigny, the

---

[1] Trans. Am. Antiq. Soc., 1836, vol. 2, p. 95.
[2] D. G. Brinton in Am. Antiquarian. March, 1885, pp. 109-114.

missionary who affirmed the affinity of the Taensa language to that of the Na'htchi, before he had visited the latter in 1699, and of Father Gravier, who also visited them. For the present, therefore, the Taensa language is considered to be a branch of the Na'htchi.

The Taensa formerly dwelt upon the Mississippi, above and close to the Na'htchi. Early in the history of the French settlements a portion of the Taensa, pressed upon by the Chicasa, fled and were settled by the French upon Mobile Bay.

PRINCIPAL TRIBES.

Na'htchi.   Taensa.

Population.—There still are four Na'htchi among the Creek in Indian Territory and a number in the Cheroki Hills near the Missouri border.

PALAIHNIHAN FAMILY.

= Palaihnih, Hale in U. S. Expl. Expd., VI, 218, 569, 1846 (used in family sense).
= Palaik, Hale in U.S. Expl. Expd., VI, 199, 218, 569, 1846 (southeast of Lutuami in Oregon), Gallatin in Trans. Am. Eth. Soc., II, pt. 1, 18, 77, 1848. Latham, Nat. Hist. Man., 325, 1850 (southeast of Lutuami). Berghaus (1851), Physik. Atlas, map 17, 1852. Latham in Proc. Philolog. Soc. Lond., VI, 82, 1854 (cites Hale's vocab). Latham in Trans. Philolog. Soc. Lond., 74, 1856 (has Shoshoni affinities). Latham, Opuscula. 310, 341, 1860. Latham, El. Comp. Phil., 407, 1862.
= Palainih, Gallatin in Trans. Am. Eth. Soc., II, pt. 1, c, 1848. (after Hale). Berghaus (1851), Physik. Atlas, map 17, 1852.
= Pulairih, Gallatin in Schoolcraft, Ind. Tribes, III, 402, 1853 (obvious typographical error; quotes Hale's Palaiks).
= Pit River, Powers in Overland Monthly, 412, May, 1874 (three principal tribes: Achomáwes, Hamefcuttelies, Astakaywas or Astakywich). Gatschet in Mag. Am. Hist., 164, 1877 (gives habitat; quotes Hale for tribes). Gatschet in Beach, Ind. Misc., 439, 1877.
= A·cho-mâ'-wi, Powell in Cont. N. A. Eth., III, 601, 1877, vocabs. of A-cho-mâ'-wi and Lutuami). Powers in ibid., 267 (general account of tribes; A-cho-mâ'-wi, Hu-mâ'-whi, Es-ta-ke'-wach, Han-te'-wa, Chu-mâ'-wa, A-tu-a'-mih, Il-mâ'-wi).
< Klamath, Keane, App. Stanford's Comp. (Cent. and So. Am.), 460, 475, 1878 (includes Palaiks).
< Shasta, Bancroft, Nat. Races, III, 565, 1882 (contains Palaik of present family).

Derivation: From the Klamath word *p'laikni*, signifying "mountaineers" or "uplanders" (Gatschet).

In two places[1] Hale uses the terms Palaihnih and Palaiks interchangeably, but inasmuch as on page 569, in his formal table of linguistic families and languages, he calls the family Palaihnih, this is given preference over the shorter form of the name.

Though here classed as a distinct family, the status of the Pit River dialects can not be considered to be finally settled. Powers speaks of the language as "hopelessly consonantal, harsh, and sesquipedalian," * * * "utterly unlike the sweet and simple lan-

[1] U. S. Expl. Expd., 1846, vol. 6, pp. 199, 218.

guages of the Sacramento." He adds that the personal pronouns show it to be a true Digger Indian tongue. Recent investigations by Mr. Gatschet lead him, however, to believe that ultimately it will be found to be linguistically related to the Sastean languages.

GEOGRAPHIC DISTRIBUTION.

The family was located by Hale to the southeast of the Lutuami (Klamath). They chiefly occupied the area drained by the Pit River in extreme northeastern California. Some of the tribe were removed to Round Valley Reservation, California.

PRINCIPAL TRIBES.

Powers, who has made a special study of the tribe, recognizes the following principal tribal divisions :[1]

Achomâ'wi.	Estake'wach.	Ilmâ'wi.
Atua'mih.	Hante'wa.	Pakamalli?
Chumâ'wa.	Humâ'whi.	

PIMAN FAMILY.

=Pima, Latham, Nat. Hist. Man, 398, 1850 (cites three languages from the Mithridates, viz, Pima proper, Opata, Eudeve). Turner in Pac. R. R. Rep., III, pt. 3, 55, 1856 (Pima proper). Latham in Trans. Philolog. Soc. Lond., 92, 1856 (contains Pima proper, Opata, Eudeve, Papagos). Latham, Opuscula, 356, 1860. Latham, El. Comp. Phil., 427, 1862 (includes Pima proper, Opata, Eudeve, Papago, Ibequi, Hiaqui, Tubar, Tarahumara, Cora). Gatschet in Mag. Am. Hist., 156, 1877 (includes Pima, Névome, Pápago). Gatschet in Beach, Ind. Misc., 429, 1877 (defines area and gives habitat).

Latham used the term Pima in 1850, citing under it three dialects or languages. Subsequently, in 1856, he used the same term for one of the five divisions into which he separates the languages of Sonora and Sinaloa.

The same year Turner gave a brief account of Pima as a distinct language, his remarks applying mainly to Pima proper of the Gila River, Arizona. This tribe had been visited by Emory and Johnston and also described by Bartlett. Turner refers to a short vocabulary in the Mithridates, another of Dr. Coulter's in Royal Geological Society Journal, vol. XI, 1841, and a third by Parry in Schoolcraft, Indian Tribes, vol. III, 1853. The short vocabulary he himself published was collected by Lieut. Whipple.

Only a small portion of the territory occupied by this family is included within the United States, the greater portion being in Mexico where it extends to the Gulf of California. The family is represented in the United States by three tribes, Pima alta, Sobaipuri, and Papago. The former have lived for at least two centuries with the

---

[1] Cont. N. A. Eth. vol. 3, p. 267.

Maricopa on the Gila River about 160 miles from the mouth. The Sobaipuri occupied the Santa Cruz and San Pedro Rivers, tributaries of the Gila, but are no longer known. The Papago territory is much more extensive and extends to the south across the border. In recent times the two tribes have been separated, but the Pima territory as shown upon the map was formerly continuous to the Gila River.

According to Buschmann, Gatschet, Brinton, and others the Pima language is a northern branch of the Nahuatl, but this relationship has yet to be demonstrated.[1]

PRINCIPAL TRIBES.

Northern group:		
Opata.	Papago.	Pima.
Southern group:		
Cahita.	Tarahumara.	Tepeguana.
Cora.		

Population.—Of the above tribes the Pima and Papago only are within our boundaries. Their numbers under the Pima Agency, Arizona,[2] are Pima, 4,464; Papago, 5,163.

PUJUNAN FAMILY.

>Pujuni, Latham in Trans. Philolog. Soc. Lond., 80, 1856 (contains Pujuni, Secumne, Tsamak of Hale, Cushna of Schoolcraft). Latham, Opuscula, 346, 1860.

>Meidoos, Powers in Overland Monthly, 420, May, 1874.

=Meidoo, Gatschet in Mag. Am. Hist., 159, 1877 (gives habitat and tribes). Gatschet in Beach, Ind. Misc., 433, 1877.

>Mai'-du, Powers in Cont. N. A. Eth., III, 282, 1877 (same as Mai'-deh; general account of; names the tribes). Powell, ibid., 586 (vocabs. of Kon'-kau, Hol-o'-lu-pai, Na'-kum, Ni'-shi-nam, "Digger," Cushna, Nishinam, Yuba or Nevada, Punjuni, Sekumne, Tsamak).

>Neeshenams, Powers in Overland Monthly, 21, Jan., 1874 (considers this tribe doubtfully distinct from Meidoo family).

>Ni-shi-nam, Powers in Cont. N. A. Eth., III, 313, 1877 (distinguishes them from Maidu family).

×Sacramento Valley, Keane, App. Stanford's Comp. (Cent. and So. Am.), 476, 1878 (Ochecumne, Chupumne, Secumne, Cosumne, Sololumne, Puzlumne, Yasumne, etc.; "altogether about 26 tribes").

The following tribes were placed in this group by Latham: Pujuni, Secumne, Tsamak of Hale, and the Cushna of Schoolcraft. The name adopted for the family is the name of a tribe given by Hale.[3] This was one of the two races into which, upon the information of Captain Sutter as derived by Mr. Dana, all the Sacramento tribes

---

[1] Buschmann, Die Pima-Sprache und die Sprache der Koloschen, pp. 321–432.

[2] According to the U. S. Census Bulletin for 1890.

[3] U. S. Expl. Exp., vi, p. 631.

were believed to be divided. "These races resembled one another in every respect but language."

Hale gives short vocabularies of the Pujuni, Sekumne, and Tsamak. Hale did not apparently consider the evidence as a sufficient basis for a family, but apparently preferred to leave its status to be settled later.

GEOGRAPHIC DISTRIBUTION.

The tribes of this family have been carefully studied by Powers, to whom we are indebted for most all we know of their distribution. They occupied the eastern bank of the Sacramento in California, beginning some 80 or 100 miles from its mouth, and extended northward to within a short distance of Pit River, where they met the tribes of the Palaihnihan family. Upon the east they reached nearly to the border of the State, the Palaihnihan, Shoshonean, and Washoan families hemming them in in this direction.

PRINCIPAL TRIBES.

Bayu.	Kū'lmeh.	Tíshum.
Boka.	Kulomum.	Toámtcha.
Eskin.	Kwatóa.	Tosikoyo.
Hélto.	Nakum.	Toto.
Hoak.	Olla.	Ustóma.
Hoankut.	Otaki.	Wapúmni.
Hololúpai.	Paupákan.	Wima.
Koloma.	Pusúna.	Yuba.
Konkau.	Taitchida.	

QUORATEAN FAMILY.

>Quoratem, Gibbs in Schoolcraft, Ind. Tribes, III, 422, 1853 (proposed as a proper name of family "should it be held one").

>Eh-nek, Gibbs in Schoolcraft, Ind. Tribes, III, 422, 1853 (given as name of a band only; but suggests Quoratem as a proper family name).

>Ehnik, Latham in Trans. Philolog. Soc. Lond., 76, 1856 (south of Shasti and Lutuami areas). Latham, Opuscula, 342, 1860.

=Cahrocs, Powers in Overland Monthly, 328, April, 1872 (on Klamath and Salmon Rivers).

=Cahrok, Gatschet in Beach, Ind. Misc., 438, 1877.

=Ka'-rok, Powers in Cont. N. A. Eth., III, 19, 1877. Powell in ibid., 447, 1877 (vocabularies of Ka'-rok, Arra-Arra, Peh'-tsik, Eh-nek).

<Klamath, Keane, App. to Stanford's Comp. (Cent. and So. Am.), 475, 1878 (cited as including Cahrocs).

Derivation: Name of a band at mouth of Salmon River, California. Etymology unknown.

This family name is equivalent to the Cahroc or Karok of Powers and later authorities.

In 1853, as above cited, Gibbs gives Eh-nek as the titular heading of his paragraphs upon the language of this family, with the remark that it is "The name of a band at the mouth of the Salmon, or Quoratem river." He adds that "This latter name may perhaps be considered as proper to give to the family, should it be held one." He defines the territory occupied by the family as follows: "The language reaches from Bluff creek, the upper boundary of the Pohlik, to about Clear creek, thirty or forty miles above the Salmon; varying, however, somewhat from point to point."

The presentation of the name Quoratem, as above, seems sufficiently formal, and it is therefore accepted for the group first indicated by Gibbs.

In 1856 Latham renamed the family Ehnik, after the principal band, locating the tribe, or rather the language, south of the Shasti and Lutuami areas.

GEOGRAPHIC DISTRIBUTION.

The geographic limits of the family are somewhat indeterminate, though the main area occupied by the tribes is well known. The tribes occupy both banks of the lower Klamath from a range of hills a little above Happy Camp to the junction of the Trinity, and the Salmon River from its mouth to its sources. On the north, Quoratean tribes extended to the Athapascan territory near the Oregon line.

TRIBES.

Ehnek.   Karok.   Pehtsik.

Population.—According to a careful estimate made by Mr. Curtin in the region in 1889, the Indians of this family number about 600.

SALINAN FAMILY.

< Salinas, Latham in Trans. Philolog. Soc. Lond., 85,1856 (includes Gioloco, Ruslen, Soledad of Mofras, Eslen, Carmel, San Antonio, San Miguel). Latham, Opuscula, 350, 1860.

> San Antonio, Powell in Cont. N. A. Eth., III, 568, 1877 (vocabulary of; not given as a family, but kept by itself).

< Santa Barbara, Gatschet in Mag. Am. Hist., 157, 1877 (cited here as containing San Antonio). Gatschet in U. S. Geog. Surv. W. 100th M., VII, 419, 1879 (contains San Antonio, San Miguel).

× Runsiens, Keane, App. Stanford's Comp. (Cent. and So. Am.), 476, 1878 (San Miguel of his group belongs here).

Derivation: From river of same name.

The language formerly spoken at the Missions of San Antonio and San Miguel in Monterey County, California, have long occupied a doubtful position. By some they have been considered distinct, not only from each other, but from all other languages. Others have held that they represent distinct dialects of the Chumashan (Santa Barbara) group of languages. Vocabularies collected in 1884 by Mr. Henshaw show clearly that the two are closely connected dialects and that they are in no wise related to any other family.

The group established by Latham under the name Salinas is a heterogeneous one, containing representatives of no fewer than four distinct families. Gioloco, which he states "may possibly belong to this group, notwithstanding its reference to the Mission of San Francisco," really is congeneric with the vocabularies assigned by Latham to the Mendocinan family. The "Soledad of Mofras" belongs to the Costanoan family mentioned on page 348 of the same essay, as also do the Ruslen and Carmel. Of the three remaining forms of speech, Eslen, San Antonio, and San Miguel, the two latter are related dialects, and belong within the drainage of the Salinas River. The term Salinan is hence applied to them, leaving the Eslen language to be provided with a name.

Population.—Though the San Antonio and San Miguel were probably never very populous tribes, the Missions of San Antonio and San Miguel, when first established in the years 1771 and 1779, contained respectively 1,400 and 1,200 Indians. Doubtless the larger number of these converts were gathered in the near vicinity of the two missions and so belonged to this family. In 1884 when Mr. Henshaw visited the missions he was able to learn of the existence of only about a dozen Indians of this family, and not all of these could speak their own language.

SALISHAN FAMILY.

>Salish, Gallatin in Trans. Am. Antiq. Soc., II, 134, 306, 1836 (or Flat Heads only). Latham in Proc. Philolog. Soc. Lond., II, 31–50, 1846 (of Duponceau. Said to be the Okanagan of Tolmie).

× Salish, Keane, App. Stanford's Comp. (Cent. and So. Am.), 460, 474, 1878 (includes Flatheads, Kalispelms, Skitsuish, Colvilles, Quarlpi, Spokanes, Pisquouse, Soaiatlpi).

= Salish, Bancroft, Nat. Races, III, 565, 618, 1882.

> Selish, Gallatin in Trans. Am. Eth. Soc. II, pt. 1, 77, 1848 (vocab. of Nsietshaws). Tolmie and Dawson, Comp. Vocabs,, 63, 78, 1884 (vocabularies of Lillooet and Kullëspelm).

> Jelish, Gallatin in Schoolcraft, Ind. Tribes, III, 402, 1853 (obvious misprint for Selish; follows Hale as to tribes).

= Selish, Gatschet in Mag. Am. Hist., 169, 1877 (gives habitat and tribes of family). Gatschet in Beach, Ind. Misc., 444, 1877.

< Selish, Dall, after Gibbs, in Cont. N. A. Eth., I, 241, 1877 (includes Yakama, which is Shahaptian).

> Tsihaili-Selish, Hale in U. S. Expl. Exp., VI, 205, 535, 569, 1846 (includes Shushwaps. Selish or Flatheads, Skitsuish, Piskwaus, Skwale, Tsihailish, Kawelitsk, Nsietshawus). Gallatin in Trans. Am. Eth. Soc., II, pt. 1, c, 10, 1848 (after Hale). Berghaus (1851), Physik. Atlas, map 17, 1852. Buschmann, Spuren der aztek. Sprache, 658–661, 1859. Latham, El. Comp. Phil., 399, 1862 (contains Shushwap or Atna Proper, Kuttelspelm or Pend d'Oreilles, Selish, Spokan, Okanagan, Skitsuish, Piskwaus, Nusdalum, Kawitchen, Cathlascou, Skwali, Chechili, Kwaintl, Kwenaiwtl, Nsietshawus, Billechula).

> Atnahs, Gallatin in Trans. Am. Antiq. Soc., II, 134, 135, 306, 1836 (on Fraser River). Prichard, Phys. Hist. Mankind, V, 427, 1847 (on Fraser River).

\> Atna, Latham in Trans. Philolog. Soc. Lond., 71, 1856 (Tsihaili-Selish of Hale and Gallatin).

✕ Nootka-Columbian, Scouler in Jour. Roy. Geog. Soc. Lond., XI, 224, 1841 (includes, among others, Billechoola, Kawitchen, Noosdalum, Squallyamish of present family).

✕ Insular, Scouler, ibid., (same as Nootka-Columbian family).

✕ Shahaptan, Scouler, ibid., 225 (includes Okanagan of this family).

✕ Southern, Scouler, ibid., 224 (same as Nootka-Columbian family).

\> Billechoola, Latham in Jour. Eth. Soc. Lond., I, 154, 1848 (assigns Friendly Village of McKenzie here). Latham, Opuscula, 250, 1860 (gives Tolmie's vocabulary).

\> Billechula, Latham, Nat. Hist. Man, 300, 1850 (mouth of Salmon River). Latham in Trans. Philolog. Soc. Lond., 72, 1856 (same). Latham, Opuscula, 339, 1860.

\> Bellacoola, Bancroft, Nat. Races, III, 564, 607, 1882 (Bellacoolas only; specimen vocabulary).

\> Bilhoola, Tolmie and Dawson, Comp. Vocabs., 62, 1884 (vocab. of Noothlākimish).

\> Bílchula, Boas in Petermann's Mitteilungen, 130, 1887 (mentions Sātsq, Nūteˌl, Nuchalkmχ, Taleómχ).

✕ Naass, Gallatin in Trans. Am. Eth. Soc. II, pt. 1, c, 77, 1848 (cited as including Billechola).

\> Tsihaili, Latham, Nat. Hist. Man, 310, 1850 (chiefly lower part of Fraser River and between that and the Columbia; includes Shuswap, Salish, Skitsuish, Piskwaus, Kawitchen, Skwali, Checheeli, Kowelits, Noosdalum, Nsietshawus).

✕ Wakash, Latham, Nat. Hist. Man, 301, 1850 (cited as including Klallems).

✕ Shushwaps, Keane, App. Stanford's Comp. (Cent. and So. Am.), 460, 474, 1878 (quoted as including Shewhapmuch and Okanagans).

✕ Hydahs, Keane, ibid., 473 (includes Bellacoolas of present family).

✕ Nootkahs, Keane, ibid., 473 (includes Komux, Kowitchans, Klallums, Kwantlums, Teets of present family).

✕ Nootka, Bancroft, Nat. Races, III, 564, 1882 (contains the following Salishan tribes: Cowichin, Soke, Comux, Noosdalum, Wickinninish, Songhie, Sanetch, Kwantlum, Teet, Nanaimo, Newchemass, Shimiahmoo, Nooksak, Samish, Skagit, Snohomish, Clallam, Toanhooch).

\< Puget Sound Group, Keane, App. Stanford's Comp. (Cent. and So. Am.), 474, 1878 (comprises Nooksahs, Lummi, Samish, Skagits, Nisqually, Neewamish, Sahmamish, Snohomish, Skeewamish, Squanamish, Klallums, Classets, Chehalis, Cowlitz, Pistchin, Chinakum; all but the last being Salishan).

\> Flatheads, Keane, ibid., 474, 1878 (same as his Salish above).

\> Kawitshin, Tolmie and Dawson, Comp. Vocabs., 39, 1884 (vocabs. of Songis and Kwantlin Sept and Kowmook or Tlathool).

\> Qauitschin, Boas in Petermann's Mitteilungen, 131, 1887.

\> Niskwalli, Tolmie and Dawson, Comp. Vocabs., 50, 121, 1884 (or Skwalliamish vocabulary of Sinahomish).

The extent of the Salish or Flathead family was unknown to Gallatin, as indeed appears to have been the exact locality of the tribe of which he gives an anonymous vocabulary from the Duponceau collection. The tribe is stated to have resided upon one of the branches of the Columbia River, "which must be either the most southern branch of Clarke's River or the most northern branch of Lewis's River." The former supposition was correct. As employed by Gallatin the family embraced only a single tribe, the Flathead tribe proper. The Atnah, a Salishan tribe, were considered by Gallatin to be distinct, and the name would be eligible as the family name ; preference, however, is given to Salish. The few words from the Friendly Village near the sources of the Salmon River given by Gallatin in Archæologia Americana, II, 1836, pp. 15, 306, belong under this family.

GEOGRAPHIC DISTRIBUTION.

Since Gallatin's time, through the labors of Riggs, Hale, Tolmie, Dawson, Boas, and others, our knowledge of the territorial limits of this linguistic family has been greatly extended. The most southern outpost of the family, the Tillamook and Nestucca, were established on the coast of Oregon, about 50 miles to the south of the Columbia, where they were quite separated from their kindred to the north by the Chinookan tribes. Beginning on the north side of Shoalwater Bay, Salishan tribes held the entire northwestern part of Washington, including the whole of the Puget Sound region, except only the Macaw territory about Cape Flattery, and two insignificant spots, one near Port Townsend, the other on the Pacific coast to the south of Cape Flattery, which were occupied by Chimakuan tribes. Eastern Vancouver Island to about midway of its length was also held by Salishan tribes, while the great bulk of their territory lay on the mainland opposite and included much of the upper Columbia. On the south they were hemmed in mainly by the Shahaptian tribes. Upon the east Salishan tribes dwelt to a little beyond the Arrow Lakes and their feeder, one of the extreme north forks of the Columbia. Upon the southeast Salishan tribes extended into Montana, including the upper drainage of the Columbia. They were met here in 1804 by Lewis and Clarke. On the northeast Salish territory extended to about the fifty-third parallel. In the northwest it did not reach the Chilcat River.

Within the territory thus indicated there is considerable diversity of customs and a greater diversity of language. The language is split into a great number of dialects, many of which are doubtless mutually unintelligible.

The relationship of this family to the Wakashan is a very interesting problem. Evidences of radical affinity have been discovered by Boas and Gatschet, and the careful study of their nature and extent now being prosecuted by the former may result in the union of the two, though until recently they have been considered quite distinct.

PRINCIPAL TRIBES.

Atnah.	Copalis.	Met'how.
Bellacoola.	Cowichin.	Nanaimo.
Chehalis.	Cowlitz.	Nanoos.
Clallam.	Dwamish.	Nehalim.
Colville.	Kwantlen.	Nespelum.
Comux.	Lummi.	Nicoutamuch.

PRINCIPAL TRIBES—continued.

Nisqualli.	Sans Puell.	Snoqualmi.
Nuksahk.	Satsop.	Soke.
Okinagan.	Sawamish.	Songish.
Pend d'Oreilles.	Sekamish.	Spokan.
Pentlatc.	Shomamish.	Squawmisht.
Pisquow.	Shooswap.	Squaxon.
Puyallup.	Shotlemamish.	Squonamish.
Quaitso.	Skagit.	Stehtsasamish.
Queniut.	Skihwamish.	Stillacum.
Queptlmamish.	Skitsuish.	Sumass.
Sacumehu.	Skokomish.	Suquamish.
Sahewamish.	Skopamish.	Swinamish.
Salish.	Sktehlmish.	Tait.
Samamish.	Smulkamish.	Tillamook.
Samish.	Snohomish.	Twana.
Sanetch.		

Population.—The total Salish population of British Columbia is 12,325, inclusive of the Bellacoola, who number, with the Hailtzuk, 2,500, and those in the list of unclassified, who number 8,522, distributed as follows:

Under the Fraser River Agency, 4,986; Kamloops Agency, 2,579; Cowichan Agency, 1,852; Okanagan Agency, 942; Williams Lake Agency, 1,918; Kootenay Agency, 48.

Most of the Salish in the United States are on reservations. They number about 5,500, including a dozen small tribes upon the Yakama Reservation, which have been consolidated with the Clickatat (Shahaptian) through intermarriage. The Salish of the United States are distributed as follows (Indian Affairs Report, 1889, and U. S. Census Bulletin, 1890):

Colville Agency, Washington, Cœur d' Alene, 422; Lower Spokane, 417; Lake, 303; Colville, 247; Okinagan, 374; Nespilem, 67; San Pueblo (Sans Puell), 300; Calispel, 200; Upper Spokane, 170.

Puyallup Agency, Washington, Quaitso, 82; Quinaielt (Queniut), 101; Humptulip, 19; Puyallup, 563; Chehalis, 135; Nisqually, 94; Squaxon, 60; Clallam, 351; Skokomish, 191; Oyhut, Hoquiam, Montesano, and Satsup, 29.

Tulalip Agency, Washington, Snohomish, 443; Madison, 144; Muckleshoot, 103; Swinomish, 227; Lummi, 295.

Grande Ronde Agency, Oregon, Tillamook, 5.

SASTEAN FAMILY.

= Saste, Hale in U. S. Expl. Exp., VI, 218, 569, 1846. Gallatin in Trans. Am. Eth. Soc., II, pt. 1, c, 77, 1848. Berghaus (1851), Physik. Atlas, map 17, 1852. Buschmann, Spuren der aztek. Sprache, 572, 1859.

= Shasty, Hale in U. S. Expl. Exp., VI, 218, 1846 (= Saste).   Buschmann, Spuren der
    aztek. Sprache, 572, 1859 (= Saste).
= Shasties, Hale in U. S. Expl. Exp., VI, 199, 569, 1846 (= Saste).   Berghaus (1851),
    Physik. Atlas, map 17, 1852.
= Shasti,Latham, Nat. Hist. Man, 325, 1850 (southwest of Lutuami).   Latham in Proc.
    Philolog. Soc., Lond., VI, 82, 1854.   Latham, ibid, 74, 1856.   Latham, Opuscula,
    310, 341, 1860 (allied to both Shoshonean and Shahaptian families).   Latham,
    El. Comp. Phil., 407, 1862.
== Shasté, Gibbs in Schoolcraft, Ind. Tribes, III, 422, 1853 (mentions Watsa-he'-wa,
    a Scott's River band).
= Sasti, Gallatin in Schoolcraft, Ind. Tribes, III, 402, 1853 (= Shasties).
= Shasta, Powell in Cont. N. A. Eth., III, 607, 1877.   Gatschet in Mag. Am. Hist., 164,
    1877.   Gatschet in Beach, Ind. Misc., 438, 1877.
= Shas-tí-ka, Powers in Cont. N. A. Eth., III, 243, 1877.
= Shasta, Gatschet in Mag. Am. Hist., 164, 1877 (==Shasteecas).
< Shasta, Bancroft, Nat. Races, III. 565, 1882 (includes Palaik, Watsahewah, Shasta).
< Klamath, Keane, App. Stanford's Comp. (Cent. and So. Am.), 475, 1878 (contains
    Shastas of present family).

Derivation : The single tribe upon the language of which Hale
based his name was located by him to the southwest of the Lutuami
or Klamath tribes.   He calls the tribe indifferently Shasties or
Shasty, but the form applied by him to the family (see pp. 218, 569)
is Saste, which accordingly is the one taken.

GEOGRAPHIC DISTRIBUTION.

The former territory of the Sastean family is the region drained
by the Klamath River and its tributaries from the western base of
the Cascade range to the point where the Klamath flows through the
ridge of hills east of Happy Camp, which forms the boundary between the Sastean and the Quoratean families.   In addition to this
region of the Klamath, the Shasta extended over the Siskiyou range
northward as far as Ashland, Oregon.

SHAHAPTIAN FAMILY.

× Shahaptan, Scouler in Jour. Roy. Geog. Soc., XI, 225, 1841 (three tribes, Shahaptan
    or Nez-percés, Kliketat, Okanagan; the latter being Salishan).
< Shahaptan, Prichard, Phys. Hist. Mankind, V, 428, 1847 (two classes, Nez-perces
    proper of mountains, and Polanches of plains; includes also Kliketat and
    Okanagan).
> Sahaptin, Hale in U. S. Expl. Expd., VI, 198, 212, 542, 1846 (Shahaptin or Nez-percés,
    Wallawallas, Pelooses, Yakemas, Klikatats).   Gallatin in Trans. Am. Eth. Soc.,
    II, pt. 1, c, 14, 1848 (follows Hale).   Gallatin, ibid., II, pt. 1, c, 77, 1848 (Nez-percés
    only).   Berghaus (1851), Physik. Atlas, map 17, 1852.   Gallatin in Schoolcraft,
    Ind. Tribes, III, 402, 1853 (Nez-perces and Wallawallas).   Dall, after Gibbs, in
    Cont. N. A. Eth., I, 241, 1877 (includes Taitinapam and Kliketat).
> Saptin, Prichard, Phys. Hist. Mankind, V, 428, 1847 (or Shahaptan).
< Sahaptin, Latham, Nat. Hist. Man, 323, 1850 (includes Wallawallas, Kliketat,
    Proper Sahaptin or Nez-percés, Pelús, Yakemas, Cayús ?).   Latham in Trans.
    Philolog. Soc. Lond., 73, 1856 (includes Waiilatpu).   Buschmann, Spuren der

aztek. Sprache, 614, 615, 1859. Latham, Opuscula, 340, 1860 (as in 1856).
Latham, El. Comp. Phil., 440, 1862 (vocabularies Sahaptin, Wallawalla, Kliketat).
Keane, App. Stanford's Comp. (Cent. and So. Am.), 460, 474, 1878 (includes Pa-
louse, Walla Wallas, Yakimas, Tairtlas, Kliketats or Pshawanwappams, Cayuse,
Mollale; the two last are Waiilatpuan).

= Sahaptin, Gatschet in Mag. Am. Hist., 168, 1877 (defines habitat and enumerates
tribes of). Gatschet in Beach, Ind. Misc., 443, 1877. Bancroft, Nat. Races, III,
565, 620, 1882.

> Shahaptani, Tolmie and Dawson, Comp. Vocabs., 78, 1884 (Whulwhaipum tribe).

> Nez-percés, Prichard, Phys. Hist. Mankind, v, 428, 1847 (see Shahaptan). Keane,
App. Stanford's Comp. (Cent. and So. Am.), 474, 1878 (see his Sahaptin).

× Selish, Dall, after Gibbs, in Cont. N. A. Eth., I, 241, 1877 (includes Yakama which
belongs here).

Derivation: From a Selish word of unknown significance.

The Shahaptan family of Scouler comprised three tribes—the Shahaptan or Nez Percés, the Kliketat, a scion of the Shahaptan, dwell-
ing near Mount Ranier, and the Okanagan, inhabiting the upper part
of Fraser River and its tributaries ; "these tribes were asserted to
speak dialects of the same language." Of the above tribes the Okinagan are now known to be Salishan.

The vocabularies given by Scouler were collected by Tolmie. The
term "Sahaptin" appears on Gallatin's map of 1836, where it doubtless
refers only to the Nez Percé tribe proper, with respect to whose linguistic affinities Gallatin apparently knew nothing at the time. At
all events the name occurs nowhere in his discussion of the linguistic
families.

GEOGRAPHIC DISTRIBUTION.

The tribes of this family occupied a large section of country along
the Columbia and its tributaries. Their western boundary was the
Cascade Mountains ; their westernmost bands, the Klikitat on the
north, the Tyigh and Warm Springs on the south, enveloping for a
short distance the Chinook territory along the Columbia which extended to the Dalles. Shahaptian tribes extended along the tributaries of the Columbia for a considerable distance, their northern
boundary being indicated by about the forty-sixth parallel, their
southern by about the forty-fourth. Their eastern extension was in-
terrupted by the Bitter Root Mountains.

PRINCIPAL TRIBES AND POPULATION.

Chopunnish (Nez Percé), 1,515 on Nez Percé Reservation, Idaho.
Klikitat, say one-half of 330 natives, on Yakama Reservation,
Washington.
Paloos, Yakama Reservation, number unknown.
Tenaino, 69 on Warm Springs Reservation, Oregon.
Tyigh, 430 on Warm Springs Reservation, Oregon.
Umatilla, 179 on Umatilla Reservation, Oregon.
Walla Walla, 405 on Umatilla Reservation, Oregon.

184   INDIAN LINGUISTIC FAMILIES.

SHOSHONEAN FAMILY.

>Shoshonees, Gallatin in Trans. and Coll. Am. Antiq. Soc., II, 120, 133, 306, 1836
(Shoshonee or Snake only). Hale in U. S. Expl. Exp., VI, 218, 1846 (Wihinasht,
Pánasht, Yutas, Sampiches, Comanches). Gallatin in Trans. Am. Eth. Soc., II,
pt. 1, c, 77, 1848 (as above). Gallatin, ibid., 18, 1848 (follows Hale; see below).
Gallatin in Schoolcraft, Ind. Tribes, III, 402, 1853. Turner in Pac. R. R. Rep., III,
pt. 3, 55, 71, 76, 1856 (treats only of Comanche, Chemehuevi, Cahuillo). Buschmann, Spuren der aztek. Sprache, 552, 649, 1859.

>Shoshoni, Hale in U. S. Expl. Exp., VI, 199, 218, 569, 1846 (Shoshóni, Wihinasht,
Pánasht, Yutas, Sampiches, Comanches). Latham in Trans. Philolog. Soc.
Lond., 73, 1856. Latham, Opuscula, 340, 1860.

>Schoschonenu Kamantschen, Berghaus (1845), Physik. Atlas, map 17, 1848. Ibid.,
1852.

>Shoshones, Prichard, Phys. Hist. Mankind, V, 429, 1847 (or Snakes; both sides
Rocky Mountains and sources of Missouri).

=Shóshoni, Gatschet in Mag. Am. Hist. 154, 1877. Gatschet in Beach, Ind. Misc., 426,
1877.

<Shoshone, Keane, App. Stanford's Comp. (Cent. and So. Am.), 460, 477, 1878 (in-
cludes Washoes of a distinct family). Bancroft, Nat. Races, III, 567, 661, 1882.

>Snake, Gallatin in Trans. and Coll. Am. Antiq. Soc., II, 120, 133, 1836 (or Sho-
shonees). Hale in U. S. Expl. Exp., VI, 218, 1846 (as under Shoshonee). Prichard, Phys. Hist. Mankind, V, 429, 1847 (as under Shoshones). Turner in Pac.
R. R. Rep., III, pt. 3, 76, 1856 (as under Shoshonees). Buschmann, Spuren der
aztek. Sprache, 552, 649, 1859 (as under Shoshonees).

<Snake, Keane, App. Stanford's Comp. (Cent. and So. Am.), 477, 1878 (contains
Washoes in addition to Shoshonean tribes proper).

>Kizh, Hale in U. S. Expl. Exp., VI, 569, 1846 (San Gabriel language only).

>Netela, Hale, ibid., 569, 1846 (San Juan Capestrano language).

>Paduca, Prichard, Phys. Hist. Mankind, V, 415, 1847 (Cumanches, Kiawas, Utas).
Latham, Nat. Hist., Man, 310, 326, 1850. Latham (1853) in Proc. Philolog. Soc.
Lond., VI, 73, 1854 (includes Wihinast, Shoshoni, Uta). Latham in Trans.
Philolog. Soc. Lond., 96, 1856. Latham, Opuscula, 300, 360, 1860.

<Paduca, Latham, Nat. Hist. Man., 346, 1850 (Wihinast, Bonaks, Diggers, Utahs,
Sampiches, Shoshonis, Kiaways, Kaskaias?, Keneways?, Bald-heads, Cumanches,
Navahoes, Apaches, Carisos). Latham, El. Comp. Phil., 440, 1862 (defines area
of; cites vocabs. of Shoshoni, Wihinasht, Uta, Comanch, Piede or Pa-uta,
Chemuhuevi, Cahuillo, Kioway, the latter not belonging here).

>Cumanches, Gallatin in Schoolcraft, Ind. Tribes, III, 402, 1853.

>Netela-Kij, Latham (1853) in Trans. Philolog. Soc. Lond., VI, 76, 1854 (composed of
Netela of Hale, San Juan Capistrano of Coulter, San Gabriel of Coulter, Kij of
Hale).

>Capistrano, Latham in Proc. Philolog. Soc. Lond., 85, 1856 (includes Netela, of San
Luis Rey and San Juan Capistrano, the San Gabriel or Kij of San Gabriel and
San Fernando).

In his synopsis of the Indian tribes' Gallatin's reference to this
great family is of the most vague and unsatisfactory sort. He speaks
of "some bands of Snake Indians or Shoshonees, living on the waters
of the river Columbia" (p. 120), which is almost the only allusion to
them to be found. The only real claim he possesses to the author-
ship of the family name is to be found on page 306, where, in his list

[1] Trans. and Coll. Am. Antiq. Soc., II, 1836.

of tribes and vocabularies, he places "Shoshonees" among his other families, which is sufficient to show that he regarded them as a distinct linguistic group. The vocabulary he possessed was by Say.

Buschmann, as above cited, classes the Shoshonean languages as a northern branch of his Nahuatl or Aztec family, but the evidence presented for this connection is deemed to be insufficient.

GEOGRAPHIC DISTRIBUTION,

This important family occupied a large part of the great interior basin of the United States. Upon the north Shoshonean tribes extended far into Oregon, meeting Shahaptian territory on about the forty-fourth parallel or along the Blue Mountains. Upon the northeast the eastern limits of the pristine habitat of the Shoshonean tribes are unknown. The narrative of Lewis and Clarke[1] contains the explicit statement that the Shoshoni bands encountered upon the Jefferson River, whose summer home was upon the head waters of the Columbia, formerly lived within their own recollection in the plains to the east of the Rocky Mountains, whence they were driven to their mountain retreats by the Minnetaree (Atsina), who had obtained firearms. Their former habitat thus given is indicated upon the map, although the eastern limit is of course quite indeterminate. Very likely much of the area occupied by the Atsina was formerly Shoshonean territory. Later a division of the Bannock held the finest portion of southwestern Montana,[2] whence apparently they were being pushed westward across the mountains by Blackfeet.[3] Upon the east the Tukuarika or Sheepeaters held the Yellowstone Park country, where they were bordered by Siouan territory, while the Washaki occupied southwestern Wyoming. Nearly the entire mountainous part of Colorado was held by the several bands of the Ute, the eastern and southeastern parts of the State being held respectively by the Arapaho and Cheyenne (Algonquian), and the Kaiowe (Kiowan). To the southeast the Ute country included the northern drainage of the San Juan, extending farther east a short distance into New Mexico. The Comanche division of the family extended farther east than any other. According to Crow tradition the Comanche formerly lived northward in the Snake River region. Omaha tradition avers that the Comanche were on the Middle Loup River, probably within the present century. Bourgemont found a Comanche tribe on the upper Kansas River in 1724. According to Pike the Comanche territory bordered the Kaiowe on the north, the former occupying the head waters of the upper Red River, Arkansas, and Rio Grande. How

---

[1] Allen ed., Philadelphia, 1814, vol. 1, p. 418.

[2] U. S. Ind. Aff., 1869, p. 289.

[3] Stevens in Pac. R. R. Rep., 1855, vol. 1, p. 329.

far to the southward Shoshonean tribes extended at this early period is not known, though the evidence tends to show that they raided far down into Texas to the territory they have occupied in more recent years, viz, the extensive plains from the Rocky Mountains eastward into Indian Territory and Texas to about 97°. Upon the south Shoshonean territory was limited generally by the Colorado River. The Chemehuevi lived on both banks of the river between the Mohave on the north and the Cuchan on the south, above and below Bill Williams Fork. The Kwaiantikwoket also lived to the east of the river in Arizona about Navajo Mountain, while the Tusayan (Moki) had established their seven pueblos, including one founded by people of Tañoan stock, to the east of the Colorado Chiquito. In the southwest Shoshonean tribes had pushed across California, occupying a wide band of country to the Pacific. In their extension northward they had reached as far as Tulare Lake, from which territory apparently they had dispossessed the Mariposan tribes, leaving a small remnant of that linguistic family near Fort Tejon.

A little farther north they had crossed the Sierras and occupied the heads of San Joaquin and Kings Rivers. Northward they occupied nearly the whole of Nevada, being limited on the west by the Sierra Nevada. The entire southeastern part of Oregon was occupied by tribes of Shoshoni extraction.

PRINCIPAL TRIBES AND POPULATION.

Bannock, 514 on Fort Hall Reservation and 75 on the Lemhi Reservation, Idaho.

Chemehuevi, about 202 attached to the Colorado River Agency, Arizona.

Comanche, 1,598 on the Kiowa, Comanche and Wichita Reservation, Indian Territory.

Gosiute, 256 in Utah at large.

Pai Ute, about 2,300 scattered in southeastern California and southwestern Nevada.

Paviotso, about 3,000 scattered in western Nevada and southern Oregon.

Saidyuka, 145 under Klamath Agency.

Shoshoni, 979 under Fort Hall Agency and 249 at the Lemhi Agency.

Tobikhar, about 2,200, under the Mission Agency, California.

Tukuarika, or Sheepeaters, 108 at Lemhi Agency.

Tusayan (Moki), 1,996 (census of 1890).

Uta, 2,839 distributed as follows : 985 under Southern Ute Agency, Colorado; 1,021 on Ouray Reserve, Utah; 833 on Uintah Reserve, Utah.

SIOUAN FAMILY.

✕ Sioux, Gallatin in Trans. and Coll. Am. Antiq. Soc., II, 121, 306, 1836 (for tribes included see text below). Prichard, Phys. Hist. Mankind, V, 408, 1847 (follows Gallatin). Gallatin in Trans. Am. Eth. Soc., II, pt. 1, xcix, 77, 1848 (as in 1836). Berghaus (1845), Physik. Atlas, map 17, 1848. Ibid., 1852. Gallatin in Schoolcraft, Ind. Tribes, III, 402, 1853. Berghaus, Physik. Atlas, map 72, 1887.

> Sioux, Latham, Nat. Hist. Man, 333, 1850 (includes Winebagoes, Dakotas, Assineboins, Upsaroka, Mandans, Minetari, Osage). Latham in Trans. Philolog. Soc. Lond., 58, 1856 (mere mention of family). Latham, Opuscula, 327, 1860. Latham, El. Comp. Phil., 458, 1862.

> Catawbas, Gallatin in Trans. and Coll. Am. Antiq. Soc., II, 87, 1836 (Catawbas and Woccons). Bancroft, Hist. U. S., III, 245, et map, 1840. Prichard, Phys. Hist. Mankind, V, 399, 1847. Gallatin in Trans. Am. Eth. Soc., II, pt. 1, xcix, 77, 1848. Keane, App. Stanford's Comp. (Cent. and So. Am.), 460, 473, 1878.

> Catahbas, Berghaus (1845), Physik. Atlas, map 17, 1848. Ibid., 1852.

> Catawba, Latham, Nat. Hist. Man., 334, 1850 (Woccoon are allied). Gallatin in Schoolcraft, Ind. Tribes, III, 401, 1853.

> Kataba, Gatschet in Am. Antiquarian, IV, 238, 1882. Gatschet, Creek Mig. Legend, I, 15, 1884. Gatschet in Science, 413, April 29, 1887.

> Woccons, Gallatin in Trans. and Coll. Am. Antiq. Soc., II, 306, 1836 (numbered and given as a distinct family in table, but inconsistently noted in foot-note where referred to as Catawban family.)

> Dahcotas, Bancroft, Hist. U.S., III, 243, 1840.

> Dakotas, Hayden, Cont. Eth. and Phil. Missouri Ind., 232, 1862 (treats of Dakotas, Assiniboins, Crows, Minnitarees, Mandans, Omahas, Iowas).

> Dacotah, Keane, App. to Stanford's Comp. (Cent. and So. Am.), 460, 470, 1878. (The following are the main divisions given: Isaunties, Sissetons, Yantons, Teetons, Assiniboines, Winnebagos, Punkas, Omahas, Missouris, Iowas. Otoes, Kaws, Quappas, Osages, Upsarocas, Minnetarees.)

> Dakota, Berghaus, Physik. Atlas, map 72, 1887.

Derivation: A corruption of the Algonkin word "nadowe-ssi-wag, "the snake-like ones," "the enemies" (Trumbull).

Under the family Gallatin makes four subdivisions, viz, the Winnebagos, the Sioux proper and the Assiniboins, the Minnetare group, and the Osages and southern kindred tribes. Gallatin speaks of the distribution of the family as follows: The Winnebagoes have their principal seats on the Fox River of Lake Michigan and towards the heads of the Rock River of the Mississippi; of the Dahcotas proper, the Mendewahkantoan or "Gens du Lac" lived east of the Mississippi from Prairie du Chien north to Spirit Lake. The three others, Wahkpatoan, Wahkpakotoan and Sisitoans inhabit the country between the Mississippi and the St. Peters, and that on the southern tributaries of this river and on the headwaters of the Red River of Lake Winnipek. The three western tribes, the Yanktons, the Yanktoanans and the Tetons wander between the Mississippi and the Missouri, extending southerly to 43° of north latitude and some distance west of the Missouri, between 43° and 47° of latitude. The "Shyennes" are included in the family but are marked as doubtfully belonging here.

Owing to the fact that "Sioux" is a word of reproach and means snake or enemy, the term has been discarded by many later writers as a family designation, and "Dakota," which signifies friend or ally, has been employed in its stead. The two words are, however, by no means properly synonymous. The term "Sioux" was used by Gallatin in a comprehensive or family sense and was applied to all the tribes collectively known to him to speak kindred dialects of a widespread language. It is in this sense only, as applied to the linguistic family, that the term is here employed. The term "Dahcota" (Dakota) was correctly applied by Gallatin to the Dakota tribes proper as distinguished from the other members of the linguistic family who are not Dakotas in a tribal sense. The use of the term with this signification should be perpetuated.

It is only recently that a definite decision has been reached respecting the relationship of the Catawba and Woccon, the latter an extinct tribe known to have been linguistically related to the Catawba. Gallatin thought that he was able to discern some affinities of the Catawban language with "Muskhogee and even with Choctaw," though these were not sufficient to induce him to class them together. Mr. Gatschet was the first to call attention to the presence in the Catawba language of a considerable number of words having a Siouan affinity.

Recently Mr. Dorsey has made a critical examination of all the Catawba linguistic material available, which has been materially increased by the labors of Mr. Gatschet, and the result seems to justify its inclusion as one of the dialects of the widespread Siouan family.

GEOGRAPHIC DISTRIBUTION.

The pristine territory of this family was mainly in one body, the only exceptions being the habitats of the Biloxi, the Tutelo, the Catawba and Woccon.

Contrary to the popular opinion of the present day, the general trend of Siouan migration has been westward. In comparatively late prehistoric times, probably most of the Siouan tribes dwelt east of the Mississippi River.

The main Siouan territory extended from about 53° north in the Hudson Bay Company Territory, to about 33°, including a considerable part of the watershed of the Missouri River and that of the Upper Mississippi. It was bounded on the northwest, north, northeast, and for some distance on the east by Algonquian territory. South of 45° north the line ran eastward to Lake Michigan, as the Green Bay region belonged to the Winnebago.[1]

---

[1] See treaty of Prairie du Chien, 1825.

It extended westward from Lake Michigan through Illinois, crossing the Mississippi River at Prairie du Chien. At this point began the Algonquian territory (Sac, etc.) on the west side of the Mississippi, extending southward to the Missouri, and crossing that river it returned to the Mississippi at St. Louis. The Siouan tribes claimed all of the present States of Iowa and Missouri, except the parts occupied by Algonquian tribes. The dividing line between the two for a short distance below St. Louis was the Mississippi River. The line then ran west of Dunklin, New Madrid, and Pemiscot Counties, in Missouri, and Mississippi County and those parts of Craighead and Poinsett Counties, Arkansas, lying east of the St. Francis River. Once more the Mississippi became the eastern boundary, but in this case separating the Siouan from the Muskhogean territory. The Quapaw or Akansa were the most southerly tribe in the main Siouan territory. In 1673[1] they were east of the Mississippi. Joutel (1687) located two of their villages on the Arkansas and two on the Mississippi one of the latter being on the east bank, in our present State of Mississippi, and the other being on the opposite side, in Arkansas. Shea says[2] that the Kaskaskias were found by De Soto in 1540 in latitude 36°, and that the Quapaw were higher up the Mississippi. But we know that the southeast corner of Missouri and the northeast corner of Arkansas, east of the St. Francis River, belonged to Algonquian tribes. A study of the map of Arkansas shows reason for believing that there may have been a slight overlapping of habitats, or a sort of debatable ground. At any rate it seems advisable to compromise, and assign the Quapaw and Osage (Siouan tribes) all of Arkansas up to about 36° north.

On the southwest of the Siouan family was the Southern Caddoan group, the boundary extending from the west side of the Mississippi River in Louisiana, nearly opposite Vicksburg, Mississippi, and running northwestwardly to the bend of Red River between Arkansas and Louisiana ; thence northwest along the divide between the watersheds of the Arkansas and Red Rivers. In the northwest corner of Indian Territory the Osages came in contact with the Comanche (Shoshonean), and near the western boundary of Kansas the Kiowa, Cheyenne, and Arapaho (the two latter being recent Algonquian intruders ?) barred the westward march of the Kansa or Kaw.

The Pawnee group of the Caddoan family in western Nebraska and northwestern Kansas separated the Ponka and Dakota on the north from the Kansa on the south, and the Omaha and other Siouan tribes on the east from Kiowa and other tribes on the west. The Omaha and cognate peoples occupied in Nebraska the lower part of the Platte River, most of the Elkhorn Valley, and the Ponka claimed the region watered by the Niobrara in northern Nebraska.

---

[1] Marquette's Autograph Map.　　[1] Disc. of Miss. Valley, p. 170, note.

There seems to be sufficient evidence for assigning to the Crows (Siouan) the northwest corner of Nebraska (i. e., that part north of the Kiowan and Caddoan habitats) and the southwest part of South Dakota (not claimed by Cheyenne[1]), as well as the northern part of Wyoming and the southern part of Montana, where they met the Shoshonean stock.[2]

The Biloxi habitat in 1699 was on the Pascogoula river,[3] in the southeast corner of the present State of Mississippi. The Biloxi subsequently removed to Louisiana, where a few survivors were found by Mr. Gatschet in 1886.

The Tutelo habitat in 1671 was in Brunswick County, southern Virginia, and it probably included Lunenburgh and Mecklenburg Counties.[4] The Earl of Bellomont (1699) says[5] that the Shateras were "supposed to be the Toteros, on Big Sandy River, Virginia," and Pownall, in his map of North America (1776), gives the Totteroy (i. e., Big Sandy) River. Subsequently to 1671 the Tutelo left Virginia and moved to North Carolina.[6] They returned to Virginia (with the Sapona), joined the Nottaway and Meherrin, whom they and the Tuscarora followed into Pennsylvania in the last century; thence they went to New York, where they joined the Six Nations, with whom they removed to Grand River Reservation, Ontario, Canada, after the Revolutionary war. The last full-blood Tutelo died in 1870. For the important discovery of the Siouan affinity of the Tutelo language we are indebted to Mr. Hale.

The Catawba lived on the river of the same name on the northern boundary of South Carolina. Originally they were a powerful tribe, the leading people of South Carolina, and probably occupied a large part of the Carolinas. The Woccon were widely separated from kinsmen living in North Carolina in the fork of the Cotentnea and Neuse Rivers.

The Wateree, living just below the Catawba, were very probably of the same linguistic connection.

PRINCIPAL TRIBES.

I. *Dakota.*

    (A) Santee: include Mde'-wa-ka^n-to^n-wa^n (Spirit Lake village, Santee Reservation, Nebraska), and Wa-qpe'-ku-te (Leaf Shooters); some on Fort Peck Reservation, Montana.

---

[1] See Cheyenne treaty, in Indian Treaties, 1873, pp. 124, 5481–5489.

[2] Lewis and Clarke, Trav., Lond., 1807, p. 25. Lewis and Clarke, Expl., 1874, vol 2, p. 390. A. L. Riggs, MS. letter to Dorsey, 1876 or 1877. Dorsey, Ponka tradition: "The Black Hills belong to the Crows." That the Dakotas were not there till this century see Corbusier's Dakota Winter Counts, in 4th Rept. Bur. Eth., p. 130, where it is also said that the Crow were the original owners of the Black Hills.

[3] Margry, Découvertes, vol. 4, p. 195.

[4] Batts in Doc. Col. Hist. N. Y., 1853, vol. 3, p. 194. Harrison, MS. letter to Dorsey, 1886.

[5] Doc. Col. Hist. N. Y., 1854, vol. 4, p. 488.

[6] Lawson, Hist. Carolina, 1714; reprint of 1860, p. 384.

I. *Dakota*—Continued.

    (B) Sisseton (Si-si′-to[n]-wa[n]), on Sisseton Reservation, South Dakota, and part on Devil's Lake Reservation, North Dakota.

    (C) Wahpeton (Wa-qpe′-to[n]-wa[n], Wa-ħpe-ton-wan); Leaf village. Some on Sisseton Reservation; most on Devil's Lake Reservation.

    (D) Yankton (I-hañk′-to[n]-wa[n]), at Yankton Reservation, South Dakota.

    (E) Yanktonnais (I-hañk′-to[n]-wa[n]-na); divided into *Upper* and *Lower*. Of the *Upper Yanktonnais*, there are some of the *Cut-head band* (Pa′-ba-ksa gens) on Devil's Lake Reservation. *Upper Yanktonnais*, most are on Standing Rock Reservation, North Dakota; *Lower Yanktonnais*, most are on Crow Creek Reservation, South Dakota, some are on Standing Rock Reservation, and some on Fort Peck Reservation, Montana.

    (F) Teton (Ti-to[n]-wa[n]); some on Fort Peck Reservation, Montana.

        (*a*) *Brulé* (Si-tca[n]′-xu); some are on Standing Rock Reservation. Most of the *Upper Brulé* (Highland Sitca[n]xu) are on Rosebud Reservation, South Dakota. Most of the *Lower Brulé* (Lowland Sitca[n]xu) are on Lower Brulé Reservation, South Dakota.

        (*b*) *Sans Arcs* (I-ta′-zip-tco′, Without Bows). Most are on Cheyenne Reservation, South Dakota; some on Standing Rock Reservation.

        (*c*) *Blackfeet* (Si-ha′sa′-pa). Most are on Cheyenne Reservation; some on Standing Rock Reservation.

        (*d*) *Minneconjou* (Mi′-ni-ko′-o-ju). Most are on Cheyenne Reservation, some are on Rosebud Reservation, and some on Standing Rock Reservation.

        (*e*) *Two Kettles* (O-o′-he-no[n]′-pa, Two Boilings), on Cheyenne Reservation.

        (*f*) *Ogalalla* (O-gla′-la). Most on Pine Ridge Reservation, South Dakota; some on Standing Rock Reservation. *Wa-ża-ża* (Wa-ja-ja, Wa-zha-zha), a gens of the Oglala (Pine Ridge Reservation); *Loafers* (Wa-glu-xe, In-breeders), a gens of the Oglala; most on Pine Ridge Reservation; some on Rosebud Reservation.

        (*g*) *Uncpapa* (1862–′63), *Uncapapa* (1880–′81), (Huñ′-kpa-pa), on Standing Rock Reservation.

II. *Assinaboin* (Hohe, Dakota name); most in British North America; some on Fort Peck Reservation, Montana.

III. *Omaha* (U-ma[n]′-ha[n]), on Omaha Reservation, Nebraska.

IV. *Ponca* (formerly *Ponka* on maps; Ponka); 605 on Ponca Reservation, Indian Territory; 217 at Santee Agency, Nebraska.

V. *Kaw* (ɥaⁿ'-ze; the Kansa Indians); on the Kansas Reservation, Indian Territory.

VI. *Osage; Big Osage* (Pa-he'-tsi, Those on a Mountain); *Little Osage* (Those at the foot of the Mountain); *Arkansas Band* (ꞩan-ɹsu-ɥȼiⁿ, Dwellers in a Highland Grove), Osage Reservation, Indian Territory.

VII. *Quapaw* (U-ɥa'-qpa; Kwapa). A few are on the Quapaw Reserve, but about 200 are on the Osage Reserve, Oklahoma. (They are the *Arkansa* of early times.)

VIII. *Iowa*, on Great Nemaha Reserve, Kansas and Nebraska, and 86 on Sac and Fox Reserve, Indian Territory.

IX. *Otoe* (Wa-to'-qta-ta), on Otoe Reserve, Indian Territory.

X. *Missouri* or *Missouria* (Ni-u'-t'a-tci), on Otoe Reserve.

XI. *Winnebago* (Ho-tcañ'-ga-ra); most in Nebraska, on their reserve; some are in Wisconsin; some in Michigan, according to Dr. Reynolds.

XII. *Mandan*, on Fort Berthold Reserve, North Dakota.

XIII. *Gros Ventres* (a misleading name; syn. *Minnetaree;* Hi-da'-tsa); on the same reserve.

XIV. *Crow* (Absáruqe, Aubsároke, etc.), Crow Reserve, Montana.

XV. *Tutelo* (Ye-saⁿ'), among the Six Nations, Grand River Reserve, Province of Ontario, Canada.

XVI. *Biloxi* (Ta'-neks ha'-ya), part on the Red River, at Avoyelles, Louisiana; part in Indian Territory, among the Choctaw and Caddo.

XVII. *Catawba.*

XVIII. *Woccon.*

Population.—The present number of the Siouan family is about 43,400, of whom about 2,204 are in British North America, the rest being in the United States. Below is given the population of the tribes officially recognized, compiled chiefly from the Canadian Indian Report for 1888, the United States Indian Commissioner's Report for 1889, and the United States Census Bulletin for 1890:

Dakota:

Mdewakantonwan and Wahpekute (Santee) on Santee Reserve, Nebraska	869
At Flandreau, Dakota	292
Santee at Devil's Lake Agency	54
Sisseton and Wahpeton on Sisseton Reserve, South Dakota	1,522
Sisseton, Wahpeton, and Cuthead (Yanktonnais) at Devil's Lake Reservation	857

Yankton:

On Yankton Reservation, South Dakota	1,725	
At Devil's Lake Agency	123	
On Fort Peck Reservation, Montana	1,121	
A few on Crow Creek Reservation, South Dakota	10	
A few on Lower Brulé Reservation, South Dakota	10	
		2,989

Dakota—Continued.
  Yanktonnais:
    Upper Yanktonnais on Standing Rock Reservation.............. 1,786
    Lower Yanktonnais on Crow Creek Reservation................. 1,058
    At Standing Rock Agency 1,739
                                                          4,583

  Teton:
    Brulé, Upper Brulé on Rosebud Reservation................. 3,245
      On Devil's Lake Reservation 2
    Lower Brulé at Crow Creek and Lower Brulé Agency......... 1,026
    Minneconjou (mostly)and Two Kettle, on Cheyenne River Reserve 2,823
    Blackfeet on Standing Rock Reservation 545
    Two Kettle on Rosebud Reservation 315
    Oglala on Pine Ridge Reservation 4,552
    Wajaja (Oglala gens) on Rosebud Reservation 1,825
    Wagluxe (Oglala gens) on Rosebud Reservation............... 1,353
    Uncapapa, on Standing Rock Reservation.. 571
    Dakota at Carlisle, Lawrence, and Hampton schools.... 169
                                                          16,426

  Dakota in British North America (tribes not stated):
    On Bird Tail Sioux Reserve, Birtle Agency, Northwest Territory. 108
    On Oak River Sioux Reserve, Birtle Agency 276
    On Oak Lake Sioux Reserve, Birtle Agency...... 55
    On Turtle Mountain Sioux Reserve, Birtle Agency.......... 34
    On Standing Buffalo Reserve, under Northwest Territory........ 184
  Muscowpetung's Agency :
    White Cap Dakota (Moose Woods Reservation)................. 105
    American Sioux (no reserve) 95
                                                          857

Assinaboin:
  On Fort Belknap Reservation, Montana................. 952
  On Fort Peck Reservation, Montana.......................... 719
  At Devil's Lake Agency..................................... 2
  The following are in British North America:
  Pheasant Rump's band, at Moose Mountain (of whom 6 at Mis-
    souri and 4 at Turtle Mountain)........ 69
  Ocean Man's band, at Moose Mountain (of whom 4 at Missouri).. 68
  The-man-who-took-the-coat's band, at Indian Head (of whom 5
    are at Milk River)... 248
  Bear's Head band, Battleford Agency......................... 227
  Chee-pooste-quahn band, at Wolf Creek, Peace Hills Agency ... 128
  Bear's Paw band, at Morleyville...... 236
  Chiniquy band, Reserve, at Sarcee Agency................ 134
  Jacob's band........ 227
                                                         3,008

Omaha:
  Omaha and Winnebago Agency, Nebraska..... 1,158
  At Carlisle School, Pennsylvania............................ 19
  At Hampton School, Virginia............................ 10
  At Lawrence School, Kansas.................. 10
                                                         1,197

Ponka:
  In Nebraska (under the Santee agent) 217
  In Indian Territory (under the Ponka agent)................... 605
  At Carlisle, Pennsylvania.................................... 1
  At Lawrence, Kansas.. 24
                                                         847

Osage:
At Osage Agency, Indian Territory	1,509	
At Carlisle, Pennsylvania	7	
At Lawrence, Kansas	65	
		1,581

Kansa or Kaw:
At Osage Agency, Indian Territory	198	
At Carlisle, Pennsylvania	1	
At Lawrence, Kansas	15	
		214

Quapaw:
On Quapaw Reserve, Indian Territory	154	
On Osage Reserve, Indian Territory	71	
At Carlisle, Pennsylvania	3	
At Lawrence, Kansas	4	
		232

Iowa:
On Great Nemaha Reservation, Kansas	165	
On Sac and Fox Reservation, Oklahoma	102	
At Carlisle, Pennsylvania	1	
At Lawrence, Kansas	5	
		273

Oto and Missouri, in Indian Territory		358

Winnebago:
In Nebraska	1,215	
In Wisconsin (1889)	930	
At Carlisle, Pennsylvania	27	
At Lawrence, Kansas	2	
At Hampton, Virginia	10	
		2,184

Mandan:
On Fort Berthold Reservation, North Dakota	251	
At Hampton, Virginia	1	
		252

Hidatsa, on Fort Berthold Reservation, North Dakota		522
Crow, on Crow Reservation, Montana		2,287
Tutelo, about a dozen mixed bloods on Grand River Reserve, Ontario, Canada. and a few more near Montreal (?), say, about		20

Biloxi:
In Louisiana, about	25	
At Atoka, Indian Territory	1	
		26

Catawba:
In York County, South Carolina, about	80	
Scattered through North Carolina, about	40?	
		120?

SKITTAGETAN FAMILY.

>Skittagets, Gallatin in Trans. and Coll. Am. Eth. Soc., II, pt. 1, c, 1848 (the equivalent of his Queen Charlotte's Island group, p. 77).

>Skittagetts, Berghaus, Physik. Atlas, map 17, 1852.

>Skidegattz, Gallatin in Schoolcraft, Ind. Tribes, III, 402, 1853 (obvious typographical error; Queen Charlotte Island).

×Haidah, Scouler in Jour. Roy. Geog. Soc. Lond., XI, 224, 1841 (same as his Northern family; see below).

=Haidah, Latham, Nat. Hist. Man, 300, 1850 (Skittegats, Massets, Kumshahas, Kyganie). Latham in Trans. Philolog. Soc. Lond., 72, 1856 (includes Skittigats,
Massetts, Kumshahas, and Kyganie of Queen Charlotte's Ids. and Prince of
Wales Archipelago). Latham, Opuscula, 339, 1860. Buschmann, Spuren der
aztek. Sprache, 673, 1859. Latham, El. Comp. Phil., 401, 1862 (as in 1856). Dall
in Proc. Am. Ass'n. 269, 1869 (Queen Charlotte's Ids. and southern part of Alex-
ander Archipelago). Bancroft, Nat. Races, III, 564, 604, 1882.

>Hai-dai, Schoolcraft, Ind. Tribes. v, 489, 1855. Kane, Wanderings of an Artist,
app., 1859, (Work's census, 1836-'41, of northwest coast tribes, classified by
language).

=Haida, Gibbs in Cont. N. A. Eth., I, 135, 1877. Tolmie and Dawson, Comp. Vocabs., 15, 1884 (vocabs. of Kaigani Sept, Masset, Skidegate, Kumshiwa dialects;
also map showing distribution). Dall in Proc. Am. Ass'n, 375, 1885 (mere mention of family).

<Hydahs, Keane, App. Stanford's Comp. (Cent. and So. Am.), 460, 473, 1878
(enumerates Massets, Klue, Kiddan, Ninstance, Skid-a-gate, Skid-a-gatees,
Cum-she-was, Kaiganies, Tsimsheeans, Nass, Skeenas, Sebasses, Hailtzas, Bellacoolas).

>Queen Charlotte's Island, Gallatin in Trans. and Coll. Am. Antiq. Soc., II, 15, 306,
1836 (no tribe indicated). Gallatin in Trans. Am. Eth. Soc., II, pt. 1, 77, 1848
(based on Skittagete language). Latham in Jour. Eth. Soc. Lond., I, 154, 1848.
Latham, Opuscula, 249, 1860.

×Northern, Scouler in Jour. Roy. Geog. Soc. Lond., XI, 219, 1841 (includes Queen
Charlotte's Island and tribes on islands and coast up to 60° N. L.; Haidas, Mas-
settes, Skittegás, Cumshawás). Prichard, Phys. Hist. Mankind, v, 433, 1847
(follows Scouler).

=Kygáni, Dall in Proc. Am. Ass'n, 269, 1869 (Queen Charlotte's Ids. or Haidahs).

×Nootka, Bancroft, Nat. Races, III, 564, 1882 (contains Quane, probably of present
family; Quactoe, Saukaulutuck).

The vocabulary referred by Gallatin[1] to "Queen Charlotte's Islands" unquestionably belongs to the present family. In addition
to being a compound word and being objectionable as a family name
on account of its unwieldiness, the term is a purely geographic one
and is based upon no stated tribe; hence it is not eligible for use in
systematic nomenclature. As it appears in the Archæologia Americana it represents nothing but the locality whence the vocabulary of
an unknown tribe was received.

The family name to be considered as next in order of date is the
Northern (or Haidah) of Scouler, which appears in volume XI, Royal
Geographical Society, page 218, et seq. The term as employed by
Scouler is involved in much confusion, and it is somewhat difficult
to determine just what tribes the author intended to cover by the
designation. Reduced to its simplest form, the case stands as follows: Scouler's primary division of the Indians of the Northwest was
into two groups, the insular and the inland. The insular (and coast
tribes) were then subdivided into two families, viz, Northern or
Haidah family (for the terms are interchangeably used, as on page
224) and the Southern or Nootka-Columbian family. Under the
Northern or Haidah family the author classes all the Indian tribes

---

[1] Archæologia Americana, 1836, II, pp. 15, 306.

in the Russian territory, the Kolchians (Athapascas of Gallatin, 1836), the Koloshes, Ugalentzes, and Tun Ghaase (the Koluscans of Gallatin, 1836); the Atnas (Salish of Gallatin, 1836); the Kenaians (Athapascas, Gallatin, 1836); the Haidah tribes proper of Queen Charlotte Island, and the Chimesyans.

It will appear at a glance that such a heterogeneous assemblage of tribes, representing as they do several distinct stocks, can not have been classed together on purely linguistic evidence. In point of fact, Scouler's remarkable classification seems to rest only in a very slight degree upon a linguistic basis, if indeed it can be said to have a linguistic basis at all. Consideration of "physical character, manners, and customs" were clearly accorded such weight by this author as to practically remove his Northern or Haidah family from the list of linguistic stocks.

The next family name which was applied in this connection is the Skittagets of Gallatin as above cited. This name is given to designate a family on page *c*, volume II, of Transactions of the Ethnological Society, 1848. In his subsequent list of vocabularies, page 77, he changes his designation to Queen Charlotte Island, placing under this family name the Skittagete tribe. His presentation of the former name of Skittagets in his complete list of families is, however, sufficiently formal to render it valid as a family designation, and it is, therefore, retained for the tribes of the Queen Charlotte Archipelago which have usually been called Haida.

From a comparison of the vocabularies of the Haida language with others of the neighboring Koluschan family, Dr. Franz Boas is inclined to consider that the two are genetically related. The two languages possess a considerable number of words in common, but a more thorough investigation is requisite for the settlement of the question than has yet been given. Pending this the two families are here treated separately.

GEOGRAPHIC DISTRIBUTION.

The tribes of this family occupy Queen Charlotte Islands, Forrester Island to the north of the latter, and the southeastern part of Prince of Wales Island, the latter part having been ascertained by the agents of the Tenth Census.[1]

PRINCIPAL TRIBES.

The following is a list of the principal villages:

Haida:

Aseguang.	Kunχit.	Skiteiget.
Cumshawa.	Massett.	Tanu.
Kayung.	New Gold Harbor.	Tartanee.
Kung.	Skedan.	Uttewas.

---

[1] See Petroff map of Alaska, 1880–'81.

Kaigani:

| Chatcheeni. | Howakan. | Shakan. |
| Clickass. | Quiahanless. | |

Population.—The population of the Haida is 2,500, none of whom are at present under an agent.

TAKILMAN FAMILY.

=Takilma, Gatschet in Mag. Am. Hist., 1882 (Lower Rogue River).

This name was proposed by Mr. Gatschet for a distinct language spoken on the coast of Oregon about the lower Rogue River. Mr. Dorsey obtained a vocabulary in 1884 which he has compared with Athapascan, Kusan, Yakonan, and other languages spoken in the region without finding any marked resemblances. The family is hence admitted provisionally. The language appears to be spoken by but a single tribe, although there is a manuscript vocabulary in the Bureau of Ethnology exhibiting certain differences which may be dialectic.

GEOGRAPHIC DISTRIBUTION.

The Takilma formerly dwelt in villages along upper Rogue River, Oregon, all the latter, with one exception, being on the south side, from Illinois River on the southwest, to Deep Rock, which was nearer the head of the stream. They are now included among the "Rogue River Indians," and they reside to the number of twenty-seven on the Siletz Reservation, Tillamook County, Oregon, where Dorsey found them in 1884.

TAÑOAN FAMILY.

>Tay-waugh, Lane (1854) in Schoolcraft, Ind. Tribes. v, 689, 1855 (Pueblos of San Juan, Santa Clara, Pojuaque, Nambe, San Il de Conso, and one Moqui pueblo). Keane, App. Stanford's Comp. (Cent. and So. Am.), 479, 1878.

>Taño, Powell in Rocky Mountain Presbyterian, Nov., 1878 (includes Sandia, Téwa, San Ildefonso, San Juan, Santa Clara, Pojoaque, Nambé, Tesuque, Sinecú, Jemez, Taos, Picuri).

>Tegua, Keane, App. Stanford's Comp. (Cent. and So. Am.), 479, 1878 (includes S. Juan, Sta. Clara, Pojuaque, Nambe, Tesugue, S. Ildefonso, Haro).

=Téwan, Powell in Am. Nat., 605, Aug., 1880 (makes five divisions: 1. Taño (Isleta, Isleta near El Paso, Sandía); 2. Taos (Taos, Picuni); 3. Jemes (Jemes); 4. Tewa or Tehua (San Ildefonso, San Juan, Pojoaque, Nambe, Tesuque, Santa Clara, and one Moki pueblo); 5. Piro).

>E-nagh-magh, Lane (1854) in Schoolcraft, Ind. Tribes, v, 689, 1855 (includes Taos, Vicuris, Zesuqua, Sandia, Ystete, and two pueblos near El Paso, Texas). Keane, App. Stanford's Comp. (Cent. and So. Am.), 479, 1878 (follows Lane, but identifies Texan pueblos with Lentis ? and Socorro ?).

>Picori, Keane, App. Stanford's Comp. (Cent. and So. Am.), 479, 1878 (or Enagh-magh).

=Stock of Rio Grande Pueblos, Gatschet in U. S. Geog. Surv. W. 100th M., VII, 415, 1879.

=Rio Grande Pueblo, Gatschet in Mag. Am. Hist., 258, 1882.

Derivation: Probably from "taínin," plural of tá-ide, "Indian," in the dialect of Isleta and Sandia (Gatschet).

In a letter[1] from Wm. Carr Lane to H. R. Schoolcraft, appear some remarks on the affinities of the Pueblo languages, based in large part on hearsay evidence. No vocabularies are given, nor does any real classification appear to be attempted, though referring to such of his remarks as apply in the present connection, Lane states that the Indians of " Taos, Vicuris, Zesuqua, Sandia, and Ystete, and of two pueblos of Texas, near El Paso, are said to speak the same language, which I have heard called E-nagh-magh," and that the Indians of "San Juan, Santa Clara, Pojuaque, Nambe, San Il de Conso, and one Moqui pueblo, all speak the same language, as it is said: this I have heard called Tay-waugh." The ambiguous nature of his reference to these pueblos is apparent from the above quotation.

The names given by Lane as those he had "heard" applied to certain groups of pueblos which "it is said" speak the same language, rest on too slender a basis for serious consideration in a classificatory sense.

Keane in the appendix to Stanford's Compendium (Central and South America), 1878, p. 479, presents the list given by Lane, correcting his spelling in some cases and adding the name of the Tusayan pueblo as Haro (Hano). He gives the group no formal family name, though they are classed together as speaking "Tegua or Tay-waugh."

The Taño of Powell (1878), as quoted, appears to be the first name formally given the family, and is therefore accepted. Recent investigations of the dialect spoken at Taos and some of the other pueblos of this group show a considerable body of words having Shoshonean affinities, and it is by no means improbable that further research will result in proving the radical relationship of these languages to the Shoshonean family. The analysis of the language has not yet, however, proceeded far enough to warrant a decided opinion.

GEOGRAPHIC DISTRIBUTION.

The tribes of this family in the United States resided exclusively upon the Rio Grande and its tributary valleys from about 33° to about 36°. A small body of these people joined the Tusayan in northern Arizona, as tradition avers to assist the latter against attacks by the Apache—though it seems more probable that they fled from the Rio Grande during the pueblo revolt of 1680—and remained to found the permanent pueblo of Hano, the seventh pueblo of the group. A smaller section of the family lived upon the Rio Grande in Mexico and Texas, just over the New Mexico border.

---

[1] Schoolcraft, Indian Tribes, 1855, vol. 5, p. 689.

Population.—The following pueblos are included in the family, with a total population of about 3,237:

Hano (of the Tusayan group).....	132	Sandia	140
Isleta (New Mexico)..............	1,059	San Ildefonso	148
Isleta (Texas).......	few	San Juan.......................	406
Jemez...........................	428	Santa Clara	225
Nambé..........................	79	Senecú (below El Paso)	few
Picuris..........................	100	Taos	409
Pojoaque......................	20	Tesuque........	91

TIMUQUANAN FAMILY.

= Timuquana, Smith in Hist. Magazine, II, 1, 1858 (a notice of the language with vocabulary; distinctness of the language affirmed). Brinton, Floridian Peninsula, 134, 1859 (spelled also Timuaca, Timagoa, Timuqua).

= Timucua, Gatschet in Proc. Am. Phil. Soc., XVI, April 6, 1877 (from Cape Cañaveral to mouth of St. John's River). Gatschet, Creek Mig. Legend I, 11–13, 1884. Gatschet in Science, 413, April 29, 1887.

= Atimuca, Gatschet in Science, ibid. (proper name).

Derivation: From ati-muca, "ruler," "master;" literally, "servants attend upon him."

In the Historical Magazine as above cited appears a notice of the Timuquana language by Buckingham Smith, in which is affirmed its distinctness upon the evidence of language. A short vocabulary is appended, which was collated from the "Confessionario" by Padre Pareja, 1613. Brinton and Gatschet have studied the Timuquana language and have agreed as to the distinctness of the family from any other of the United States. Both the latter authorities are inclined to take the view that it has affinities with the Carib family to the southward, and it seems by no means improbable that ultimately the Timuquana language will be considered an offshoot of the Carib linguistic stock. At the present time, however, such a conclusion would not be justified by the evidence gathered and published.

GEOGRAPHIC DISTRIBUTION.

It is impossible to assign definite limits to the area occupied by the tribes of this family. From documentary testimony of the sixteenth and seventeenth centuries the limits of the family domain appear to have been about as follows: In general terms the present northern limits of the State of Florida may be taken as the northern frontier, although upon the Atlantic side Timuquanan territory may have extended into Georgia. Upon the northwest the boundary line was formed in De Soto's time by the Ocilla River. Lake Okeechobee on the south, or as it was then called Lake Sarrape or Mayaimi, may be taken as the boundary between the Timuquanan tribes proper and the Calusa province upon the Gulf coast and the Tegesta province upon the Atlantic side. Nothing whatever of the languages spoken in these two latter provinces is available for comparison. A number of the local names of these provinces given by Fontanedo (1559) have terminations similar to many of the Timuquanan local names. This slender evidence is all that we have from which to infer the Timuquanan relationship of the southern end of the peninsula.

PRINCIPAL TRIBES.

The following settlements appear upon the oldest map of the regions we possess, that of De Bry (Narratio; Frankf. a. M. 15, 1590):

(A) Shores of St. John's River, from mouth to sources :

Patica.	Utina.
Saturiwa.	Patchica.
Atore.	Chilili.
Homolua or Molua.	Calanay.
Alimacani.	Onochaquara.
Casti.	Mayarca.
Malica.	Mathiaca.
Melona.	Maiera.
Timoga or Timucua.	Mocoso.
Enecaqua.	Cadica.
Choya.	Eloquale.
Edelano (island).	Aquonena.
Astina.	

(B) On a (fictitious) western tributary of St. John's River, from mouth to source :

Hicaranaou.	Potanou.
Appalou.	Ehiamana.
Oustaca.	Anouala.
Onathcaqua.	

(C) East Floridian coast, from south to north :

Mocossou.	Hanocoroucouay.
Oathcaqua.	Marracou.
Sorrochos.	

(D) On coast north of St. John's River :
Hiouacara.

(E) The following are gathered from all other authorities, mostly from the accounts of De Soto's expedition :

Acquera.	San Mateo (1688).
Aguile.	Santa Lucia de Acuera (SE.
Basisa or Vacissa (1688).	coast).
Cholupaha.	Tacatacuru.
Hapaluya.	Tocaste.
Hirrihiqua.	Tolemato.
Itafi (perhaps a province).	Topoqui.

Itara
Machaua (1688).
Napetuca.
Osile (Oxille).
San Juan de Guacara (1688).

Tucururu (SE. coast)
Ucita.
Urriparacuxi.
Yupaha (perhaps a province).

TONIKAN FAMILY.

=Tunicas, Gallatin in Trans. and Coll. Am. Antiq. Soc., II, 115, 116, 1836 (quotes Dr.
Sibley, who states they speak a distinct language). Latham, Nat. Hist. Man,
341, 1850 (opposite mouth of Red River; quotes Dr. Sibley as to distinctness of
language).
=Tonica, Gatschet, Creek Mig. Legend, I, 39, 1884 (brief account of tribe).
=Tonika, Gatschet in Science, 412, April 29, 1887 (distinctness as a family asserted; the tribe calls itself Túniχka).

Derivation: From the Tonika word óni, "man," "people;" t- is a
prefix or article; -ka,-χka a nominal suffix.

The distinctness of the Tonika language, has long been suspected,
and was indeed distinctly stated by Dr. Sibley in 1806.[1] The statement to this effect by Dr. Sibley was quoted by Gallatin in 1836, but
as the latter possessed no vocabulary of the language he made no
attempt to classify it. Latham also dismisses the language with the
same quotation from Sibley. Positive linguistic proof of the position of the language was lacking until obtained by Mr. Gatschet in
1886, who declared it to form a family by itself.

GEOGRAPHIC DISTRIBUTION.

The Tonika are known to have occupied three localities: First,
on the Lower Yazoo River (1700); second, east shore of Mississippi
River (about 1704); third, in Avoyelles Parish, Louisiana (1817).
Near Marksville, the county seat of that parish, about twenty-five
are now living.

TONKAWAN FAMILY.

=Tonkawa, Gatschet, Zwölf Sprachen aus dem Südwesten Nordamerikas, 76, 1876
(vocabulary of about 300 words and some sentences). Gatschet, Die Sprache der
Tonkawas, in Zeitschrift für Ethnologie, 64, 1877. Gatschet (1876), in Proc. Am.
Philosoph. Soc., XVI, 318, 1877.

Derivation: the full form is the Caddo or Wako term tonkawéya,
"they all stay together" (wéya, "all").

After a careful examination of all the linguistic material available for comparison, Mr. Gatschet has concluded that the language
spoken by the Tonkawa forms a distinct family.

---

[1] President's message, February 19, 1806.

The Tónkawa were a migratory people and a *colluvies gentium*, whose earliest habitat is unknown. Their first mention occurs in 1719; at that time and ever since they roamed in the western and southern parts of what is now Texas. About 1847 they were engaged as scouts in the United States Army, and from 1860–'62 (?) were in the Indian Territory; after the secession war till 1884 they lived in temporary camps near Fort Griffin, Shackelford County, Texas, and in October, 1884, they removed to the Indian Territory (now on Oakland Reserve). In 1884 there were seventy-eight individuals living; associated with them were nineteen Lipan Apache, who had lived in their company for many years, though in a separate camp. They have thirteen divisions (partly totem-clans) and observe mother-right.

UCHEAN FAMILY.

=Uchees, Gallatin in Trans. and Coll. Am. Antiq. Soc., II., 95, 1836 (based upon the Uchees alone). Bancroft, Hist. U. S., III., 247, 1840. Gallatin in Trans. Am. Eth. Soc. II., pt. 1, xcix, 77, 1848. Keane, App. Stanford's Comp. (Cent. and So. Am.), 472, 1878 (suggests that the language may have been akin to Natchez).

=Utchees, Gallatin in Trans. and Coll, Am. Antiq. Soc., II., 306, 1836. Gallatin in Schoolcraft, Ind. Tribes, III., 401, 1853. Keane, App. Stanford's Comp. (Cent. and So. Am.), 472, 1878.

=Utschies, Berghaus (1845), Physik. Atlas, map 17, 1848. Ibid., 1852.

=Uché, Latham, Nat. Hist. Man, 338, 1850 (Coosa River). Latham in Trans. Philolog. Soc. Lond., II., 31–50, 1846. Latham, Opuscula, 293, 1860.

=Yuchi, Gatschet, Creek Mig. Legend, I, 17, 1884. Gatschet in Science, 413, April 29, 1887.

The following is the account of this tribe given by Gallatin (probably derived from Hawkins) in Archæologia Americana, page 95:

The original seats of the Uchees were east of Coosa and probably of the Chatahoochee; and they consider themselves as the most ancient inhabitants of the country. They may have been the same nation which is called Apalaches in the accounts of De Soto's expedition, and their towns were till lately principally on Flint River.

The pristine homes of the Yuchi are not now traceable with any degree of certainty. The Yuchi are supposed to have been visited by De Soto during his memorable march, and the town of Cofitachiqui chronicled by him, is believed by many investigators to have stood at Silver Bluff, on the left bank of the Savannah, about 25 miles below Augusta. If, as is supposed by some authorities, Cofitachiqui was a Yuchi town, this would locate the Yuchi in a section which, when first known to the whites, was occupied by the Shawnee. Later the Yuchi appear to have lived somewhat farther down the Savannah, on the eastern and also the western side, as far as the Ogeechee River, and also upon tracts above and below Augusta, Georgia. These tracts were claimed by them as late as 1736.

In 1729 a portion of the Yuchi left their old seats and settled among the Lower Creek on the Chatahoochee River; there they established three colony villages in the neighborhood, and later on a Yuchi settlement is mentioned on Lower Tallapoosa River, among the Upper Creek.[1] Filson[2] gives a list of thirty Indian tribes and a statement concerning Yuchi towns, which he must have obtained from a much earlier source: " Uchees occupy four different places of residence—at the head of St. John's, the fork of St. Mary's, the head of Cannouchee, and the head of St. Tillis" (Satilla), etc.[3]

Population.—More than six hundred Yuchi reside in northeastern Indian Territory, upon the Arkansas River, where they are usually classed as Creek. Doubtless the latter are to some extent intermarried with them, but the Yuchi are jealous of their name and tenacious of their position as a tribe.

WAIILATPUAN.

= Waiilatpu, Hale. in U. S. Expl. Exp., VI, 199, 214, 569, 1846 (includes Cailloux or Cayuse or Willetpoos, and Molele). Gallatin, after Hale, in Trans. Am. Eth. Soc., II, pt. 1, c, 14, 56, 77, 1848 (after Hale). Berghaus (1851), Physik. Atlas, map 17, 1852. Buschmann, Spuren der aztek. Sprache, 628, 1859. Bancroft, Nat. Races, III, 565, 1882 (Cayuse and Mollale).

= Wailatpu, Gallatin in Schoolcraft, Ind. Tribes, III, 402, 1853 (Cayuse and Molele).

× Sahaptin, Latham, Nat. Hist. Man, 323, 1850 (cited as including Cayús ?).

× Sahaptins, Keane, App. Stanford's Comp. (Cent. and So. Am.), 474, 1878 (cited because it includes Cayuse and Mollale).

= Molele, Latham, Nat. Hist. Man, 324, 1850 (includes Molele, Cayús?).

> Cayús?, Latham, ibid.

= Cayuse, Gatschet in Mag. Am. Hist., 166, 1877 (Cayuse and Moléle). Gatschet in Beach, Ind. Misc., 442, 1877.

Derivation: Wayíletpu, plural form of Wa-ílet, " one Cayuse man " (Gatschet).

Hale established this family and placed under it the Cailloux or Cayuse or Willetpoos, and the Molele. Their headquarters as indicated by Hale are the upper part of the Walla Walla River and the country about Mounts Hood and Vancouver.

GEOGRAPHIC DISTRIBUTION.

The Cayuse lived chiefly near the mouth of the Walla Walla River, extending a short distance above and below on the Columbia, between the Umatilla and Snake Rivers. The Molále were a mountain tribe and occupied a belt of mountain country south of the Columbia River, chiefly about Mounts Hood and Jefferson.

PRINCIPAL TRIBES.

Cayuse.   Molále.

---

[1] Gatschet, Creek Mig. Legend, I, 21–22, 1884.

[2] Discovery, etc., of Kentucky, 1793, II, 84–7.

[3] Gatschet, Creek Mig. Legend, I, p. 20.

Population.—There are 31 Molále now on the Grande Ronde Reservation, Oregon,[1] and a few others live in the mountains west of Klamath Lake. The Indian Affairs Report for 1888 credits 401 and the United States Census Bulletin for 1890, 415 Cayuse Indians to the Umatilla Reservation, but Mr. Henshaw was able to find only six old men and women upon the reservation in August, 1888, who spoke their own language. The others, though presumably of Cayuse blood, speak the Umatilla tongue.

WAKASHAN FAMILY.

>Wakash, Gallatin in Trans. and Coll. Am. Antiq. Soc., II, 15, 306, 1836 (of Nootka Sound; gives Jewitt's vocab.). Gallatin in Trans. Am. Eth. Soc., II, pt. 1, 77, 1848 (based on Newittee). Berghaus (1851), Physik. Atlas, map 17, 1852. Gallatin in Schoolcraft, Ind. Tribes, III, 402, 1853 (includes Newittee and Nootka Sound). Latham in Trans. Philolog. Soc. Lond., 73, 1856 (of Quadra and Vancouver's Island). Latham, Opuscula, 340, 1860. Latham, El. Comp. Phil., 403, 1862 (Tlaoquatsh and Wakash proper; Nútka and congeners also referred here).

×Wakash, Latham, Nat. Hist. Man, 301, 1850 (includes Naspatle, proper Nutkans, Tlaoquatsh. Nittenat, Klasset, Klallems ; the last named is Salishan).

×Nootka-Columbian, Scouler in Jour. Roy. Geog. Soc., XI, 221, 1841 (includes Quadra and Vancouver Island, Haeeltzuk, Billechoola, Tlaoquatch, Kawitchen, Noosdalum, Squallyamish, Cheenooks). Prichard, Phys. Hist. Mankind, V, 435, 1847 (follows Scouler). Latham in Jour. Eth. Soc. Lond., I, 162, 1848 (remarks upon Scouler's group of this name). Latham, Opuscula, 257, 1860 (the same).

<Nootka, Hale in U. S. Expl. Exp., VI, 220, 569, 1846 (proposes family to include tribes of Vancouver Island and tribes on south side of Fuca Strait).

>Nutka, Buschmann, Neu-Mexico, 329, 1858.

>Nootka, Gatschet in Mag. Am. Hist., 170, 1877 (mentions only Makah, and Classet tribes of Cape Flattery). Gatschet in Beach, Ind. Misc., 446, 1877.

×Nootkahs, Keane, App. Stanford's Comp. (Cent. and So. Am.), 473, 1878 (includes Muchlahts, Nitinahts, Ohyahts, Manosahts, and Quoquoulths of present family, together with a number of Salishan tribes).

×Nootka, Bancroft, Nat. Races, III, 564, 607, 1882 (a heterogeneous group, largely Salishan, with Wakashan, Skittagetan, and other families represented).

>Straits of Fuca, Gallatin in Trans. and Coll. Am. Antiq. Soc., II, 134, 306, 1836 (vocabulary of, referred here with doubt; considered distinct by Gallatin).

×Southern, Scouler in Jour. Roy. Geog. Soc., XI, 224, 1841 (same as his Nootka-Columbian above).

×Insular, Scouler ibid. (same as his Nootka-Columbian above).

×Haeltzuk, Latham in Jour. Eth. Soc. Lond., I, 155, 1848 (cities Tolmie's vocab. Spoken from 50° 30′ to 53° 30′ N. L.). Latham, Opuscula, 251, 1860 (the same).

>Haeeltsuk and Hailtsa, Latham, Nat. Hist. Man, 300, 1850 (includes Hyshalla, Hyhysh, Esleytuk, Weekenoch, Nalatsenoch, Quagheuil. Tlatla-Shequilla, Lequeeltoch).

>Hailtsa, Latham in Trans. Philolog. Soc. Lond.,72,1856. Buschmann, Neu-Mexico, 322, 1858. Latham, Opuscula, 339, 1860. Latham, El. Comp. Phil., 401, 1862 (includes coast dialects between Hawkesbury Island, Broughton's Archipelago, and northern part of Vancouver Island).

>Ha-eelb-zuk, Schoolcraft, Ind. Tribes, V, 487, 1855. Kane, Wand. of an Artist, app., 1859 (or Ballabola; a census of N. W. tribes classified by language).

---

[1] U. S. Ind. Aff., 1889.

>Ha-ilt'-zŭkh, Dall, after Gibbs, in Cont. N. A. Eth., I, 144, 1877 (vocabularies of Bel-bella of Milbank Sound and of Kwákiŭtl').

<Nass, Gallatin in Trans. Am. Eth. Soc., II, pt 1, c, 1848.

<Naass, Gallatin in Trans. Am. Eth. Soc.. II, pt. 1, 77, 1848 (includes Hailstla, Haceltzuk, Billechola, Chimeysan). Gallatin in Schoolcraft, Ind. Tribes, III, 402, 1853 (includes Huitsla).

×Nass, Bancroft, Nat. Races, III, 564, 606, 1882 (includes Hailtza of present family).

>Aht, Sproat, Savage Life, app., 312, 1868 (name suggested for family instead of Nootka-Columbian).

>Aht, Tolmie and Dawson, Comp. Vocabs., 50, 1884 (vocab. of Kaiookwāht).

×Puget Sound Group, Keane, App. Stanford's Comp. (Cent. and So. Am.), 460, 474, 1878.

×Hydahs. Keane, App. Stanford's Comp. (Cent. and So. Am.), 473, 1878 (includes Hailtzas of the present family).

>Kwakiool, Tolmie and Dawson, Comp. Vocabs., 27 48, 1884 (vocabs. of Haishilla, Hailtzuk, Kwiha, Likwiltoh, Septs ; also map showing family domain).

>Kwä'kiŭtl. Boas in Petermann's Mitteilungen, 130, 1887 (general account of family with list of tribes).

Derivation: Waúkash, waukash, is the Nootka word " good " " good." When heard by Cook at Friendly Cove, Nootka Sound, it was supposed to be the name of the tribe.

Until recently the languages spoken by the Aht of the west coast of Vancouver Island and the Makah of Cape Flattery, congeneric tribes, and the Haeltzuk and Kwakiutl peoples of the east coast of Vancouver Island and the opposite mainland of British Columbia, have been regarded as representing two distinct families. Recently Dr. Boas has made an extended study of these languages, has collected excellent vocabularies of the supposed families, and as a result of his study it is now possible to unite them on the basis of radical affinity. The main body of the vocabularies of the two languages is remarkably distinct, though a considerable number of important words are shown to be common to the two.

Dr. Boas, however, points out that in both languages suffixes only are used in forming words, and a long list of these shows remarkable similarity.

The above family name was based upon a vocabulary of the Wakash Indians, who, according to Gallatin, "inhabit the island on which Nootka Sound is situated." The short vocabulary given was collected by Jewitt. Gallatin states[1] that this language is the one "in that quarter, which, by various vocabularies, is best known to us." In 1848[2] Gallatin repeats his Wakash family, and again gives the vocabulary of Jewitt. There would thus seem to be no doubt of his intention to give it formal rank as a family.

The term "Wakash" for this group of languages has since been generally ignored, and in its place Nootka or Nootka-Columbian has been adopted. "Nootka-Columbian" was employed by Scouler in 1841 for a group of languages, extending from the mouth of Salmon

---

[1] Archæologia Americana, II, p. 15.   [2] Trans. Am. Eth. Soc. II, p. 77.

River to the south of the Columbia River, now known to belong to several distinct families. "Nootka family" was also employed by Hale in 1846, who proposed the name for the tribes of Vancouver Island and those along the south side of the Straits of Fuca.

The term "Nootka-Columbian" is strongly condemned by Sproat.[2] For the group of related tribes on the west side of Vancouver Island this author suggests Aht, "house, tribe, people," as a much more appropriate family appellation.

Though by no means as appropriate a designation as could be found, it seems clear that for the so-called Wakash, Newittee, and other allied languages usually assembled under the Nootka family, the term Wakash of 1836 has priority and must be retained.

GEOGRAPHIC DISTRIBUTION.

The tribes of the Aht division of this family are confined chiefly to the west coast of Vancouver Island. They range to the north as far as Cape Cook, the northern side of that cape being occupied by Haeltzuk tribes, as was ascertained by Dr. Boas in 1886. On the south they reached to a little above Sooke Inlet, that inlet being in possession of the Soke, a Salishan tribe.

The neighborhood of Cape Flattery, Washington, is occupied by the Makah, one of the Wakashan tribes, who probably wrested this outpost of the family from the Salish (Clallam) who next adjoin them on Puget Sound.

The boundaries of the Haeltzuk division of this family are laid down nearly as they appear on Tolmie and Dawson's linguistic map of 1884. The west side of King Island and Cascade Inlet are said by Dr. Boas to be inhabited by Haeltzuk tribes, and are colored accordingly.

PRINCIPAL AHT TRIBES.

Ahowsaht.	Kyoquaht.	Ohiaht.
Ayhuttisaht.	Macaw.	Opechisaht.
Chicklesaht.	Manosaht.	Pachenaht.
Clahoquaht.	Mowachat.	Seshaht.
Hishquayquaht.	Muclaht.	Toquaht.
Howchuklisaht.	Nitinaht.	Yuclulaht.
Kitsmaht.	Nuchalaht.	

Population.—There are 457 Makah at the Neah Bay Agency, Washington.[3] The total population of the tribes of this family under the West Coast Agency, British Columbia, is 3,160.[4] The grand total for this division of the family is thus 3,617.

---

[1] U. S. Expl. Expd., vol. 6, p. 220.   [3] U. S. Census Bulletin for 1890.
[2] Savage Life, 312.   [4] Canada Ind. Aff. Rep. for 1888.

PRINCIPAL HAELTZUK TRIBES.

Aquamish.	Keimanoeitoh.	Nakwahtoh.
Belbellah.	Kwakiutl.	Nawiti.
Clowetsus.	Kwashilla.	Nimkish.
Hailtzuk.	Likwiltoh.	Quatsino.
Haishilla.	Mamaleilakitish.	Tsawadinoh.
Kakamatsis.	Matelpa.	

Population.—There are 1,898 of the Haeltzuk division of the family under the Kwawkewlth Agency, British Columbia. Of the Bellacoola (Salishan family) and Haeltzuk, of the present family, there are 2,500 who are not under agents. No separate census of the latter exists at present.

WASHOAN FAMILY.

= Washo, Gatschet in Mag. Am. Hist., 255, April, 1882.

< Shoshone, Keane, App. Stanford's Comp. (Cent. and So. Am.), 477, 1878 (contains Washoes).

< Snake, Keane, ibid. (Same as Shoshone, above.)

This family is represented by a single well known tribe, whose range extended from Reno, on the line of the Central Pacific Railroad, to the lower end of the Carson Valley.

On the basis of vocabularies obtained by Stephen Powers and other investigators, Mr. Gatschet was the first to formally separate the language. The neighborhood of Carson is now the chief seat of the tribe, and here and in the neighboring valleys there are about 200 living a parasitic life about the ranches and towns.

WEITSPEKAN FAMILY.

= Weits-pek, Gibbs in Schoolcraft, Ind. Tribes, III, 422, 1853 (a band and language on Klamath at junction of Trinity). Latham, El. Comp. Phil., 410, 1862 (junction of Klamatl and Trinity Rivers). Gatschet in Mag. Am. Hist., 163, 1877 (affirmed to be distinct from any neighboring tongue). Gatschet in Beach, Ind. Misc., 438, 1877.

< Weitspek, Latham in Trans. Philolog. Soc. Lond., 77, 1856 (junction of Klamatl and Trinity Rivers; Weyot and Wishosk dialects). Latham, Opuscula, 343, 1860.

= Eurocs, Powers in Overland Monthly, VIII, 530, June, 1872 (of the Lower Klamath and coastwise; Weitspek, a village of).

= Eurok, Gatschet in Mag. Am. Hist., 163, 1877. Gatschet in Beach, Ind. Misc., 437, 1877.

= Yu'-rok, Powers in Cont. N. A. Eth., III, 45, 1877 (from junction of Trinity to mouth and coastwise). Powell, ibid., 460 (vocabs. of Al-i-kwa, Klamath, Yu'-rok.)

× Klamath, Keane, App. Stanford's Comp. (Cent. and So. Am.), 475, 1878 (Eurocs belong here).

Derivation: Weitspek is the name of a tribe or village of the family situated on Klamath River. The etymology is unknown.

Gibbs was the first to employ this name, which he did in 1853, as

above cited. He states that it is "the name of the principal band
on the Klamath, at the junction of the Trinity," adding that "this
language prevails from a few miles above that point to the coast, but
does not extend far from the river on either side." It would thus
seem clear that in this case, as in several others, he selected the name
of a band to apply to the language spoken by it. The language thus
defined has been accepted as distinct by later authorities except Latham, who included as dialects under the Weitspek language, the
locality of which he gives as the junction of the Klamath and Trinity
Rivers, the Weyot and Wishosk, both of which are now classed under
the Wishoskan family.

By the Karok these tribes are called Yurok, "down" or "below,"
by which name the family has recently been known.

GEOGRAPHIC DISTRIBUTION.

For our knowledge of the range of the tribes of this family we are
chiefly indebted to Stephen Powers.[1] The tribes occupy the lower
Klamath River, Oregon, from the mouth of the Trinity down. Upon
the coast, Weitspekan territory extends from Gold Bluff to about 6
miles above the mouth of the Klamath. The Chillúla are an offshoot
of the Weitspek, living to the south of them, along Redwood Creek
to a point about 20 miles inland, and from Gold Bluff to a point
about midway between Little and Mad Rivers.

PRINCIPAL TRIBES.

Chillúla, Redwood Creek.
Mita, Klamath River.
Pekwan, Klamath River.
Rikwa, Regua, fishing village at outlet of Klamath River.
Sugon, Shragoin, Klamath River.
Weitspek, Klamath River (above Big Bend).

WISHOSKAN FAMILY.

> Wish-osk, Gibbs in Schoolcraft, Ind. Tribes, III, 422, 1853 (given as the name of a
    dialect on Mad River and Humboldt Bay).

= Wish-osk, Powell in Cont. N. A. Eth., III, 478, 1877 (vocabularies of Wish-osk,
    Wi-yot, and Ko-wilth). Gatschet in Mag. Am. Hist., 162, 1877 (indicates area
    occupied by family). Gatschet in Beach, Ind. Misc., 437, 1877.

> Wee-yot, Gibbs in Schoolcraft, Ind. Tribes, III, 422, 1853 (given as the name of a
    dialect on Eel River and Humboldt Bay).

× Weitspek, Latham in Trans. Philolog. Soc. Lond., 77, 1856 (includes Weyot and
    Wishosk). Latham, Opuscula, 343, 1860.

< Klamath, Keane, App. Stanford's Comp. (Cent. and So. Am.), 475, 1878 (cited as
    including Patawats, Weeyots, Wishosks).

Derivation: Wish-osk is the name given to the Bay and Mad River
Indians by those of Eel River.

---

[1] Cont. N. A., Eth., 1877, vol. 3, p. 44.

This is a small and obscure linguistic family and little is known concerning the dialects composing it or of the tribes which speak it.

Gibbs[1] mentions Wee-yot and Wish-osk as dialects of a general language extending "from Cape Mendocino to Mad River and as far back into the interior as the foot of the first range of mountains," but does not distinguish the language by a family name.

Latham considered Weyot and Wishosk to be mere dialects of the same language, i. e., the Weitspek, from which, however, they appeared to him to differ much more than they do from each other. Both Powell and Gatschet have treated the language represented by these dialects as quite distinct from any other, and both have employed the same name.

GEOGRAPHIC DISTRIBUTION.

The area occupied by the tribes speaking dialects of this language was the coast from a little below the mouth of Eel River to a little north of Mad River, including particularly the country about Humboldt Bay. They also extended up the above-named rivers into the mountain passes.

TRIBES.

Patawat, Lower Mad River and Humboldt Bay as far south as Arcata.

Weeyot, mouth of Eel River.

Wishosk, near mouth of Mad River and north part of Humboldt Bay.

YAKONAN FAMILY.

> Yakones, Hale in U. S. Expl. Exp., VI, 198, 218, 1846 (or Iakon, coast of Oregon). Buschmann, Spuren der aztek. Sprache, 612, 1859.

> Iakon, Hale in U. S. Expl. Exp., VI, 218, 569, 1846 (or Lower Killamuks). Buschmann, Spuren der aztek. Sprache, 612, 1859.

> Jacon, Gallatin in Trans. Am. Eth. Soc., II, pt. 1, c, 77, 1848.

> Jakon, Gallatin in Trans. Am. Eth. Soc., II, pt. 1, 17, 1848. Berghaus (1851), Physik. Atlas, map 17, 1852. Gallatin in Schoolcraft, Ind. Tribes, III, 402, 1853 (language of Lower Killamuks). Latham in Trans. Philolog. Soc. Lond., 73, 1856. Latham, Opuscula, 340, 1860.

> Yakon, Latham, Nat. Hist. Man, 324, 1850. Gatschet, in Mag. Am. Hist., 166, 1877. Gatschet in Beach, Ind. Misc., 441, 1877. Bancroft, Nat. Races, III, 565, 640, 1882.

> Yákona, Gatschet in Mag. Am. Hist., 256, 1882.

> Southern Killamuks, Hale in U. S. Expl. Exp., VI, 218, 569, 1846 (or Yakones). Gallatin in Trans. Am. Eth. Soc., II, 17, 1848 (after Hale).

> Süd Killamuk, Berghaus (1851), Physik. Atlas, map 17, 1852.

> Sainstskla, Latham, Nat. Hist. Man, 325, 1850 ("south of the Yakon, between the Umkwa and the sea").

> Sayúskla, Gatschet in Mag. Am. Hist., 257, 1882 (on Lower Umpqua, Sayúskla, and Smith Rivers).

> Killiwashat, Latham, Nat. Hist. Man, 325, 1850 ("mouth of the Umkwa").

× Klamath, Keane, App. Stanford's Comp. (Cent. and So. Am.), 475, 1878 (cited as including Yacons).

---

[1] Schoolcraft, Ind. Tribes, 1853, vol. 3, p. 422.

Derivation: From yakwina, signifying "spirit" (Everette).

The Yakwina was the leading tribe of this family. It must have been of importance in early days, as it occupied fifty-six villages along Yaquina River, from the site of Elk City down to the ocean. Only a few survive, and they are with the Alsea on the Siletz Reservation, Tillamook County, Oregon. They were classed by mistake with the Tillamook or "Killamucks" by Lewis and Clarke. They are called by Lewis and Clarke[1] Youikcones and Youkone.[2]

The Alsea formerly dwelt in villages along both sides of Alsea River, Oregon, and on the adjacent coast. They are now on the Siletz Reservation, Oregon. Perhaps a few are on the Grande Ronde Reservation, Oregon.

The Siuslaw used to inhabit villages on the Siuslaw River, Oregon. There may be a few pure Siuslaw on the Siletz Reservation, but Mr. Dorsey did not see any of them. They are mentioned by Drew,[3] who includes them among the "Kat-la-wot-sett" bands. At that time, they were still on the Siuslaw River. The Ku-itc or Lower Umpqua villages were on both sides of the lower part of Umpqua River, Oregon, from its mouth upward for about 30 miles. Above them were the Upper Umpqua villages, of the Athapascan stock. A few members of the Ku-itc still reside on the Siletz Reservation, Oregon.

This is a family based by Hale upon a single tribe, numbering six or seven hundred, who live on the coast, north of the Nsietshawus, from whom they differ merely in language. Hale calls the tribe Iakon or Yakones or Southern Killamuks.

The Sayúsklan language has usually been assumed to be distinct from all others, and the comments of Latham and others all tend in this direction. Mr. Gatschet, as above quoted, finally classed it as a distinct stock, at the same time finding certain strong coincidences with the Yakonan family. Recently Mr. Dorsey has collected extensive vocabularies of the Yakonan, Sayúskla, and Lower Umpqua languages and finds unquestioned evidence of relationship.

GEOGRAPHIC DISTRIBUTION.

The family consists of four primary divisions or tribes: Yakwina, Alsea, Siuslaw, and Ku-itc or Lower Umpqua. Each one of these comprised many villages, which were stretched along the western part of Oregon on the rivers flowing into the Pacific, from the Yaquina on the north down to and including the Umpqua River.

TRIBES.

Alsea (on Alseya River).	Yakwĭ′na.	Kuitc.	Siuslaw.

---

[1] Allen, ed. 1814, vol. 2, p. 473.
[2] Ibid., p. 118.

[3] U. S. Ind. Aff. Rept., 1857, p. 359.

Population.—The U. S. Census Bulletin for 1890 mentions thirty-one tribes as resident on the Siletz Reservation with a combined population of 571. How many Yakwina are among this number is not known. The breaking down of tribal distinctions by reason of the extensive intermarriage of the several tribes is given as the reason for the failure to give a census by tribes.

YANAN FAMILY.

=Nó-zi, Powers in Cont. N. A. Eth., III, 275, 1877 (or No-si; mention of tribe; gives numerals and states they are different from any he has found in California).

=Noces, Gatschet in Mag. Am. Hist., 160, March, 1877 (or Nozes; merely mentioned under Meidoo family).

Derivation: Yana means " people " in the Yanan language.

In 1880 Powell collected a short vocabulary from this tribe, which is chiefly known to the settlers by the name Noje or Nozi. Judged by this vocabulary the language seemed to be distinct from any other. More recently, in 1884, Mr. Curtin visited the remnants of the tribe, consisting of thirty-five individuals, and obtained an extensive collection of words, the study of which seems to confirm the impression of the isolated position of the language as regards other American tongues.

The Nozi seem to have been a small tribe ever since known to Europeans. They have a tradition to the effect that they came to California from the far East. Powers states that they differ markedly in physical traits from all California tribes met by him. At present the Nozi are reduced to two little groups, one at Redding, the other in their original country at Round Mountain, California.

GEOGRAPHIC DISTRIBUTION.

The eastern boundary of the Yanan territory is formed by a range of mountains a little west of Lassen Butte and terminating near Pit River; the northern boundary by a line running from northeast to southwest, passing near the northern side of Round Mountain, 3 miles from Pit River. The western boundary from Redding southward is on an average 10 miles to the east of the Sacramento. North of Redding it averages double that distance or about 20 miles.

YUKIAN FAMILY.

=Yuki, Powers in Cont. N. A. Eth., III, 125–138, 1877 (general description of tribe).

=Yú-ki, Powell in ibid., 483 (vocabs. of Yu'-ki, Hūchnōm, and a fourth unnamed vocabulary).

=Yuka, Powers in Overland Monthly, IX, 305, Oct., 1872 (same as above). Gatschet in Mag. Am. Hist., 161, 1877 (defines habitat of family; gives Yuka, Ashochemies or Wappos, Shumeias, Tahtoos). Gatschet in Beach, Ind. Misc., 435, 1877. Bancroft, Nat. Races, III, 566, 1882 (includes Yuka, Tahtoo, Wapo or Ashochemie).

=Uka, Gatschet in Mag. Am. Hist., 161, 1877.   Gatschet in Beach, Ind. Misc., 435,
    1877 (same as his Yuka).
×Klamath, Keane, App. Stanford's Comp. (Cent. and So. Am.), 475, 1878 (Yukas of
    his Klamath belong here).

Derivation: From the Wintun word yuki, meaning "stranger;"
secondarily, " bad " or " thieving."

A vocabulary of the Yuki tribe is given by Gibbs in vol. III of
Schoolcraft's Indian Tribes, 1853, but no indication is afforded that
the language is of a distinct stock.

Powell, as above cited, appears to have been the first to separate
the language.

GEOGRAPHIC DISTRIBUTION.

Round Valley, California, subsequently made a reservation to receive the Yuki and other tribes, was formerly the chief seat of the
tribes of the family, but they also extended across the mountains to
the coast.

PRINCIPAL TRIBES.

Ashochimi (near Healdsburgh).
Chumaya (Middle Eel River).
Napa (upper Napa Valley).
Tatu (Potter Valley).
Yuki (Round Valley, California).

YUMAN FAMILY.

>Yuma, Turner in Pac. R. R. Rep., III, pt. 3, 55, 94, 101, 1856 (includes Cuchan, Coco-
    Maricopa, Mojave, Diegeño).   Latham in Trans. Philolog. Soc. Lond., 86, 1856.
    Latham, Opuscula, 351, 1860 (as above).   Latham in addenda to Opuscula, 392,
    1860 (adds Cuchan to the group).   Latham, El. Comp. Phil., 420, 1862 (includes
    Cuchan, Cocomaricopa, Mojave, Dieguno).   Gatschet in Mag. Am. Hist., 156,
    1877 (mentions only U. S. members of family).   Keane, App. Stanford's Comp.
    (Cent. and So. Am.), 460, 479, 1878 (includes Yumas, Maricopas, Cuchans, Mojaves,
    Yampais, Yavipais, Hualpais).   Bancroft, Nat. Races, III, 569, 1882.
=Yuma, Gatschet in Beach, Ind. Misc., 429, 1877 (habitat and dialects of family).
    Gatschet in U. S. Geog. Surv. W. 100th M., VII, 413, 414, 1879.
>Dieguno, Latham (1853) in Proc. Philolog. Soc. Lond., VI, 75, 1854 (includes mission
    of San Diego, Dieguno, Cocomaricopas, Cuchañ, Yumas, Amaquaquas.)
>Cochimi, Latham in Trans. Philolog. Soc. Lond., 87, 1856 (northern part peninsula
    California).   Buschmann, Spuren der aztek.   Sprache, 471, 1859 (center of
    California peninsula).   Latham, Opuscula, 353, 1860.   Latham, El. Comp. Phil.,
    423, 1862.   Orozco y Berra, Geografía de las Lenguas de México, map, 1864.
    Keane, App. Stanford's Comp. (Cent. and So. Am.), 476, 1878 (head of Gulf to
    near Loreto).
>Layamon, Latham in Trans. Philolog. Soc. Lond., 88, 1856 (a dialect of Waikur ?).
    Latham, Opuscula, 353, 1860.   Latham, El. Comp. Phil., 423, 1862.
>Waikur, Latham in Trans. Philolog. Soc. Lond., 90, 1856 (several dialects of).
    Latham, Opuscula, 353, 1860.   Latham, El. Comp. Phil., 423, 1862.
>Guaycura, Orozco y Berra, Geografía de las Lenguas de México, map, 1864.
>Guaicuri, Keane, App. Stanford's Comp. (Cent. and So. Am.), 476, 1878 (between
    26th and 23d parallels).

>Ushiti, Latham in Trans. Philolog. Soc. Lond., 88, 1856 (perhaps a dialect of Wai-
    kur). Latham, Opuscula, 353, 1860.

>Utshiti, Latham, El. Comp. Phil., 423, 1862 (same as Ushiti).

>Pericú, Latham in Trans. Philolog. Soc. Lond., 88, 1856. Latham, Opuscula, 353,
    1860. Orozco y Berra, Geografía de las Lenguas de México, map, 1864.

>Pericui, Keane, App. Stanford's Comp. (Cent. and So. Am.), 476, 1878 (from 23° N.
    L. to Cape S. Lucas and islands).

>Seri, Gatschet in Zeitschr. für Ethnologie, xv, 129, 1883, and xviii, 115, 1886.

Derivation: A Cuchan word signifying "sons of the river"
(Whipple).

In 1856 Turner adopted Yuma as a family name, and placed under
it Cuchan, Coco-Maricopa, Mojave and Diegeno.

Three years previously (1853) Latham[1] speaks of the Dieguno language, and discusses with it several others, viz, San Diego, Cocomari-
copa, Cuchañ, Yuma, Amaquaqua (Mohave), etc. Though he seems
to consider these languages as allied, he gives no indication that he
believes them to collectively represent a family, and he made no
formal family division. The context is not, however, sufficiently
clear to render his position with respect to their exact status as precise as is to be desired, but it is tolerably certain that he did not
mean to make Dieguéño a family name, for in the volume of the
same society for 1856 he includes both the Dieguéño and the other
above mentioned tribes in the Yuma family, which is here fully set
forth. As he makes no allusion to having previously established a
family name for the same group of languages, it seems pretty certain that he did not do so, and that the term Dieguéño as a family
name may be eliminated from consideration. It thus appears that
the family name Yuma was proposed by both the above authors during the same year. For, though part 3 of vol. iii of Pacific Railroad
Reports, in which Turner's article is published, is dated 1855, it appears from a foot-note (p. 84) that his paper was not handed to Mr.
Whipple till January, 1856, the date of title page of volume, and
that his proof was going through the press during the month of
May, which is the month (May 9) that Latham's paper was read before the Philological Society. The fact that Latham's article was not
read until May 9 enables us to establish priority of publication in
favor of Turner with a reasonable degree of certainty, as doubtless
a considerable period elapsed between the presentation of Latham's
paper to the society and its final publication, upon which latter
must rest its claim. The Yuma of Turner is therefore adopted as
of precise date and of undoubted application. Pimentel makes
Yuma a part of Piman stock.

GEOGRAPHIC DISTRIBUTION.

The center of distribution of the tribes of this family is generally
considered to be the lower Colorado and Gila Valleys. At least this

---

[1] Proc. London Philol. Soc., vol. 6, 75, 1854.

is the region where they attained their highest physical and mental development. With the exception of certain small areas possessed by Shoshonean tribes, Indians of Yuman stock occupied the Colorado River from its mouth as far up as Cataract Creek where dwell the Havasupai. Upon the Gila and its tributaries they extended as far east as the Tonto Basin. From this center they extended west to the Pacific and on the south throughout the peninsula of Lower California. The mission of San Luis Rey in California was, when established, in Yuman territory, and marks the northern limit of the family. More recently and at the present time this locality is in possession of Shoshonean tribes.

The island of Angel de la Guardia and Tiburon Island were occupied by tribes of the Yuman family, as also was a small section of Mexico lying on the gulf to the north of Guaymas.

PRINCIPAL TRIBES.

Cochimi.	Maricopa.
Cocopa.	Mohave.
Cuchan or Yuma proper.	Seri.
Diegueño.	Waicuru.
Havasupai.	Walapai.

Population.—The present population of these tribes, as given in Indian Affairs Report for 1889, and the U. S. Census Bulletin for 1890, is as follows:

Of the Yuma proper there are 997 in California attached to the Mission Agency and 291 at the San Carlos Agency in Arizona.

Mohave, 640 at the Colorado River Agency in Arizona ; 791 under the San Carlos Agency ; 400 in Arizona not under an agency.

Havasupai, 214 in Cosnino Cañon, Arizona.

Walapai, 728 in Arizona, chiefly along the Colorado.

Diegueño, 555 under the Mission Agency, California.

Maricopa, 315 at the Pima Agency, Arizona.

The population of the Yuman tribes in Mexico and Lower California is unknown.

ZUÑIAN FAMILY.

=Zuñi, Turner in Pac. R. R. Rep., III, pt. 3, 55, 91–93, 1856 (finds no radical affinity between Zuñi and Keres). Buschmann, Neu-Mexico, 254, 266, 276–278, 280–296, 302, 1858 (vocabs. and general references). Keane, App. Stanford's Com. (Cent. and So. Am.), 479, 1878 (" a stock language "). Powell in Rocky Mountain Presbyterian, Nov., 1878 (includes Zuñi, Las Nutrias, Ojo de Pescado). Gatschet in Mag. Am. Hist., 260, 1882.

=Zuñian, Powell in Am. Nat., 604, August, 1880.

Derivation: From the Cochití term Suinyi, said to mean "the people of the long nails," referring to the surgeons of Zuñi who always wear some of their nails very long (Cushing).

Turner was able to compare the Zuñi language with the Keran, and his conclusion that they were entirely distinct has been fully substantiated. Turner had vocabularies collected by Lieut. Simpson and by Capt. Eaton, and also one collected by Lieut. Whipple.

The small amount of linguistic material accessible to the earlier writers accounts for the little done in the way of classifying the Pueblo languages. Latham possessed vocabularies of the Moqui, Zuñi, A'coma or Laguna, Jemez, Tesuque, and Taos or Picuri. The affinity of the Tusayan (Moqui) tongue with the Comanche and other Shoshonean languages early attracted attention, and Latham pointed it out with some particularity. With the other Pueblo languages he does little, and attempts no classification into stocks.

GEOGRAPHIC DISTRIBUTION.

The Zuñi occupy but a single permanent pueblo, on the Zuñi River, western New Mexico. Recently, however, the summer villages of Tâiakwin, Heshotatsína, and K'iapkwainakwin have been occupied by a few families during the entire year.

Population.—The present population is 1,613.

CONCLUDING REMARKS.

The task involved in the foregoing classification has been accomplished by intermittent labors extending through more than twenty years of time. Many thousand printed vocabularies, embracing numerous larger lexic and grammatic works, have been studied and compared. In addition to the printed material, a very large body of manuscript matter has been used, which is now in the archives of the Bureau of Ethnology, and which, it is hoped, will ultimately be published. The author does not desire that his work shall be considered final, but rather as initiatory and tentative. The task of studying many hundreds of languages and deriving therefrom ultimate conclusions as contributions to the science of philology is one of great magnitude, and in its accomplishment an army of scholars must be employed. The wealth of this promised harvest appeals strongly to the scholars of America for systematic and patient labor. The languages are many and greatly diverse in their characteristics, in grammatic as well as in lexic elements. The author believes it is safe to affirm that the philosophy of language is some time to be greatly enriched from this source. From the materials which have been and may be gathered in this field the evolution of language can be studied from an early form, wherein words are usually not parts of speech, to a form where the parts of speech are somewhat differentiated; and where the growth of gender, number, and case systems, together with the development of tense and mode systems can be observed. The evolution of mind in the endeavor to express thought, by coining, combining, and contracting words and by organizing logical sentences through the development of parts of speech and their syntactic arrangement, is abundantly illustrated. The languages are very unequally developed in their several parts. Low gender systems appear with high tense systems, highly evolved case systems with slightly developed mode systems; and there is scarcely any one of these languages, so far as they have been studied, which does not exhibit archaic devices in its grammar.

The author has delayed the present publication somewhat, expecting to supplement it with another paper on the characteristics of those languages which have been most fully recorded, but such supplementary paper has already grown too large for this place and is yet unfinished, while the necessity for speedy publication of the present results seems to be imperative. The needs of the Bureau of Ethnology, in directing the work of the linguists employed in it, and especially in securing and organizing the labor of a large body of collaborators throughout the country, call for this publication at the present time.

In arranging the scheme of linguistic families the author has proceeded very conservatively. Again and again languages have been thrown together as constituting one family and afterwards have been separated, while other languages at first deemed unrelated have ultimately been combined in one stock. Notwithstanding all this care, there remain a number of doubtful cases. For example, Buschmann has thrown the Shoshonean and Nahuatlan families into one. Now the Shoshonean languages are those best known to the author, and with some of them he has a tolerable speaking acquaintance. The evidence brought forward by Buschmann and others seems to be doubtful. A part is derived from jargon words, another part from adventitious similarities, while some facts seem to give warrant to the conclusion that they should be considered as one stock, but the author prefers, under the present state of knowledge, to hold them apart and await further evidence, being inclined to the opinion that the peoples speaking these languages have borrowed some part of their vocabularies from one another.

After considering the subject with such materials as are on hand, this general conclusion has been reached: That borrowed materials exist in all the languages; and that some of these borrowed materials can be traced to original sources, while the larger part of such acquisitions can not be thus relegated to known families. In fact, it is believed that the existing languages, great in number though they are, give evidence of a more primitive condition, when a far greater number were spoken. When there are two or more languages of the same stock, it appears that this differentiation into diverse tongues is due mainly to the absorption of other material, and that thus the multiplication of dialects and languages of the same group furnishes evidence that at some prior time there existed other languages which are now lost except as they are partially preserved in the divergent elements of the group. The conclusion which has been reached, therefore, does not accord with the hypothesis upon which the investigation began, namely, that common elements would be discovered in all these languages, for the longer the study has proceeded the more clear it has been made to appear that the grand process of linguistic development among the tribes of North America has been toward unification rather than toward multiplication, that is, that the multiplied languages of the same stock owe their origin very largely to absorbed languages that are lost. The data upon which this conclusion has been reached can not here be set forth, but the hope is entertained that the facts already collected may ultimately be marshaled in such a manner that philologists will be able to weigh the evidence and estimate it for what it may be worth.

The opinion that the differentiation of languages within a single stock is mainly due to the absorption of materials from other stocks, often to the extinguishment of the latter, has grown from year to year as the investigation has proceeded. Wherever the material has been sufficient to warrant a conclusion on this subject, no language has been found to be simple in its origin, but every language has been found to be composed of diverse elements. The processes of borrowing known in historic times are those which have been at work in prehistoric times, and it is not probable that any simple language derived from some single pristine group of roots can be discovered.

There is an opinion current that the lower languages change with great rapidity, and that, by reason of this, dialects and languages of the same stock are speedily differentiated. This widely spread opinion does not find warrant in the facts discovered in the course of this research. The author has everywhere been impressed with the fact that savage tongues are singularly persistent, and that a language which is dependent for its existence upon oral tradition is not easily modified. The same words in the same form are repeated from generation to generation, so that lexic and grammatic elements have a life that changes very slowly. This is especially true where the habitat of the tribe is unchanged. Migration introduces a potent agency of mutation, but a new environment impresses its characteristics upon a language more by a change in the sematic content or meaning of words than by change in their forms. There is another agency of change of profound influence, namely, association with other tongues. When peoples are absorbed by peaceful or militant agencies new materials are brought into their language, and the affiliation of such matter seems to be the chief factor in the differentiation of languages within the same stock. In the presence of opinions that have slowly grown in this direction, the author is inclined to think that some of the groups herein recognized as families will ultimately be divided, as the common materials of such languages, when they are more thoroughly studied, will be seen to have been borrowed.

In the studies which have been made as preliminary to this paper, I have had great assistance from Mr. James C. Pilling and Mr. Henry W. Henshaw. Mr. Pilling began by preparing a list of papers used by me, but his work has developed until it assumes the proportions of a great bibliographic research, and already he has published five bibliographies, amounting in all to about 1,200 pages. He is publishing this bibliographic material by linguistic families, as classified by myself in this paper. Scholars in this field of research will find their labors greatly abridged by the work of Mr. Pilling. Mr. Henshaw began the preparation of the list of tribes, but his work also has developed into an elaborate system of research into the synonymy of the North American tribes, and when his work is published it will constitute a great and valuable contribution to the subject. The present paper is but a preface to the works of Mr. Pilling and Mr. Henshaw, and would have been published in form as such had not their publications assumed such proportions as to preclude it. And finally, it is needful to say that I could not have found the time to make this classification, imperfect as it is, except with the aid of the great labors of the gentlemen mentioned, for they have gathered the literature and brought it ready to my hand. For the classification itself, however, I am wholly responsible.

I am also indebted to Mr. Albert S. Gatschet and Mr. J. Owen Dorsey for the preparation of many comparative lists necessary to my work.

The task of preparing the map accompanying this paper was greatly facilitated by the previously published map of Gallatin. I am especially indebted to Col. Garrick Mallery for work done in the early part of its preparation in this form. I have also received assistance from Messrs. Gatschet, Dorsey, Mooney and Curtin. The final form which it has taken is largely due to the labors of Mr. Henshaw, who has gathered many important facts relating to the habitat of North American tribes while preparing a synonymy of tribal names.

ADDENDA I.

Concordance of Names

POWELL	HOIJER
Adaizan	included under Caddo
Athapascan	Athapaskan
Attacapan	Atakapa
Chimarikan	Chimariko
Chimnesyan	Tsimshian
Chinookan	Chinook
Coahuiltecan	Coahuilteco
Copehan	Wintun
Eskimauan	Eskimo-Aleut
Kalapooian	Kalapuya
Karankawan	Karankawa
Kitunahan	Kutenai
Koluschan	Tlingit
Kulanapan	Pomo
Kusan	Coos
Mariposan	Yokuts
Moquelumnan	Miwok
Muskhogean	Natchez-Muskogean
Natchesan	Natchez-Muskogean
Palaihnihan	Shasta-Achomawi
Piman	Uto-Aztecan
Pujunan	Maidu
Quoratean	Karok
Sastean	Shasta-Achomawi
Shoshonean	Uto-Aztecan
Skittagetan	Haida
Takilman	Takelma
Tonikan	Tunican
Tonkawan	Tonkawa
Uchean	Yuchi
Weitspekan	Yurok
Wishoskan	Wiyot
Yakonan	Siuslaw and Yakonan
Yukian	Yuki
Zunian	———

ADDENDA II.

Apachean: Hoijer (p. 11) "The Southern Athapaskan
languages (now called Apachean)—Western,
Apachean (which includes Navajo, San Carlos Apache—Chiricahua Apache, and Mescalero Apache); and Eastern Apachean (which
includes Jicarilla, Lipan, and Kiowa-Apache)
. . ."

Eyak: Hoijer (p. 11) "A recently discovered language spoken by about 200 people on the
Copper River delta in Alaska. Its classification is as yet uncertain, but it may turn out to
be a link between Athapaskan and Tlingit."

Hokan-Siouan: see Sapir's listing below. Also Hoijer (p. 17)
under Chumashan and p. 21 under Timu-
quan.

Na-Dene: Hoijer (p. 12) "Athapaskan, Tlingit, and
Haida were grouped together by Sapir in
1915 under the name . . . Na-Dene . . ."

Penutian: Hoijer (p. 14) "In 1913 Dixon and Kroeber
combined Miowk, Costanoan, Yokuts, Maidu
and Wintun into a single genetically related
group which they called Penutian."
——— (p. 15) "In 1918 Frachtenberg published a paper comparing Takelma, Kalapuya
and Chinook . . . Sapir in 1921, suggested
that these languages together with certain
others constituted the Oregon Penutian
family . . ."

Ritwan: Hoijer (p. 13) "A similarity between Wiyot
and Yurok has long been noted. Dixon and
Kroeber, in 1913, classed the two together
under the name Ritwan."

Sahaptin: Hoijer (pp. 15–16) "In 1931 Jacobs suggested that Powell's Shahaptian, Waiilatpuan and Lutuamian stocks be tentatively combined into a single linguistic stock for which he proposed the name. Sahaptin."

Tunican: Hoijer (p. 19) "In 1917 Swanton . . . compared . . . Tunican, Chitimacha, and Atakapa . . . he . . . gave the new stock the name Tunican."

Uto-Aztecan: Hoijer (p. 21) "This stock, which includes the Powell stocks Piman and Shoshonean, as well as a number of Mexican families, was first clearly defined in Sapir's papers on Southern Paiute and Nahuatl."